PRE

A manual of concept analysis and subject indexing

SECOND EDITION

DEREK AUSTIN
PhD FLA
with assistance from Mary Dykstra

THE BRITISH LIBRARY
BIBLIOGRAPHIC SERVICES DIVISION
2 Sheraton Street, London W1A 4BH
1984

ISBN 0 7123 1008 8

British Library Cataloguing in Publication Data

Austin, Derek

PRECIS.—2nd ed.
1. PRECIS (Indexing system)
I. Title II. Dykstra, Mary
025.4′82 Z695.9

ISBN 0–7123–1008–8

PRECIS feature: Documents. Subject indexing.
Schemes: PRECIS—*Manuals*

Derek Austin, Head of the Subject Systems Office, British Library Bibliographic Services Division, has worked with PRECIS since its beginnings in 1969.

Mary Dykstra teaches PRECIS at the School of Library Service, Dalhousie University, and was involved in setting up the PRECIS data base (in English and French) used by the National Film Board of Canada.

Printed in Great Britain
at the University Press, Oxford

Foreword

This edition of the *Manual* developed out of a project, initiated by Mary Dykstra and involving Derek Austin as joint author, to write a students' introduction or *Primer* for PRECIS. Their work encountered a dilemma after the first few chapters. It became clear that the *Primer* should not describe, in a simplified form, the system presented in the first edition of the *Manual*; that would mean ignoring a number of developments over the past ten years, most of which are contained in reports, discussion papers and program specifications held in the British Library. Nor should the *Primer* set out to cover these developments in a fully systematic fashion; it would then become too long and complex for its intended use as a students' introduction. The dilemma was resolved by opting for two new works: firstly, the present *Manual*, offering a completely new description of the system, including all important developments since the first edition; secondly, a *Primer* intended for students, based on the updated *Manual*. This may help to explain why these two works are likely to show resemblances, at least in their first few chapters.

PRECIS is now taught in library schools all over the world, and practical courses and workshops have been held in several countries, attended by indexers with a wide range of languages. This teaching experience has affected the present edition, which sets out to answer, in anticipation, questions that are regularly raised on these courses.

Two developments in the fields of indexing and index use have occurred since the first edition was published ten years ago. Firstly, subject enquiries are handled more frequently by on-line access to a computer rather than searching through printed indexes. PRECIS was conceived as a printed page index, but experience has shown that its controlled pre-coordination has a part to play in improving the effectiveness of on-line searches, and this aspect of the system is exploited by the British Library and the National Film Board of Canada. Secondly, research on an international scale, supported by Unesco, has led to a series of international (and national) standards dealing with subject analysis, vocabulary control and thesaurus construction. These have not shown the need for any changes to PRECIS; on the contrary, it could be said that the general principles on which the standards are based have been present in the system since its beginnings.

The principal changes found in this edition can be traced to two main sources. The first is entirely pragmatic, and relates to ten years use of PRECIS in the British Library and other agencies. This experience revealed the need for a limited number of extra procedures, including some new codes, to deal with day-to-day situations that were not sufficiently covered in the first edition. These new codes allow not only shorter input strings but also easier indexing, since they offer standard routines to deal with otherwise difficult situations. Despite the introduction of these extra codes, the present edition is noticeably shorter, mainly because a number of relatively complex solutions to indexing problems (called 'stratagems' in the first edition) are now unnecessary and have been excluded.

The second source of changes can be traced to a growing interest in PRECIS among agencies, including national libraries, working in other languages. Experiments in new languages have also revealed the need for extra codes and procedures, but these deal with language features not found in English (such as inflections) rather than problems related to subject analysis. Most of the codes developed for this purpose have been tested and programmed, but they are not described in this version of the *Manual*, which is offered as a standard account of the English-language system. These experiments have nevertheless affected the system as a whole, in two main ways. Firstly, the search for solutions to problems encountered in new languages sometimes pointed the way to simpler solutions to related problems in English. Secondly, these practical experiments were necessarily accompanied by a concomitant search for language-independent explanations. This has led to a generalization of the principles on which PRECIS is based, which allows, in its turn, a simpler approach to both application and teaching.

It should be stressed that neither the basic techniques of PRECIS, nor its underlying logic, have been affected by these contacts with new languages. To understand why, we have to distinguish between two different levels within an indexing (or any other) language. On a completely general level, language deals with sets of concepts linked by a limited number of elementary relationships that are regarded by linguists as 'universals', meaning that they occur in all human languages. These basic relationships are conveyed in statements (including sentences and index entries) by surface conventions and mechanisms, such as prepositions, inflections, etc., that tend to vary from language to language. The extra codes developed to deal with new languages are all concerned with these surface mechanisms. The basic relationships, represented in PRECIS by the role operators, have not been affected, and the logic on which the system is based has, in fact, been confirmed and reinforced by these contacts with new languages.

These various developments mean that the status of the *Manual* changes with this edition. When the first edition was published in 1974 it described the whole of the system as conceived at that time. The present edition deals fully with those basic relationships that occur in all languages, but covers only a subset of the available procedures for dealing with surface features—essentially, those that are needed for indexing in a non-inflected, preposition-using language such as English or French. This edition of the *Manual* might serve as a model for other accounts of the system, but it is unlikely to last for another ten years as the only authoritative account.

Acknowledgements

Special thanks are due to—

—Ross Trotter (BL/BSD) and Martin Nail (BL/BSD) for reading the *Manual* in its various drafts, detecting errors and omissions, and offering useful suggestions;

—Fred Smith (Loughborough University) for checking the Algorithms in Appendix 5;

—and particularly Jutta Austin, for preparing the index, selecting or devising many of the examples, offering insights into indexing and language problems, and a good deal more.

Remaining errors are entirely the responsibility of the author.

Derek Austin
Subject Systems Office
The British Library

Contents

1. What PRECIS is (and what it is not)

PRECIS is an acronym for the *PRE*served *C*ontext *I*ndex *S*ystem, a technique for subject indexing developed originally for the *British National Bibliography* (*BNB*), and adopted since by a number of indexing agencies throughout the world. A PRECIS index is usually produced by a computer †, but the system does not belong to the class of automatic indexes in which terms, intended for use as keywords in retrieval, are extracted from texts entirely by computer. The production of a PRECIS index can be considered in two stages, the first performed by a human indexer, and the second by a machine. The indexer is responsible for intellectual tasks, such as examining the document ‡, selecting appropriate indexing terms and deciding how these terms are interrelated. These decisions call for the use of finely-honed skills and they cannot yet be delegated to a machine. The terms selected by the indexer are recorded in the form of an *input string*, where each term is prefixed by a code that indicates, for example, whether or not the term should function as a user's access point, or *lead*, in the printed index. These strings are input to the computer, which then takes over the various clerical jobs which indexers tend to find irksome for the same reason that computers do them so well: they consist of repetitive, step-by-step routines which can be described in algorithms and translated into programs. This is the stage when entries are generated out of the input strings, and the appropriate *See* and *See also* references are extracted from a machine-held thesaurus. Finally, these entries and references are interfiled ready for output in various forms, such as printed indexes, COM authority files, etc. It could be said that

---

† Some bibliographic agencies produce their PRECIS indexes without computer assistance, but this is unusual.

‡ 'Document' is used in its widest sense throughout this *Manual*, and refers to any medium, printed or otherwise, for the transfer of information.

PRECIS represents an example of job-sharing between the indexer and the machine. PRECIS is a relatively new system, and it may be useful at this stage to compare and contrast it briefly with some other (possibly more familiar) systems, especially those that represent types of index to which PRECIS does *not* belong.

PRECIS is *not* a subject heading system, although it can be used to organise entries in an alphabetical subject catalogue in much the same way as traditional subject headings. The reader who is familiar with the use of a list such as *Sears* or *Library of Congress Subject Headings (LCSH)* is advised to set this experience to one side for the present, and approach PRECIS, if not with a *tabula rasa*, then at least with an open mind. Teaching experience has shown that a student who starts by regarding PRECIS as a kind of subject heading system runs a risk of confusion or even frustration. An example will illustrate some of the more obvious differences. A film called *Confrontation Paris 1968* dealt with the student protest movements active in Paris during that year. An indexer using LCSH might select the following headings for a subject catalogue:

Radicalism — France
Students — Political activity
France — Politics and government

Two points about these headings should be noted:

— Although a term such as 'Protest movements' may be in current use, it should not be used as a heading for this film until it has appeared in the list of approved subject headings;

— Each heading functions independently as an access point to the catalogue, and no attempt is made to interrelate the separate headings. Consequently, the reader who is interested in, say, French student protest movements, and who checks the catalogue at 'Students — Political activity', must then search through titles etc. for possible clues to the French connection.

This approach can now be contrasted with the PRECIS entries for this film that appeared in an issue of *Audio-visual Materials for Higher Education* (published in London by the British Universities Film & Video Council):

France
  Paris. Students. Protest movements, *1968*

Paris. France
  Students. Protest movements, *1968*

Students. Paris. France
  Protest movements, *1968*

Protest movements. Students. Paris. France
  1968

These entries would be supported by references such as:

Political movements
  See also
    Protest movements

Apart from the fact that the various entries in the PRECIS index were not copied from a list, but were generated by a computer from a single input string, they also differ from the subject headings in both content and terminology. PRECIS is based on the concept of an *open-ended vocabulary*, which means that a new term such as 'Protest movements' can be admitted into the indexing vocabulary as soon as it has been encountered in documents. It should also be noted that the whole of the subject has been stated in a summary form (a mini-précis) under each of the PRECIS leads.

PRECIS is *not*, as some writers have suggested, a variety of chain indexing. The step-by-step analysis of a subject usually associated with chain indexing is also employed in PRECIS, but the basis of this analysis, as well as the form of output, differ in some significant ways. These can again be demonstrated by examples. *BNB*, before adopting PRECIS, produced a chain index based on its modified version of the 14th edition of the Dewey Decimal Classification (DDC). Using this system, the subject 'Working conditions of children in mines' would have been classed at 331.3822 †. A number of hierarchical steps are embedded within this number:

330	Economics
331	Labour economics
331.3	Young people
331.38	In specific industries
331.3822	Mining industries

† A slightly different hierarchy occurs in later editions of the DDC, but this does not affect the principles illustrated above.

Each step in a hierarchy is expressed, where possible, by an entry in the chain index, such as the following (modelled on entries in the 1969 annual volume of *BNB*):

Economics	330
Labour: Economics	331
Employment: Economics	331
Youth: Labour: Economics	331.3
Young people: Labour: Economics	331.3
Mines: Youth: Employment: Economics	331.3822

The topics expressed by some of these entries, such as 'Economics' and 'Labour: Economics', are wider than that of the document, which means that a reader interested in, say, 'Economics', could be misled into supposing that works on this general topic can be found at class 330 in that particular issue of the bibliography. The final entry, beginning with 'Mines', comes closest to the subject, but certain terms, such as 'Children' and 'Working conditions', are nevertheless missing, mainly because these concepts cannot (or should not) be specified at that position in the DDC schedules. Consequently, some of the entries in the chain index refer to concepts that did not occur in the document, and certain concepts which did occur, and which might have provided useful access points in the index, were excluded. The examples above should now be seen in contrast to the following PRECIS entries based on models in the current files of *BNB*

Mining industries
  Personnel: Children. Working conditions

Children. Personnel. Mining industries
  Working conditions

Working conditions. Children. Personnel. Mining industries

It will be seen that a general term, such as 'Young persons' (rather than 'Children'), does not appear in these entries, whereas certain heavily-used terms, such as 'Industries' and 'Personnel', occurred in the entries but were not used as leads. These entries would be supported, however, by references such as:

Young persons
  See also
    Children

Personnel
  See also
    Personnel *under names of specific industries*

Industries
See also
Names of specific industries

A further point of contrast between PRECIS and the chain index should also be noted. In the final entry of the chain index:

Mines: Youth: Employment: Economics

— the order of terms appears to be somewhat unnatural, and this may sometimes disturb the user's immediate understanding. This occasional lack of clarity (sometimes ambiguity) can be attributed directly to the fact that terms in a chain index entry are set down in an order that is supposed to reflect the hierarchical structure of a clasification scheme, without regard for the ways in which the terms might be related in a natural language statement. We shall see later that PRECIS is based on different principles, and uses a kind of indexing 'grammar' to ensure that terms are organised consistently into 'meaningful' sequences.

The first of the PRECIS entries shown above, i.e.

Mining industries
Personnel: Children. Working conditions

- resembles an entry in a KWOC index, at least to the extent that the term in the lead was 'lifted out' of the string and printed above on a separate line. PRECIS is *not*, however, a member of that class of computer-produced indexes which includes KWIC, KWOC and their variants. Input to these keyword systems usually consists of unedited titles, which means that their production calls for minimal intellectual effort on the part of the indexer. The choice of leads may be controlled, either by the use of a 'stop list' which prevents the generation of entries under common words (such as articles and prepositions), or by the insertion of tags which label those words that should be printed as leads, but no attempt is usually made to control the vocabulary or to regulate the order of terms in entries. These systems are easy to use, and they are capable of producing quick results (for, say, a current awareness service) in fields where titles are generally expressive and most of the terms are unambiguous — such as reports and journal articles in the harder sciences. A title such as 'Testing the relationship between food intake and sexual arousal in the albino rat' lends itself readily to keyword indexing. This favourable situation would not occur, however, when indexing a documentary film such as *'Still in one piece, anyway'*, which deals with the navigation of a heavily-laden supertanker into Chedabucto Bay in Nova Scotia. Even when titles are reasonably expressive, keyword systems can still be confusing when applied to collections of documents covering several disciplines, where the meaning of a term (such as 'groups') can vary according to its context (e.g. social groups *vs* mathematical groups). It would, of course, be possible to improve the performance of a keyword system by applying controls at the input stage, either by regulating the vocabulary or by adding extra terms so that the input consists of an 'enriched' title. If this is done, however, the *raison d'être* of keyword indexing, mainly its speed and simplicity, will have been seriously undermined.

So what *is* PRECIS? It can be described in very general terms as two interrelated sets of working procedures, each concerned with a particular group of inter-term relationships. The first refers to the organization of terms in input strings and their manipulation into entries. Since the order of terms in strings and entries is regulated by a kind of 'grammar', we might call this the *syntactical* side of the system. The second set of procedures deals with *thesaural* relationships between indexing terms and their synonyms, broader terms, narrower terms, etc. These are organized as machine-held networks that serve as the sources of *See* and *See also* references in the printed index. These two sets of relationships, the syntactical and thesaural, together with their associated procedures, are treated separately in the *Manual*. Chapters 2 to 14 deal mainly with the techniques of subject analysis and string writing and the manipulation of strings into entries. Thesaurus construction is covered in Chapters 15 to 18.

One feature of PRECIS should be noted at this point. In some respects the system could be described as prescriptive. It is, for example, based on rules which determine:

— how concepts should be ordered in strings and entries according to their roles in the subject (such as 'location', 'action', 'performer', etc.);

— whether compound terms, such as 'library management' and 'rolled steel joists', should be retained in their compound forms or factored into separate noun components (such as 'libraries' and 'management').

Nevertheless, the system does not prescribe *which* term should be used to represent a given concept in the index; there is no equivalent to a list of 'approved' subject headings. We shall also see examples where the same subject has been analysed and indexed in slightly different ways, each equally valid according to the rules of the system. The indexer is then expected to choose, from among the allowed options, whichever procedure appears most likely to generate an index tuned to the needs of its users. The examples in the *Manual* usually reflect a general approach — one that would be appropriate for, say, the index to a large collection covering several disciplines — but it should be borne in mind that other approaches are sometimes possible and are not necessarily 'wrong'. Some grounds for choosing among these allowed options are surveyed briefly in Appendix 3.

Further reading

The evolution of PRECIS, from a background of classification theory and automated cataloguing, is described in:

Austin, Derek. The development of PRECIS: a theoretical and technical history. *Journal of Documentation*, 30(1), March 1974, p 47-102

2. How PRECIS works

Before examining the separate parts of PRECIS and their interrelationships we need to glance briefly over the system as a whole. For the sake of simpler explanations, two liberties will be taken in this and most of the following chapters. Firstly, we shall refer to the initial stage of indexing, starting with the examination of a document and ending with the writing of a string, as though it consists of a sequence of separate steps. It is realised, however, that an experienced indexer does not work in this pedestrian fashion; the string is usually formulated in the course of examining the document. As one indexer explained, "... discerning the subject matter of a document and indexing it are simultaneous mental exercises" (1). Secondly, we shall not yet attempt to describe or use the full range of manipulation codes that serve as machine instructions in a computerized system. This coding system is explained in Chapter 14, and it will then be seen that each term in a string is preceded by a code containing a number of fixed positions, each of which records a specific decision by the indexer. For example, one position indicates the status of the following term as 'lead' or 'non-lead'. There is nothing difficult about this coding system, but it appears rather cumbersome at first sight, and the same decisions will therefore be indicated in most of the following examples by the simpler and shorter conventions described in the next chapter.

Examining the document and writing the string

We shall start our overview of the indexing operation by assuming that the indexer, after examining a document, has reached a point where its subject (and also, perhaps, its form) could be expressed in a

---

(1) Bakewell, K G B *& others*. A study of indexers' reactions to the PRECIS indexing system. Liverpool, Liverpool Polytechnic, Department of Library and Information Studies, 1978

summary phrase such as 'This is an *atlas of France*', or 'This is about the *management of Canadian libraries*'. The words in italic in each of these phrases form what is called a *subject statement*. These statements are clearly similar to titles, and the title of a document can, indeed, offer useful clues when formulating its subject statement, but it must be remembered that PRECIS is not a kind of title or keyword indexing. This statement is next analysed into separate terms, and the indexer also considers the *role* of each term. This search for roles might be described as the search for answers to straightforward questions such as:

— *Did anything happen?*
— *If yes, to whom or what did it happen?*
— *Who or what did it?*
— *Where did it happen?*

In effect, the indexer is engaged at this stage in a kind of grammatical analysis, similar to parsing a sentence. Other questions deal with logical rather than grammatical roles, e.g.

— *Are any of the concepts in the statement related as whole-to-part?*

Not all these questions will necessarily lead to answers; that depends on the document in hand. For example, we could hardly say that anything *happened* when dealing with an 'Atlas of France'. When an answer occurs, however, it will be found that the question provides a clue to the role of the term that forms its answer. This is illustrated in the table below, which shows three questions related to the subject statement, 'Management of Canadian libraries', followed by the terms that form their answers and also an indication of their roles:

Question	Answer	Role
What happened?	management	*action*
To whom/what did it happen?	libraries	*object of action*
Where?	Canada	*location*

The roles in the table should now be checked against the list of *role operators* shown in the right-hand panel of Appendix 1 (the fold-out appendix on p 307). A glance down this list will show that:

— an *action* can be matched by the operator '2';
— the *object of an action* should be indicated by the operator '1';
— a *location* can be matched by the operator '0'.

When roles can be matched by numbers selected from the set of *primary operators* (as in this example), the order of terms in the input string is generally determined by the filing values of these operators. Since '0' files before '1', and '1' before '2', the terms should be set down in the order:

(0) Canada
(1) libraries
(2) management

We should pause at this point and note some typical features of this string:

— each term is preceded by its operator written within parentheses (this is one of the conventions mentioned earlier);
— except for proper names, such as 'Canada', terms have been written with lower case initials. An upper case initial may be needed in the printed output, but this is left to the computer;
— each concept, including the action, is expressed by a noun. PRECIS, like other controlled language systems, consistently chooses nouns or noun phrases as indexing terms, avoiding verbs (e.g. 'manage') and participles (e.g. 'managed'), etc..

The use of the operators to regulate the filing order of terms ensures that different indexers (including the same indexer on different occasions) consistently achieve the same results in their strings. It also ensures that terms are set down in a *context dependent order*. In the present example this means that:

— the string begins with the name of the location, 'Canada', which sets all the remaining terms into their wider context;
— the following term, 'libraries', then establishes the context in which the act of 'management' occurred.

When terms have been organised in this way, they frequently form what is called a *one-to-one related sequence*; this simply means that each of the terms in the string is directly related to its neighbour. These two characteristics (*context dependency*, leading to terms linked by *one-to-one relations*) play important parts in conveying the meaning of an index entry and avoiding the more obvious kinds of ambiguity. If the order of terms is changed, a risk of ambiguity may arise. For example, a sequence of terms such as:

Canada - management - libraries

— might refer to 'Management of Canadian libraries' or 'Canadian libraries of management'.

To complete the present stage, the indexer selects those terms that should serve as *leads* in the printed index. For the present, a lead will be indicated by adding a check mark (√) over each term:

(0) Canada
(1) libraries
(2) management

It has been assumed in this example that the indexer wishes to generate an entry under each term in the string. It is realised, however, that an indexer in Canada, dealing with a subject of this kind, might not want a lead under the name of the location — otherwise 'Canada' could become a heavily overused term. In that case the first term in the string would not have been marked as a lead, but it would still appear in each of the other entries. As far as the syntactical side of the system is concerned, the indexer's job is finished, and the computer can now take over.

The generation of entries

The string above would be manipulated by the computer into three entries:

Canada
  Libraries. Management

Libraries. Canada
  Management

Management. Libraries. Canada

Some characteristic features of PRECIS can be seen in these entries:

— each of the entries is *co-extensive* with the subject as perceived by the indexer: that is to say, the whole of the subject has been stated under every term.

— the lead in each entry is emphasised by the use of a distinctive type face. In the examples above the leads were printed in a bolder face, but upper case is used in some published indexes.

— the order of terms in the first entry (under 'Canada') corresponds to the order of the original string. Terms in the final entry (under 'management') are printed in the reverse of their input order. This change of order has been made deliberately to ensure that the original one-to-one relations are not disturbed in either of these entries.

— one-to-one relationships are also retained in the entry under 'libraries', but a different mechanism was used in this case. A study of this entry will show that terms have been assigned to three different positions. It is these positions that are linked by one-to-one relations, as seen in the following diagram:

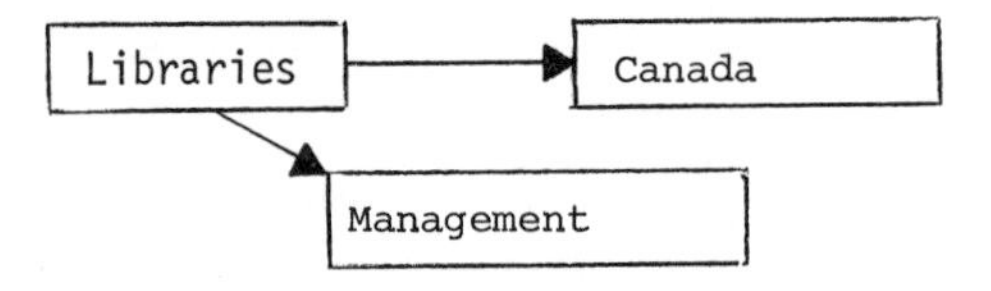

These three positions, which occur in many PRECIS entries, have been given specific names:

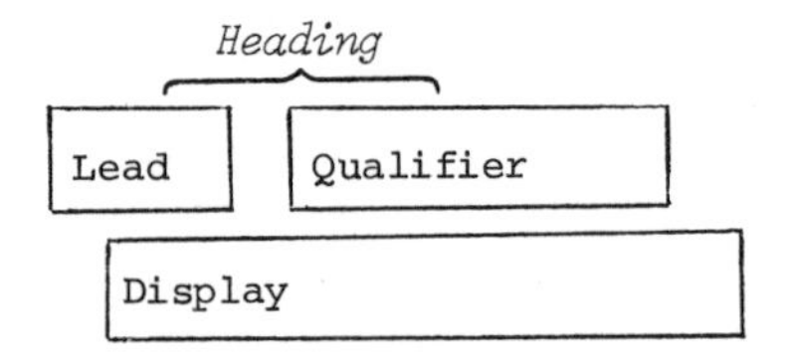

Each position has a part to play in conveying the meaning of a subject to the user:

— the *lead* is offered as the reader's access point in the index;

— the *qualifier* contains the term (or terms) that sets the lead into its wider context. Terms in the qualifier are usually printed in the reverse of their input order, which means that the *heading* (the lead plus the qualifier) consists of terms set down in a narrower-to-wider context order. The qualifier position is not always occupied; for example, the entry under 'Canada' does not contain a qualifier. If the terms in the qualifier overrun to an extra line, this line is indented eight spaces from the start of the lead.

— the *display* contains those terms which rely upon the heading for their context. These terms are usually printed in their original or input order, although we shall later see examples where a different order occurs. The display position can sometimes be empty; for example, the entry under 'management' does not contain a display. The display is indented two spaces from the start of the lead, and a display overrun, if necessary, is indented an extra space.

— the *heading* consists of the lead plus the qualifier (if any). In some situations two or more different strings can generate exactly the same heading. For example, a string such as:

(0) Canada
(1) libraries
(2) automation

- would generate three entries:

Canada
  Libraries. Automation

Libraries. Canada
  Automation

Automation. Libraries. Canada

The headings in the first two entries exactly match those produced from the earlier string:

Canada
  Libraries. Management

Libraries. Canada
  Management

If these two strings occur as part of the input for the same index, the computer will recognize the common headings, and it will automatically cancel the second and any subsequent occurrence of the same heading. The various displays will then be organised alphabetically under a common heading:

Canada
  Libraries. Automation
  Libraries. Management

Libraries. Canada
  Automation
  Management

We can, from a study of the entry under 'Libraries', begin to perceive how a user probably reads a PRECIS index. We need to assume that the reader had the term 'libraries' in mind before approaching the index, and therefore registered a hit on finding this term in the lead. In this case, however, the lead is immediately qualified by the name of the location, 'Canada'. In some circumstances this qualification might cause the user to reject the entry without bothering to read the displays; the reader may be interested only in 'libraries in general', or 'libraries outside North America'. If, however, the heading as a whole appears to be acceptable, there is no need to remember all (or any) of its terms. The reader can simply register the entry as 'Relevant so far' before going on to scan the sequence of displays, testing each display in turn for relevance or non-relevance. Reading the index is thus perceived as a set of discrete steps, each involving a relatively simple decision ('relevant' or 'non-relevant') which was prompted partly by the structure of the entry, but especially by the context-establishing relationships between its parts.

Each of the entries shown above illustrates what is called the *standard format*, generated by a technique known as *shunting*. To see how this works we need to visualise the three parts of a PRECIS entry as positions in a railway yard, and imagine that a string of index terms, in input order, is marshalled in the display position ready for shunting:

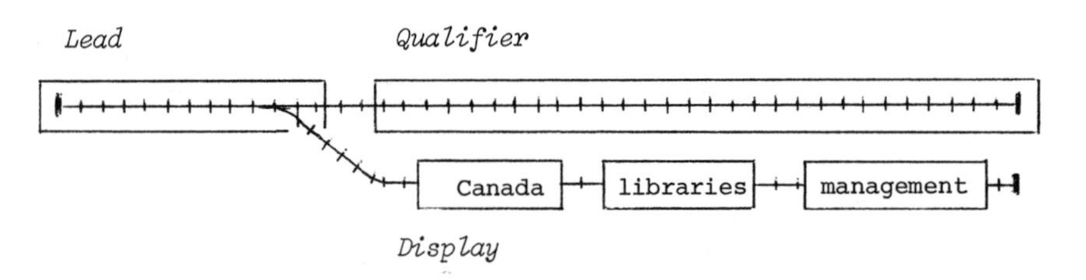

Note that neither the lead nor qualifier is occupied at the start of the shunting operation. The generation of entries then proceeds in mechanical steps as follows:

To generate the entry under 'Canada'

Step 1. Shunt the first (or next) available lead from the display and into the lead position.

Step 2. Any term(s) remaining in the display are shunted up to the standard indentation level (that is, they are left-aligned).

Output: Canada
Libraries. Management

To generate the entry under 'libraries'

Step 3. Shunt the term in the lead across to the qualifier.

Repeat Steps 1 and 2 (in that order)

Output: Libraries. Canada
Management

To generate the entry under 'management' (or any subsequent entry in the standard format

Repeat Steps 3, 1 and 2 (in that order)

Output: Management. Libraries. Canada

Further refinements of the standard format are available. For example:

— the program includes routines which allow the generation of entries under any word or words selected from a compound term such as 'Reinforced concrete floors';

— terms that are written as separate elements in a string are sometimes linked by prepositions into pre-coordinated phrases in the entry.

These routines, together with some different formats, are described in later chapters. It is worth noting, however, that the shunting technique described above, leading to entries in the standard format, accounts for most of the entries in any PRECIS index.

Other examples of subject analysis and entry generation are shown below (Examples 1 to 4). When studying these, note how the various tasks are shared between the indexer and the computer. To recapitulate:

The indexer is responsible for: (i) analysing the document; (ii) selecting terms, and organising them into a string where the role of each term is indicated by its operator, and the values of the primary operators determine the filing order.

The computer shunts the terms through three basic positions to generate entries in the standard format.

When studying the entries, note how: (i) an entry can sometimes occupy two lines; (ii) one-to-one relationships between the terms in the string, based on the idea of context-dependency, are preserved in each of the entries.

Example 1

Subject statement (indexer): Environment planning of new towns in Sweden

String (indexer): (0) Sweden
(1) new towns
(2) environment planning

Entries (computer): Sweden
New towns. Environment planning

New towns. Sweden
Environment planning

Environment planning. New towns. Sweden

Example 2

Subject: Training hospital chaplains in Canada

String: (0) Canada
(1) hospitals
(p) chaplains
(2) training

Note: The operator 'p' indicates a part or property of the preceding concept. The whole (e.g. 'hospitals') is always written before its part.

Entries: Canada
Hospitals. Chaplains. Training

Hospitals. Canada
Chaplains. Training

Chaplains. Hospitals. Canada
Training

Training. Chaplains. Hospitals. Canada

Example 3

Subject: Family life of the aborigines in the deserts of Western Australia

String: (0) Western Australia
(p) deserts
(1) aborigines
(2) family life

Entries: Western Australia
Deserts. Aborigines. Family life

Deserts. Western Australia
Aborigines. Family life

Aborigines. Deserts. Western Australia
Family life

Family life. Aborigines. Deserts. Western Australia

Example 4

Subject: The life styles of women in Cuba

String: (0) Cuba
(1) women
(p) life styles

Entries: Cuba
Women. Life styles

Women. Cuba
Life styles

Life styles. Women. Cuba

Introduction of supporting references

The entries used as examples above express their subjects as pre-coordinated summaries but make no concessions to readers who might be interested in these and similar topics and enter the index with other words in mind. For example, a user who would regard the entry under 'Training' as possibly relevant might enter at the broader term 'Education'. The exclusion of a broader concept from a string that deals with its narrower concept is a matter of deliberate policy in PRECIS, and is expressed in the general rule:

> Two terms should not be written as adjacent elements in a string if the first serves only to indicate the class of which the second is usually regarded as a member.

Links between these related terms are provided by references such as:

Education
See also
Training

Similar references were attached to some of the examples seen in Chapter 1, e.g.

Political movements
See also
Protest movements

Young persons
See also
Children

These references, which are interfiled with entries in the printed index, are not written by indexers, but are constructed by the computer, as and when they are needed, from data in a machine-held thesaurus. The techniques used to build this thesaurus are described in Chapters 15 to

18, and it is sufficient for the present to identify only the principal features of this component of PRECIS.

Two kinds of reference are provided in a PRECIS index. Each has its own purpose and its own form of output:

(a) A *See* reference directs the user from a *non-preferred term* to its *preferred synonym*. When a term has one or more synonyms, only one of the terms in this synonym set is chosen for use in strings, to ensure that entries on a given concept are consistently brought together in the alphabetical index. The user who enters the index at a non-preferred term is then directed by a reference such as:

Aves *See* Birds
Ceylon *See* Sri Lanka

These references usually occupy single lines (with a necessary allowance for overruns), and their parts are named as follows:

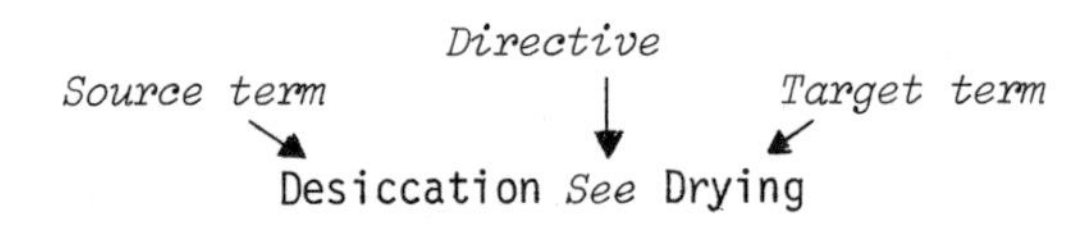

(b) A *See also* reference occupies three lines on the printed page (more if an overrun occurs), and its parts are named as follows:

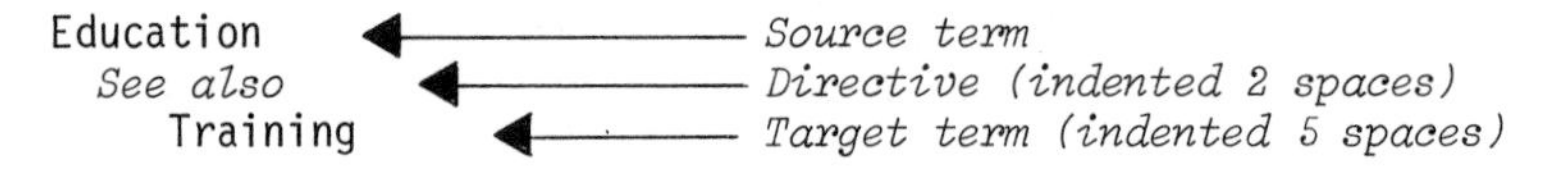

These references direct a user from one preferred term (which may occur as a lead in its own right), to another preferred term.

In a given issue of an index, two or more different terms may call for references from the same source term. This would occur, for example, if the index contains leads under 'Vegetables' and 'Shrubs', each of which calls for a *See also* reference from 'Plants'. When this situation arises, the computer 'recognises' the identical parts of the references (that is, the source term and the directive), and it then:

— cancels the second and any subsequent appearance of these common elements;

— arranges the various target terms as an alphabetical column, e.g.

Plants
See also
Botany
Shrubs
Vegetables
etc.

The different formats of *See* and *See also* references, and also the different words chosen as their directives, help to convey their different purposes to the user. A *See* reference functions as a definite instruction, and indicates that relevant documents can be traced only if the directive is followed. A *See also* reference is offered more as an *aide memoire*; it allows a reader to scan a sequence of related terms, selecting those that might be relevant and rejecting others.

The merging of entries and references

Figure 1 (page 20) shows part of a page from the PRECIS index to an issue of the *British Catalogue of Audiovisual Materials (BCAVM)*. This represents a typical layout after index entries and references have been brought together and merged as a single alphabetical sequence. The sample includes many features of PRECIS covered in this and the previous chapter:

— A *See* reference from Contests to Competitions.

— A *See also* reference from Cooperatives to the associated concept Communes.

— Copying equipment occurred as the common source term for two *See also* references. These were brought together, and their narrower terms, Duplicating machines and Photoreproduction equipment, were organised as an alphabetical column.

— The sample contains a number of entries generated by shunting, e.g.

Contaminants. Food
Microorganisms

Cornwall
Mining & quarrying
Tin mines. Machinery — *Illustrations*

THE BRITISH CATALOGUE OF AUDIOVISUAL MATERIALS

Conquests
See also
Norman Conquest
Conrad, Joseph. Fiction in English
— *Critical studies* 823'.9'12
Conservation. Buildings of historical importance. Great Britain 720'.941
Conservation. Energy resources 333.7'2
Conservation. Environment 301.31
Conservation. Environment. Great Britain 301.31
Conservation. Matter 531'.62
Conservation. Water. Natural resources. Developing countries
Intermediate technology 333.9'1'091724
Conservation. Wildlife 639'.9

Conservative and Unionist Party. Great Britain
1832-1902 329.9'41
Constable, John, *b.1776.* English paintings
— *Illustrations* 759.2
Constantinople *See* **Istanbul**
Constellations
See also
Ursa Major
Constellations
Identification 523.8
Construction
See also
Construction *under* Names of specific objects constructed
Structural engineering
Construction
Sites 624
Construction materials
See also
Building materials
Construction trades
See also
Building trades
Consumer behaviour
See also
Purchase
Consumer goods. Great Britain
Purchase & sale 339.4'7
Consumer protection. Great Britain
Legal aspects 343'.41'07
Consumption
See also
Consumer behaviour
Consumption. Alcoholic drinks
Health aspects 613.8'1
Consumption. Energy resources 339.4'8'3337
Contact inhibition. Movement. Fibroblasts. Vertebrates 596'.08'764
Contact process. Manufacture. Sulphuric acid 661'.22
Containers
See also
Cans
Contaminants. Food
Microorganisms 576'.163
Contaminants. Milk
Antibiotics. Testing. Laboratory techniques 637'.127'7
Microorganisms. Testing. Laboratory techniques 637'.127'7

Contests *See* **Competitions**
Contour lines. Maps
Interpretation 912'.0148
Contrabasses *See* **Double basses**
Contraception
See also
Sterilisation
Contraception. Man 613.9'4
Contraction. Skeletal muscles. Animals
Laboratory techniques — *Study examples: Frogs. Gastrocnemius* 597'.8
Contracts. Great Britain
Legal aspects 346'.41'02

Cooling
See also
Deep freezing
Heating
Cooper, James Fenimore. American writers. Fiction in English
— *Critical studies* 813'.2
Cooperatives
See also
Communes
Cooperatives. China
Agricultural cooperatives, *1957-1958* 334'.683'0951
Cooperatives. Tanzania
Agricultural cooperatives: Ujamaas 334'.683'09678
Agricultural cooperatives: Ujamaas. Social life 967.8
Coordination. Physical fitness. Children
Exercises 613.7'1
Copenhagen. Denmark
Description & travel 914.89'1
Coppelia. Delibes, Leo. Ballet
— *Plot outlines* 792.8'4
Copper
Refining 669'.3
Copying equipment
See also
Duplicating machines
Photoreproduction equipment
Copying processes
See also
Photoreproduction
Printing
Coral reefs
See also
Atolls
Great Barrier Reef
Coral reefs
Geological features 551.4'2
Marine animals 591.9'09'42
Marine animals. Mutualism 591.5'2636
Organisms 574.909'42
Corbusier, *Le.* Architectural design
— *Critical studies* 720'.92'4
Cordage
See also
String
Coriolanus. Shakespeare, William. Drama in English
— *Critical studies* 822.3'3
Corn. Maize *See* **Maize**
Corn flakes 664'.756
Cornets
Care 788'.1'2
Cornflakes *See* **Corn flakes**
Cornwall
Mining & quarrying 622'.094237
Tin mines. Machinery — *Illustrations* 622'.345'3
Coronation. Elizabeth II, *Queen of Great Britain* 941.085'092'4
Corpora allata. Colorado beetles
Removal. Effects on behaviour 595.7'64
Corporations *See* **Companies**
Corries *See* **Cirques**
Corrosion
See also
Rusting
Corrosion
Causes & control 620.1'1223
Corsican pine trees 585'.2
Cortés, Hernándo. Spain
Conquest of Mexico 972'.02'0924
Cosmetics
Manufacture 668'.55
Cosmonauts *See* **Astronauts**
Costume
See also
Wigs
Women's costume

Figure 1. Part of a page from the PRECIS index to *British Catalogue of Audiovisual Materials* (published by the British Library)

The second of these entries shows the layout produced when a common heading is cancelled and the displays are organised as an alphabetical column.

Each entry in the sample in Figure 1 is followed by a class mark which directs the user to a position in a separate classified file where the full citations are printed. This form of output is typical of a classified catalogue or bibliography — the main sequence of citations in *BCAVM* (and also in the British and Australian national bibliographies) is arranged by the Dewey Decimal Classification. Other kinds of output are also used, however, and alternative arrangements are described in a later chapter.

3. String writing codes and conventions

Introduction

In a computerized system a PRECIS input string consists of a sequence of terms preceded by *manipulation codes* which record, as machine-readable instructions, how each term should be handled when the entries are produced. A fully-coded string can appear to be quite complicated to the uninitiated, e.g.

```
$z 1 103 0$a microscopes $21 electron
$z 2 003 0$a design $w of
$z s 003 0$a applications $v of $w in
$z 3 103 0$a computer systems
```

This string contains two kinds of codes which need to be clearly distinguished:

(a) A *primary manipulation code* containing nine positions, e.g. '$z 1 103 0$a', precedes each term in the string. Three of these nine positions are pre-printed; the remainder contain specific instructions written by the indexer.
(b) *Secondary codes*, such as '$21' and '$v', precede parts of terms (such as adjectives), or adjuncts (such as prepositions).

An experienced indexer quickly learns to read a string of this kind, and can see at a glance the subject it expresses and the entries it will produce.

All these codes are suppressed from the printed index, and the order of terms in an entry may differ from that in a string. The string above, for example, would generate the entries:

Microscopes
  Electron microscopes. Design. Applications of computer systems
Electron microscopes
  Design. Applications of computer systems

Computer systems
  Applications in design of electron microscopes

As noted in Chapter 1, we shall not yet attempt to use or explain the full range of manipulation codes. The secondary codes will be covered in detail in this and the following chapters, but the primary codes will be replaced for the present by a set of standard *conventions* which express the same information in a shorter and more mnemonic form. The primary codes are covered separately in Chapter 14. It will then be found that the explanations are easier to follow once the conventions have become familiar. These conventions have been a standard feature of PRECIS since its beginnings. Apart from their use in teaching, they are regularly used as a convenient shorthand by indexers when discussing or comparing their strings. As they stand, the conventions are not intended to function as computer instructions †, but they are sufficiently explicit to serve as entry generation instructions if an agency does not have access to a computer and intends to produce its indexes manually.

Some of these conventions have already been used in previous chapters. For example, each term in the strings seen earlier was preceded by its *role operator* written between parentheses. An operator has various functions. It specifies the role of the following term, and this in its turn determines:

(a) The order in which the terms should be written in the string;

(b) The order and positions of terms in the printed entries;

(c) The typeface of the term when it appears in the qualifier or display. Remember that leads are always printed in the same distinctive form (for example, roman bold).

(d) The punctuation mark that should *precede* the term when it appears in the qualifier or display.

All these points are illustrated later by specific examples. Do not be over-concerned at this stage about the exact meanings of the operators

---

† Nevertheless, a PRECIS program developed at the library school of Loughborough University (England) allows students to use the standard conventions when entering their strings on-line. These are then translated automatically into full manipulation strings.

in the examples that follow; these are fully explained in later chapters. Note, too, that these examples have been chosen especially to demonstrate the conventions. They are not offered as indexing models, and it will sometimes be found that the same subject has been treated in more than one way.

Conventions governing the choice of leads, or the deletion of terms from selected parts of an entry

****

√ = Lead
(LO) = Lead only
(NU) = Not up
(ND) = Not down

****

Leads were indicated in earlier examples by adding a tick or check mark over the chosen term, but this is only one of four conventions (listed above) which regulate the appearance or non-appearance of terms in pre-selected positions within an entry. Apart from their status as leads, most terms in a string are *not* accompanied by one of these conventions, which means that they could potentially appear in any position.

√ = Lead

Whether or not a term should appear in the lead is determined entirely by the indexer, not by the system or the computer. Significant or sought terms are usually led, but not diffuse or over-used terms. General decisions concerning leads may be taken within an agency and recorded as policy statements, e.g.

Testing: *Do not lead in the context of a named thing or activity being tested*

Policies of this kind may vary from one agency to another depending on the kind of material being indexed and the community of users served by the index. They are independent of PRECIS as an indexing system. The use of this convention is best explained through an example. The following string:

(1) children
(2) growth

- contains two terms, either or both of which could be considered as potential leads. If you wish to generate leads under both terms, the string should be marked:

(1) children
(2) growth

This will generate the entries:

Children
  Growth

Growth. Children

If for some reason you decide that an entry is *not* wanted under 'growth' the string should be marked:

(1) children
(2) growth

Only the first entry will then be produced.

(LO) = Lead only

This code is used relatively infrequently. It marks a term that should appear in the lead *but in no other part of the entry*. It is then known as a 'lead only' term. It might be used in a case such as the following:

(1) man
(p) eyes (LO)
(2) glaucoma

Note that the term 'eyes' was provided as a useful access point to this subject, but it occurs only as the lead in the second entry. It is strictly redundant in the other two entries.

(NU) = Not up

When a string is written in the list form used in these examples, the words 'up' and 'down' refer to the direction in which the string is being read when terms are selected and assigned to their positions in an entry. The 'Not up' instruction operates only when a *later* term appears in the lead. The term marked 'Not up' may be useful for showing context in entries under earlier terms, but it can be suppressed from entries under later terms if it appears to be redundant. The following string:

(1) man
(p) eyes
(2) glaucoma

- will produce the following entry under 'man':

Man
Eyes. Glaucoma

The choice of 'eyes' as the first term in the display helps to collocate all the entries that relate to the human eye, e.g. its anatomy, injuries, etc. This term may also merit a lead in its own right:

Eyes. Man
Glaucoma

Clearly, however, 'eyes' should be regarded as redundant in the third entry:

Glaucoma. Eyes. Man

- since it is implied by 'glaucoma'. The redundant term can then be suppressed from the final entry, using the 'Not up' instruction:

(1) man
(p) eyes (NU)
(2) glaucoma

This will not affect the entries under 'man' and 'eyes', but the final entry will be different:

Glaucoma. Man

A further complication occurs in the string:

(1) man
(p) eyes (NU)
(2) glaucoma
(2) therapy

— since the extra term, 'therapy', is also marked as a lead. This will generate the entries:

Man
  Eyes. Glaucoma. Therapy

Eyes. Man
  Glaucoma. Therapy

Glaucoma. Man
  Therapy

Therapy. Glaucoma. Man

Note that 'eyes' is then suppressed from *two* of the entries, since the 'Not up' instruction is encountered twice when entries are being generated.

(ND) = Not down

This instruction, which is basically similar to (NU), is used to suppress terms from the entries generated under *earlier* terms. This instruction is rarely needed when indexing in English, but examples are shown later when we deal with the coding of 'Upward-reading substitutes'.

Summary of conventions regulating the appearance of terms in entries

The four conventions considered so far regulate the appearance or suppression of selected terms:

1. *Lead terms* are indicated by ✓. Any term, whether marked as a lead or not, will be assigned to its position within an entry unless it has been suppressed by a definite instruction. This is the 'standard' situation, and is not marked by a special convention.

2. *Not-up terms*, indicated by (NU), are suppressed from entries when *later* terms appear in the lead.

3. *Not-down terms*, indicated by (ND), are suppressed from entries when *earlier* terms appear in the lead.

4. *Lead only*, indicated by the convention (LO) attached to a lead, causes this term to be suppressed from entries under later and also earlier terms. A 'lead only' instruction can therefore be seen as an intersection of the 'not up' and 'not down' instructions. Such a term *must* contain at least one part (focus or difference) marked as a lead — or it should not have been written in the first place.

Substitutes

It is sometimes necessary, for the sake of clarity, to select a set of terms written as separate components in a string, and combine them into a pre-coordinated phrase when a term outside the set appears in the lead. Phrases can be constructed in two ways: either by the use of *connectives* (described below), or by the insertion of a *substitute phrase* into the string. Two forms of substitute are available, and are distinguished by the following conventions:

****

(sub n↑) = Upward-reading substitute: the substitute phrase replaces 'n' earlier terms when a *later* term is in the lead

****

(sub n↓) = Downward-reading substitute: the substitute phrase replaces 'n' later terms when an *earlier* term is in the lead

****

A substitute is never marked as a lead. It must be preceded by an operator to express the role of the phrase as a whole, since this affects the position of the substitute in the printed entry.

Upward-reading substitute (sub n↑)

This phrase suppresses and replaces 'n' earlier terms when an entry is generated under a later term. The substitute is indicated by the convention shown above, except that 'n' would be replaced by a number within the range 1 to 9 which shows how many terms should be replaced. The set of terms indicated by the number are known as the *substitute block*. Upward-reading substitutes are always ignored when a string is read in a 'downward' direction, and they are therefore marked 'Not down' in the full manipulation code. These substitutes carry the following print instructions:

	Print when reading 'down' — i.e. when earlier term(s) in lead?	Print in lead?	Print when reading 'up' — i.e. when later term(s) in lead?
(sub n↑)	*NO*	*NO*	*YES* — substitute replaces 'n' earlier terms

The need for an upward-reading substitute would occur if a lead is needed under 'planning' when indexing a document on 'Planning of agricultural research'. The following string does *not* include a substitute:

```
*(2) agriculture
 (p) research
 (2) planning
```

- and would generate the entries

Agriculture
  Research. Planning
*Planning. Research. Agriculture

The second of these entries is ambiguous, and the ambiguity can be attributed to a blurring of the one-to-one relationships considered earlier. The reader cannot immediately tell whether 'research' was being conducted into 'planning' or 'agriculture'. A stronger bond between 'research' and 'agriculture' can be established by inserting an upward-reading substitute into the string:

```
         (2) agriculture  ]
         (p) research     ]—— substitute block
(sub 2↑) (2) agricultural research
         (2) planning
```

This phrase replaces the first two terms in the string when the later term, 'planning', appears in the lead:

Planning. Agricultural research

The first entry will not be affected, since an upward-reading substitute is 'invisible' when the string is read in a downward direction.

A similar situation occurs when indexing the subject 'Forecasting population growth in Europe'. To avoid ambiguity when the final term, 'forecasting', appears in the lead, the indexer should insert a substitute as follows:

---

* Following a standard convention in linguistics, an asterisk (*) is used consistently throughout the *Manual* to mark an example that is regarded as invalid or unacceptable

```
          (0) Europe
          (1) population  ]── substitute block
          (2) growth      ]
(sub 2↑)  (2) population growth
          (2) forecasting
```

This will generate the entries:

Europe
  Population. Growth. Forecasting

Population. Europe
  Growth. Forecasting

Forecasting. Population growth. Europe

Without the substitute, the string would have produced the potentially ambiguous entry:

*Forecasting. Growth. Population. Europe

Downward-reading substitute (sub n↓)

The need for a substitute arose in the examples above because a later term, marked as a lead, referred to a set of earlier terms rather than the next adjacent earlier term. The same situation can arise when a string is read in the other direction. Two or more terms which should be written as separate elements in the string, each a potential lead preceded by its own operator, should nevertheless be combined into a phrase to express a single idea when an *earlier* term appears in the lead. This is handled by a *downward-reading substitute*. Except for a change in the direction of the arrow, these are indicated by the same convention as upward-reading substitutes, and they are subject to similar conditions:

(a) they are never marked as leads;

(b) they are not printed in entries generated under later terms (they are therefore marked (NU) in the full manipulation code).

These substitutes carry the print instructions shown as a grid at the top of the next page.

The need for a downward-reading substitute would occur when indexing a subject such as 'Pollution of the atmosphere by car exhaust

(sub n↓)	Print when reading down - i.e. when earlier term(s) in lead ?	Print in lead ?	Print when reading up - i.e. when later term(s) in lead ?
	YES (substitutes for 'n' later terms)	*NO*	*NO*

fumes'. This would be expressed by the following string:

```
           (1) atmosphere
           (2) pollution $v by $w of
  (sub 2↓) (3) car exhaust fumes
           (1) cars                ]
           (p) exhaust fumes       ]—— substitute block
```

- which would generate the following entries †:

Atmosphere
  Pollution by car exhaust fumes

Pollution. Atmosphere
  By car exhaust fumes

Cars
  Exhaust fumes. Pollution of atmosphere

Exhaust fumes. Cars
  Pollution of atmosphere

'Car exhaust fumes' forms a single semantic unit from the viewpoints of 'atmosphere' and 'pollution', and this unity is conveyed by the substitute. But the phrase then amounts to a mini-subject which should be analysed into separate terms, each a potential lead in its own right. These terms, preceded by their own operators, were therefore written as a *block* below the substitute. In fact, the operators in the block are those that would have been used to index 'Car exhaust fumes' as a separate topic, with no reference to atmospheric pollution:

(1) cars
(p) exhaust fumes

This would generate the entries:

---

† Do not worry at this stage about the unfamiliar format of some of these entries.

Cars
  Exhaust fumes

Exhaust fumes. Cars

- which collocate exactly with those produced from the substitute block in the earlier string. The block below a downward-reading substitute is, in a sense, a string-within-a-string.

Combinations of substitutes

The need for both an upward- and downward-reading substitute can occur within the same string. This might arise when indexing a subject such as 'Effects of cigarette smoking on athletic performance', which would be expressed by the string:

```
          (1) ✓athletes       ]
          (p) ✓performance    ]— substitute block
(sub 2↑)  (1) athletic performance
          (s) effects $v of $w on
(sub 2↓)  (3) cigarette smoking
          (1) ✓cigarettes     ]
          (2) ✓smoking        ]— substitute block
```

This string would generate the entries:

Athletes
  Performance. Effects of cigarette smoking

Performance. Athletes
  Effects of cigarette smoking

Cigarettes
  Smoking. Effects on athletic performance

Smoking. Cigarettes
  Effects on athletic performance

Blank substitutes

The convention 'Not up' was used in an earlier example to delete the term 'eyes' from the entry when 'glaucoma' appeared in the lead, on the grounds that users who enter the index at 'glaucoma' would regard 'eyes' as redundant. The 'Not up' instruction effectively deletes a single redundant term, but it cannot always be applied successfully if two or more consecutive terms are regarded as redundant and should be deleted. This could occur when indexing a 'Visitor's guide to Stonehenge', which might be expressed in the string:

(0) Wiltshire
(1) henge monuments
(q) Stonehenge
(6) visitors' guides

It could be argued that the user who enters the index at 'Stonehenge' already knows that this unique henge monument is located in Witshire; consequently, the first and second terms could be deleted from the entry under 'Stonehenge'. If we tried to achieve this by marking these terms 'Not up', e.g.

*(0) Wiltshire (NU)
(1) henge monuments (NU)
(q) Stonehenge
(6) visitors' guides

- we would generate the entries:

Wiltshire
Henge monuments: Stonehenge — *Visitors' guides*

*Henge monuments
Stonehenge — *Visitors' guides*

Stonehenge
— *Visitors' guides*

This successfully deletes the redundant term from the 3rd entry, but it also inadvertently removes the qualifier, 'Wiltshire', from the entry under 'henge monuments', which means that this entry will no longer collocate with those produced for more general works on 'The henge monuments of Wiltshire', e.g.

Henge monuments. Wiltshire

The desired entries can be achieved, however, by inserting a *blank substitute* into the string: that is, a substitute containing no data that nevertheless replaces 'n' other terms elsewhere in the string:

(0) Wiltshire
(1) henge monuments
(sub 2↑) (1)
(q) Stonehenge
(6) visitors' guides

This will generate the entries:

Wiltshire
Henge monuments: Stonehenge — *Visitors' guides*

Henge monuments. Wiltshire
  Stonehenge — *Visitors' guides*

Stonehenge
  — *Visitors' guides*

General notes on substitutes

1. Note that a substitute is needed *ONLY* if a lead is marked —
— on a later term in the case of upward-reading substitutes;
— on an earlier term for downward-reading substitutes.

2. Two kinds of substitute have been encountered in practice:
(a) A phrase inserted into a string to assist understanding or avoid ambiguity when a later or earlier term appears in the lead (as in the examples above). We might call these *logically necessary substitutes*.
(b) A phrase introduced to improve the 'style' of some entries, even though they would not be misleading or ambiguous without the substitute. This would apply to a string such as:

```
          *(1) cars
           (p) doors
(sub 2↑)(1) car doors
           (2) painting
```

— which would generate the entries:

Cars
  Doors. Painting

Doors. Cars
  Painting

*Painting. Car doors

We might refer to these as *stylistic substitutes*. As a matter of general policy, stylistic substitutes should be avoided as far as possible. They usually involve subjective judgements which can vary from one indexer to another and therefore give rise to inconsistencies. Consequently, the subject above should be handled by the simpler string:

```
(1) cars
(p) doors
(2) painting
```

This would generate an unambiguous final entry:

Painting. Doors. Cars

The first two entries would remain the same.

Connectives

Substitutes were introduced into the strings above to ensure that concepts expressed by separate terms at one point in a string could be brought together and printed as a phrase in an entry produced under another term. All these substitutes involved some kind of structural change to the terms in the string, so that 'athletes', for example, was replaced by its adjectival form in the substitute 'athletic performance'. In many cases, however, this kind of change is quite unnecessary — a satisfactory phrase can be constructed out of the elements in a string by linking them together with prepositions. When this is feasible, there is no need to write a substitute. The phrase can be constructed more easily, and from a shorter string, by using the connective codes.

****

$v = Downward-reading connective

****

$w = Upward-reading connective

****

These are not strictly 'conventions' in the sense used earlier. They belong instead to the class of *secondary manipulation codes* (see Appendix 1), and they are written in the forms shown above in machine-readable strings. A connective code does not indicate the syntactical role of its following term, but introduces an adjunct (usually a preposition) which plays a part in phrase construction. Phrases can be constructed when reading either 'up' or 'down' a string, and each code contains a useful mnemonic: the letter 'v' in the code '$v' forms a *downward-pointing* arrow; the letter 'w' contains an embedded *upward-pointing* arrow. The instructions associated with these codes are summarised as a table at the top of page 36.

The need for an upward-reading connective would arise when indexing the subject 'Radioactive materials as constituents of water'. A string which lacks a connective:

	Print when reading down — i.e. when *earlier* term(s) in lead ?	Print when reading up — i.e. when *later* term(s) in lead ?
$v	*YES*	*NO*
$w	*NO*	*YES*

General instructions:

1. A full phrase linked by connectives consists of: (i) the term to which the connective is attached; (ii) the connective; (iii) the next adjacent term (up or down) in the string. This phrase is printed with no intervening punctuation. Only the first word has an upper case initial (except for proper names).
2. When the term to which the connective is attached appears in the lead:
   (i) the display *can* begin with a connective;
   (ii) the qualifier *never* begins with a connective.
3. When both connectives are attached to the same term, they must be written in the order $v before $w.

---

*(1) water
(p) constituents
(q) radioactive materials

- would generate three entries (assuming, for the sake of demonstration, that 'constituents' was marked as a lead):

Water
  Constituents: Radioactive materials

Constituents. Water
  Radioactive materials

*Radioactive materials. Constituents. Water

The first and second entries convey their meanings correctly and without difficulty. In the first entry, the relationship between 'constituents' and 'radioactive materials' is expressed by the colon used in its usual sense to mean *being* or *kind of*; this is generated automatically by the operator 'q'. The close relationship between 'water' and 'constituents' is conveyed in the second entry by the two-line format; both terms are printed in the heading, so they are separated from 'radioactive materials'. The third entry is ambiguous, however; the reader cannot easily tell whether the radioactive materials are constituents of water or the other way round. This ambiguity can be removed by inserting an upward-reading connective:

(l) water
(p) constituents $w of
(q) radioactive materials

The first and second entries will remain the same, since a preposition introduced by $w is invisible when entries are generated under earlier terms. The final entry will be different, however:

Radioactive materials. Constituents of water

Note that the qualifier does *not* begin with 'of' when constituents is in the lead (see General instruction 2 in the Table above).

A subject such as 'Evaluation of the professional education of nurses' resembles in some respects those used earlier to demonstrate substitutes, since it contains an action term, 'evaluation', which takes as its object a set of two earlier terms, 'professional education' and 'nurses'. Unless the bond between these two terms is conveyed to the user by adding a substitute or connective, the entry under 'evaluation' is likely to be ambiguous. A string which lacks either a connective or substitute, i.e.

*(1) nurses
(2) professional education
(2) evaluation

- will generate the entries:

Nurses
Professional education. Evaluation

Professional education. Nurses
Evaluation

*Evaluation. Professional education. Nurses

The first and second entries convey their meanings clearly enough, but the third could be misinterpreted as 'Evaluation *as part of* the professional education of nurses'. The correct interpretation can be suggested by using a $w connective to bind 'professional education' more closely to 'nurses' in the final entry:

(1) nurses
(2) professional education $w of
(2) evaluation

The first and second entries will be unchanged, but the third entry will appear as:

Evaluation. Professional education of nurses

The code $v is used in practice less often than $w, and it frequently occurs in conjunction with $w: that is, both connectives are attached to the same term. This combination would typically be used when stringing a subject such as 'Industrial exploitation of natural resources':

(1) nátural resources
(2) exploitation $v by $w of
(3) industries

— which leads to the entries:

Natural resources
  Exploitation by industries

Exploitation. Natural resources
  By industries

Industries
  Exploitation of natural resources

Note that the display in the second entry begins with the connective 'by', whereas 'of' is *not* printed as the first word in the qualifier.

General notes on connectives and substitutes

1. Substitutes and connectives serve the same general purpose: they link together closely bound concepts that should be presented as a set when some other term is in the lead. From the viewpoints of indexer effort and string complexity, connectives are far more economical than substitutes, and they should be preferred whenever possible. The difference can be demonstrated quite simply by writing two strings for the subject 'Monitoring pesticide hazards to children's health', first using substitutes:

(1) children
(p) health
(sub 2↑) (1) health of children
(3) hazards
(sub 4↑) (3) hazards to health of children
(q) pesticides
(2) monitoring

— and then connectives:

(1) children
(p) health $w of
(3) hazards $w to
(q) pesticides
(2) monitoring

Both strings will generate exactly the same entries:

Children
Health. Hazards: Pesticides. Monitoring

Health. Children
Hazards: Pesticides. Monitoring

Hazards. Health of children
Pesticides. Monitoring

Pesticides. Hazards to health of children
Monitoring

Monitoring. Pesticides. Hazards to health of children

Connectives were more effective in this case because the required phrases consist of terms selected from the string and linked by prepositions without changing their order or spellings. This is not always possible, in which case a substitute has to be used.

2. Connectives, like substitutes, are extremely useful devices, but they should not be used unnecessarily. Most entries are sufficiently clear without the use of either connectives or substitutes provided that terms in the string are set down correctly in a context-dependent order. These mechanisms sometimes appear to improve the 'style' of an entry, especially when the same code, e.g. '$w', is attached to consecutive terms (such as 'health' and 'hazards' in the example above). The program then 'runs through' a sequence of connectives and generates a relatively long phrase. We should remember, however, that our job is to produce intelligible index entries, not to write prose or tell a story.

3. In most of the examples above, the need to introduce an upward-reading substitute or connective arose because the string contained the name of a *second action*: that is, an action such as 'planning', 'forecasting' or 'monitoring' which takes as its object a *set* of earlier terms (including an earlier action). Second actions are considered again later, but it should be noted at this point that any string

containing a second or subsequent action, introduced by the operator '2' and marked as a lead, is likely to need a substitute or connective.

Conventions indicating type of term

****

Term type	*Character in 9th position of manipulation code*	*Convention*
Common noun	a	-
Proper name of 'class-of-one'	c	c
Place name	d	d

****

When manipulation coding is covered in a later chapter it will be seen that the final (9th) position in the primary code is occupied by one of three letters: 'a', 'c' or 'd'. These indicate the type of term that follows, and they are used to distinguish between:

Common nouns (term code 'a')

Proper names ('c' for names other than places; 'd' for place names).

A proper name identified by 'c' or 'd' can be accompanied by one or more special secondary codes that regulate the typography of the coded part and its status as a filing element, ensuring that proper names appear in the subject index in the same form as in a name index. These codes are listed as a table below:

Typographic code	*Instruction*
$e	Non-filing part in italic preceded by comma
$f	Filing part in italic preceded by comma
$g	Filing part in roman, no preceding punctuation
$h	Filing part in italic preceded by full point
$i	Filing part in italic, no preceding punctuation

We would need to use a term convention and one of the typographic codes when indexing a biography of Queen Elizabeth II. This would be expressed in the string:

✓c
(1) Elizabeth II $f Queen of Great Britain
(6) biographies

Note that the term coded 'c' is written above the term, in the same way the ✓ is used to indicate a lead. This string would generate the entry:

Elizabeth II, *Queen of Great Britain*
— *Biographies*

The special typographic code, $f, generated a comma after 'Elizabeth II' and caused 'Queen of Great Britain' to be printed in italic, following the standard practice set down in cataloguing codes. Other examples will be introduced later; it is sufficient, for the present, to know that proper names should be identified. *No special convention is used to indicate common nouns.*

Theme interlinks

The subject of a document can usually be perceived and expressed as a single theme, even though the string can sometimes appear quite complicated. Some documents, however, cover two or more distinct topics. The indexer can handle these by writing a separate string for each, or these *coordinate themes* can be stacked into a single string and distinguished by the *theme interlink codes.*

****

(x) = First element in a coordinate theme

(y) = Second or subsequent element in a coordinate theme

(z) = Element common to all themes

****

These characters are listed among the *primary codes* in the schema shown as Appendix 1, and they occupy the second position in the full manipulation code. Every term in a string must be preceded by one of these codes when input is prepared for the computer. For the present, single-theme strings (such as all the examples used so far) will not be indicated, and the theme interlinks will be added to a string only when it contains two or more topics. The codes 'x', 'y' and 'z' will then be written between parentheses in front of the operators.

We could use these codes to deal with a document on two separate themes, 'Freezing of cod' and 'Drying of herrings'. This can be expressed in a single string as follows:

Theme 1 — (x) (1) cód — *1st element in Theme 1*
(y) (2) fŕeezing — *subsequent element in Theme 1*

Theme 2 — (x) (1) hérrings — *1st element in Theme 2*
(y) (2) dŕying — *subsequent element in Theme 2*

Each theme will then be treated as a separate string, leading to the entries:

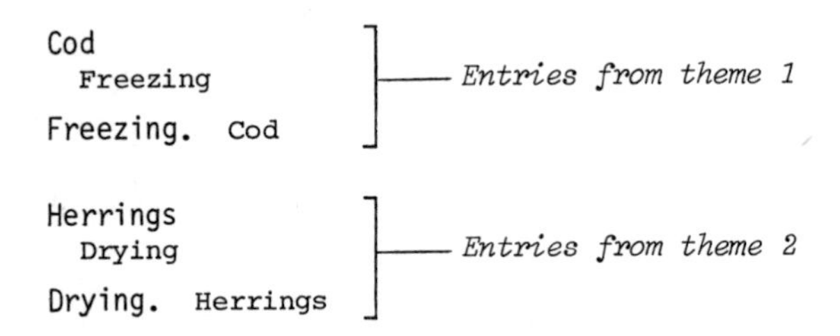

Elements common to *all* the coordinate themes in a string can be introduced at the beginning and/or end of a string, but *not* in the middle of a string. If a document deals with 'Beekeeping', and (in a separate part) 'The marketing of honey', and both occurred in 'Nova Scotia', this could be expressed in the string:

(z) (0) Nóva Scotia — *Common element*
(x) (2) béekeeping — *Element of theme 1*
(x) (1) hóney — *Elements of theme 2*
(y) (2) márketing

The code (z) which precedes 'Nova Scotia' indicates that this term is common to both the coordinate themes which follow. If a common element is marked as a lead, it will automatically generate as many entries as there are terms coded (x) in the string. The string above will therefore be treated for practical purposes as though it consists of two strings, i.e.

(0) Nova Scotia
(2) beekeeping

AND

(0) Nova Scotia
(1) honey
(2) marketing

— which would generate the entries:

Nova Scotia
  Beekeeping

Beekeeping. Nova Scotia

Nova Scotia
  Honey. Marketing

Honey. Nova Scotia
  Marketing

Marketing. Honey. Nova Scotia

Remember that when two headings are identical, one of them is deleted and their displays are organised as an alphabetical column. Consequently, the entries under 'Nova Scotia' seen above will be reduced in the final output to:

Nova Scotia
  Beekeeping
  Honey. Marketing

Common terms would occur at both the beginning and end of the string when indexing a 'Report on the costs of beekeeping *and* the costs of marketing honey in Nova Scotia'. This can be handled by the string:

(z)(0) Nova Scotia ——— *Common term 1*
(x)(2) beekeeping ——— *Element of theme 1*
(x)(1) honey] ——— *Elements of theme 2*
(y)(2) marketing]
(z)(p) costs ——— *Common term 2*
(z)(6) reports ——— *Common term 3*

- which will generate the entries:

Nova Scotia
  Beekeeping. Costs — *Reports*

Beekeeping. Nova Scotia
  Costs — *Reports*

Costs. Beekeeping. Nova Scotia
  — *Reports*

Nova Scotia
  Honey. Marketing. Costs — *Reports*

Honey. Nova Scotia
  Marketing. Costs — *Reports*

Marketing. Honey. Nova Scotia
  Costs — *Reports*

Costs. Marketing. Honey. Nova Scotia
  — *Reports*

'Nova Scotia' again occurs as part of a common heading, and deletion will therefore lead to the output:

Nova Scotia
  Beekeeping. Costs — *Reports*
  Honey. Marketing. Costs — *Reports*

The term 'costs' also occurred as a common element marked as a lead, but the qualifiers are different when this term appears in the lead, so deletion does not take place.

EXERCISES (For answers, see Appendix 4, p 321)

Exercise 1

Add conventional marks to the terms in the following strings to generate the entries in the right hand column.

Example:

(1) buildings ✓
(p) heating systems ✓
(2) installation
	Buildings
	  Heating systems. Installation
	
	Heating systems. Buildings
	  Installation

(a)	(1) children
	(2) mental development
	(2) assessment
		Children
		  Mental development. Assessment
		
		Mental development. Children
		  Assessment

(b)	(0) France
	(p) Paris
	(1) art galleries
		France
		  Paris. Art galleries
		
		Paris
		  Art galleries
		
		Art galleries. Paris

(c)	(0) Cornwall
	(1) castles
	(q) Pendennis Castle
	(6) visitors' guides
		Cornwall
		  Pendennis Castle — *Visitors' guides*
		
		Castles. Cornwall
		  Pendennis Castle — *Visitors' guides*
		
		Pendennis Castle. Cornwall
		  — *Visitors' guides*

Exercise 2

Write out the entries (in the standard format) that would be generated by the following strings. Unmarked terms do not appear as leads.

Example:

(0) ✓India (1) ✓urban regions (p) ✓population (2) forecasting	India Urban regions. Population. Forecasting Urban regions. India Population. Forecasting Population. Urban regions. India Forecasting

---

(a)
(1) ✓coal
(2) ✓mining
(sub 2↑) (2) coal mining
(2) ✓operations research

(b)
(1) ✓films
(2) ✓indexing $w of
(2) ✓automation

(c)
(z) (1) ✓offices
(x) (p) ✓electronic equipment
(y) (2) maintenance
(x) (p) ✓stationery
(y) (2) ✓purchasing

4. Differencing

Before we consider how the terms in a string are interrelated we need to look more closely at the terms themselves. In some examples in the previous chapter the indexing terms consisted of more than one word, such as 'henge monuments' and 'professional education'. We can write a *compound term* of this kind in natural language order if we wish to generate a lead under the first word only, or if we decide that no part of the term should appear in the lead. In many cases, however, terms of this kind raise the question: 'How can we serve the user who searches for this topic under the second (or later) word in the term ?'. When dealing with 'professional education', for example, how do we provide access under 'education' ?

Compound terms have been recognised for a long time as a source of problems in indexing. In traditional subject heading lists some multiword headings are artificially inverted; for example, 'Libraries, University and college'. This can lead to difficulties and inconsistencies when other headings are not inverted, e.g. 'School libraries'. The problem is largely avoided in indexing languages which prefer single-word terms (e.g. 'schools' and 'libraries'), perhaps as keywords intended for post-coordinate searching, but another kind of problem can then arise. When a compound term is factored into separate words, each expressed as a noun, the meaning of the original term is sometimes lost. For example, 'cruise missiles' is not clearly expressed by a combination of 'cruises' (or 'cruising') and 'missiles'.

PRECIS has tried to find answers to these problems. Terms in PRECIS are always printed in their natural language order — there are *no* inverted headings. Nevertheless, the indexer can provide access under any of the words in a compound term without distorting the meaning of the term as a whole. This is achieved by a technique known as *differencing*.

Distinction between focus and difference

In order to understand this technique, we need to consider how the words in a compound term (its building blocks) are related one-to-another to express a particular idea. A distinction is made in PRECIS between the *focus* and the *difference*. All terms contain a focus; this is the part of a term which indicates the general *class* of things, properties or events to which the term as a whole refers. The focus is always expressed as a noun. In a one-word term, such as 'timber' or 'milk', the word *is* the focus. The focal noun may also be accompanied by one or more differences. These words refer to attributes possessed by *some* (but not all) members of the focal class, and they therefore indicate (or *differentiate*) particular kinds or species of the focus. For example, we can indicate a special kind of 'milk' by adding the difference 'powdered', giving the compound term 'powdered milk'. Differences are frequently adjectives, as in 'Danish pastry' and 'powdered milk', but other words or phrases can serve the same logical purpose. It is convenient to refer to all of these differentiating words or phrases as 'differences'. They belong to two general types: those which precede the focus *(preceding differences)*, and those printed after the focus *(following differences)*. The distinction between these parts of a compound term is illustrated in the table below; the focus is printed in italic in each case.

Single-word term as focus	Modifying word expressed as an adjective and used as preceding difference	Modifying word or phrase used as following difference
Children	Children's *stories*	*Games* for children
France	French *music*	*Essays* in French

Preceding differences: the 'standard' codes

If the indexer wishes to generate entries under more than one part of a compound term, the parts are written in the input string in the *reverse of natural language order*. Natural language order is then restored by the computer at output. The indexer records certain decisions concerning the form of the term, including the choice of leads, by writing a special instruction code in front of each difference. This technique is best explained through an example. When indexing a document on 'premature babies', it may be decided that entries should be generated under the focal noun 'babies' and also under the whole of the term. This would be achieved by the following codes:

String: (1) ✓babies $21 premature

Entries: Babies
Premature babies

Premature babies

Two points should be noted about these entries:

(a) when the lead contains only part of the term (e.g. the focus 'babies'), the *whole* of the term is printed in the display;

(b) the compound term, 'premature babies', always appears in natural language order in the ouput, although its parts were set down in the order focus-before-difference in the input string.

The entries above were generated in response to, firstly, the *lead* mark over the focus, and, secondly, the *differencing code*, $21, which precedes 'premature' in the string. This code consists of three characters, i.e. the sign ($) which identifies an instruction code, followed by two numbers. The first of these numbers is selected from the grid shown below.

****

First number in standard differencing code

	Space-generating	Close-up
Non-lead	0	1
Lead	2	3

****

The numbers in this table indicate, in a machine-readable form, the result of two decisions which have to be taken when dealing with compound terms:

(1) The indexer must decide whether the difference that follows the code should serve as an access point in the index — that is, should it occur as the *first* word in the lead ? —

— If *YES*, the first figure should be either '2' or '3'
— If *NO*, the first figure should be either '0' or '1'. A non-lead difference will appear in other positions within the entry, and it may also form part of the lead, but it cannot *begin* the lead.

(2) The indexer needs to indicate whether or not a space should be left between the difference and the following part of the term —
— Spaces occur in most adjective-noun combinations in English, e.g. 'hair brushes', 'soup spoons' and 'dining rooms', in which case the first number in the code should be either '0' or '2';
— The same relationship between a focus and its difference also occurs in single-word compounds such as 'toothbrushes', 'teaspoons' and 'bedrooms', including hyphenated words such as 'arc-welded' (as in 'arc-welded girders'). These *close-up differences* can be handled in the same way as adjectives. They would be indicated by the choice of '1' or '3' as the first figure in the code.

If these decisions are related to the example above:

(1) b✓abies $21 premature

— it can be seen that the figure '2' in the differencing code calls for a space between the words 'premature' and 'babies', and it also marks 'premature' as a lead difference.

Second number in the differencing code: levels of differences

This number indicates the *level* of a difference, also referred to as its *distance from the focus*. It indicates whether the difference —

— *directly modifies the focus*, in which case it functions as *first level difference* and is identified by the figure '1';

— *modifies some other difference* but does not refer directly to the focus, in which case it would have a distance of more than one, and the indexer would write the appropriate figure within the range 2 to 9.

The notion of *levels of differences* is illustrated in the diagram below, which shows the analysis of the compound term 'quick-frozen peas'. The words are written in natural language order:

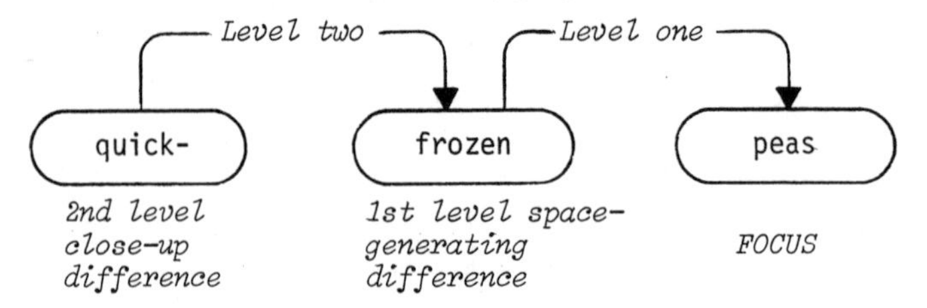

This shows that the adjective 'frozen' refers directly to the focus: we would regard 'frozen peas' as a logical subclass of 'peas'. The adjective 'quick', however, does not relate directly to the focus (these are not 'quick peas'), but refers instead to the first level difference 'frozen'. It therefore functions as a *second level difference*. If we wish to generate leads beginning with each of these words, we should code the input as follows:

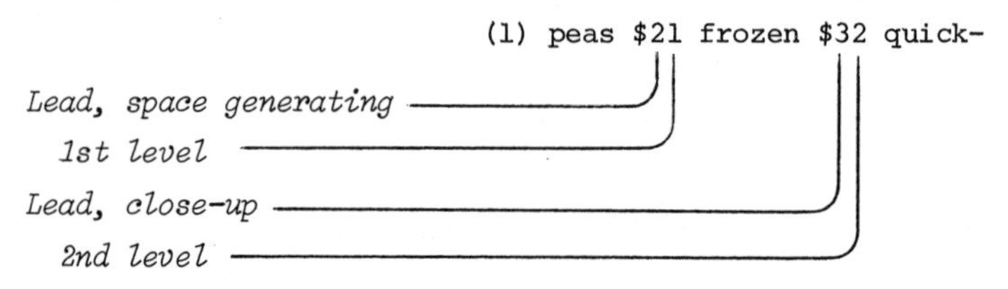

The instructions built into these codes will lead to the production of the following entries:

Peas
  Quick-frozen peas
Frozen peas
  Quick-frozen peas
Quick-frozen peas

The following points should be noted about these entries:

(a) Except when the whole of a differenced term is in the lead (as in the third entry), the full form of the term always appears in the display.

(b) The choice of leads is completely under the control of the indexer. If the indexer decides, for example, that the word 'quick' should not be offered as a lead, the coding would be changed as follows:

(1) peas $21 frozen $12 quick-

The third entry above would not then be printed; the other two entries would be unaffected. Further examples of differenced terms (becoming progressively more complex) are illustrated below.

The subject 'skimmed milk' is expressed by a compound term consisting of a focal noun 'milk' and a difference 'skimmed'. The stages in decision-making could be described as follows:

— It is decided that both words should function as access points in the index. *This reduces the choice of first number to '2' or '3'.*

— A space should appear between the adjective and noun. *The first number must therefore be '2'.*

— Since 'skimmed' refers directly to the focus, 'milk', it must be coded as a *first level difference.*

These decisions would be expressed in the following string and entries:

String: (1) ✓milk $21 skimmed

Entries: Milk
  Skimmed milk

Skimmed milk

A different situation arises when indexing the subject 'partially skimmed milk'. The adjective 'partially' relates to the first-level difference 'skimmed' but not to the focus (we are not concerned with 'partially milk') — it is therefore a *second level difference.* The word 'partially' is somewhat diffuse and has little value as a lead, but it would still be needed in other entries to specify the subject correctly. Each of these words should be followed by a space. These decisions are expressed as follows:

String: (1) ✓milk $21 skimmed $02 partially

Entries: Milk
  Partially skimmed milk

Skimmed milk
  Partially skimmed milk

Since neither of these leads contains the whole of the term, the term is printed in full in both displays.

The same focus occurs again in the compound term 'powdered skimmed milk', but in this case the milk is both 'skimmed' *and* 'powdered', which means that each adjective functions as a first-level difference:

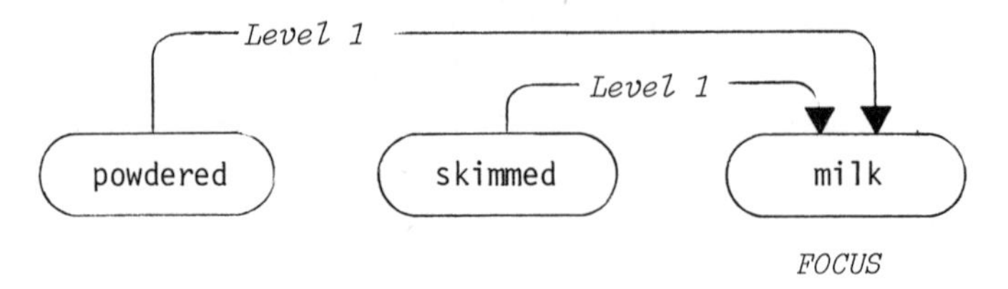

This should be indicated in the string as follows:

String: (1) m̌ilk $21 skimmed $21 powdered

When a term contains two or more differences at the same level, they are written in the order that produces the most 'natural' output †.

Entries: Milk
  Powdered skimmed milk

Skimmed milk
  Powdered skimmed milk

Powdered milk
  Powdered skimmed milk

Note that a first-level difference is always followed immediately by the focus in the lead. Consequently, the lead can never contain the whole of a term if its focus is modified by *two or more differences at the same level*. The display in each of the entries above therefore contains the whole of the term.

A document on 'quick-frozen garden peas' could justify a lead under each of its four components. The term contains one close-up difference ('quick-'), and two space generating differences ('frozen' and 'garden'). Their levels are shown in the diagram below:

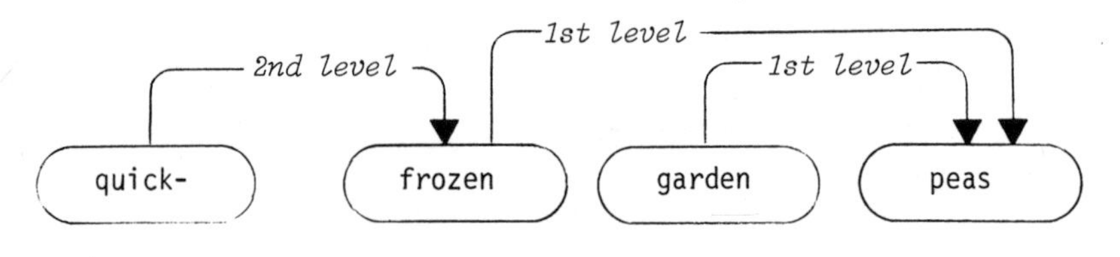

---

† Some general observations on word order in English adjectival compounds are offered in Appendix 2 (p 309).

These decisions should be expressed as follows:

String: (1) peas $21 garden $21 frozen $32 quick-

Entries: Peas
Quick-frozen garden peas

Garden peas
Quick-frozen garden peas

Frozen peas
Quick-frozen garden peas

Quick-frozen peas
Quick-frozen garden peas

A document on 'Arc-welded steel containers' might also call for a lead under each of its four components, but the analysis would then be different. The term contains one close-up difference ('arc-'), and two space-generating differences ('welded' and 'steel'). In this case, however, each element occupies a progressively higher level:

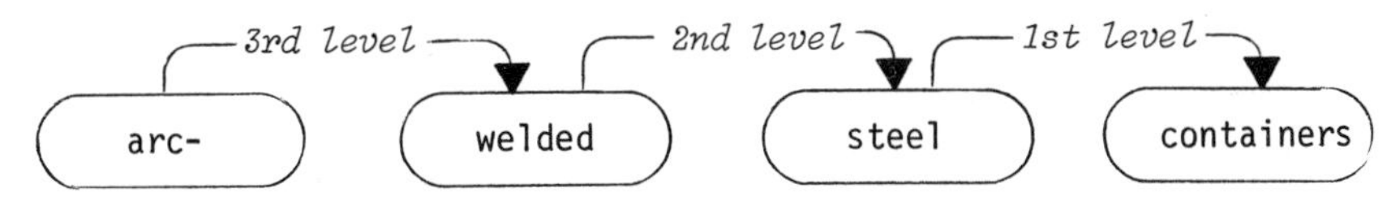

This information would be conveyed in the following string and entries:

String: (1) containers $21 steel $22 welded $33 arc-

Entries: Containers
Arc-welded steel containers

Steel containers
Arc-welded steel containers

Welded steel containers
Arc-welded steel containers

Arc-welded steel containers

The close-up differencing codes

These codes are frequently needed in languages, such as German, where complex ideas are commonly expressed as single words. They can also be used in English whenever the same kind of construction occurs. This applies not only to hyphenated words, such as those in the examples above, but also to single words if these are amenable to factoring into elements which logically represent a focus and difference. This could apply to a term such as 'buttermilk' if leads are needed under the embedded noun 'milk' and also the whole of the term:

String: (1) milk $31 butter

Entries: Milk
  Buttermilk

Buttermilk

Differenced terms in multi-term strings

We have concentrated so far on single terms consisting of foci and one or more differences. Compound terms often occur, however, in multi-term strings, in which case the differencing procedures are completed *before* the remaining terms are assigned to their positions in the entry. This situation occurs quite commonly in PRECIS, and is illustrated by two examples below:

Subject: Storage of powdered milk

String: (1) milk $21 powdered
(2) storage

Entries: Milk
  Powdered milk. Storage

Powdered milk
  Storage

Storage. Powdered milk

Subject: Marketing of powdered skimmed milk in Mexico

String: (0) Mexico
(1) milk $21 skimmed $21 powdered
(2) marketing

Entries: Mexico
  Powdered skimmed milk. Marketing

Milk. Mexico
  Powdered skimmed milk. Marketing

Skimmed milk. Mexico
  Powdered skimmed milk. Marketing

Powdered milk. Mexico
  Powdered skimmed milk. Marketing

Marketing. Powdered skimmed milk. Mexico

The 'Rules of differencing'

Not all the compound terms encountered in documents can be accepted as candidates for differencing. Too much freedom of choice would inevitably lead to a lowering of consistency in the indexing language. For example, some indexers might decide to represent the subject 'Church roof repair' as a compound term, using the differencing procedures:

*(2) repair $21 roof $22 church

— while others would rather express this topic as two terms:

*(1) róofs $21 church
(2) repair

— and others as three terms:

(1) chúrches
(p) róofs
(2) repair

This potential source of inconsistency is regulated in PRECIS by rules which determine whether a complex concept should be expressed as a single term (consisting of a focus and one or more differences), or as two or more separate nouns or noun phrases, each assigned to its own position in a string and introduced by its own operator. These four *Rules of differencing* are logical and straightforward, and indexers quickly learn to spot situations that call for one kind of treatment rather than another. Each rule is explained and illustrated separately below, followed in each case by notes on a converse situation that defines a class of compounds usually retained in their unfactored forms. *Rule 1 is binding in all circumstances.* Rules 2, 3 and 4 are regarded as strong recommendations rather than mandatory instructions, for reasons considered later.

Rule 1. Do not difference a part or property by the entity or action which possesses it.

This means that an indexer faced by a multi-word term, such as 'church roofs', should first consider how the words are related, then recognize that 'roofs' refers to a part, and 'church' (used here as an adjective) refers to its possessing whole. *This concept should therefore be factored into separate elements*, and re-expressed as two nouns:

(1) chúrches
(p) roófs

It should not be differenced as:

*(1) roófs $21 church

Note: The operator 'p', which introduces a part or property, is explained in the next chapter.

The same situation occurs when dealing with a concept such as 'motorcycle noise'. Differencing offers a mechanism for coding this adjective-noun combination as a focus and difference, but the term should nevertheless be factored into separate noun components, on the grounds that 'noise' is a property *possessed* by 'motorcycles'. This subject should therefore be handled as two separate terms:

String: (1) mótorcycles
(p) nóise

Entries: Motorcycles
Noise

Noise. Motorcycles

— *not* as a focus and difference:

*(1) nóise $21 motorcycle

Although this rule states that parts or properties may not be differenced by the names of their wholes, differencing a whole by one or more of its parts, properties or materials is permitted and relatively common. This *converse condition* means that the following terms should be retained in their unfactored forms. The differencing codes can then be used, if necessary, to generate leads under selected parts of the compounds:

— (1) cárs $01 four-door
— (1) pártitions $21 brick
— (1) cúps $21 paper

Rule 2. Do not difference a transitive action by the name of the entity on which the action was performed.

This rule would call for the factoring of a compound term such as 'roof repair', since the focus, 'repair', refers to a transitive action, and the difference, 'roof', refers to its object. The term should therefore be analysed into two components, each expressed (or re-expressed if necessary) as a noun or noun phrase. These components should then be assigned to separate positions in the string, each preceded by its own operator. This means that the compound term considered earlier, 'church roof repair', is subject to two of the differencing rules, and should be expressed as a string of three terms:

String: (1) chu✓rches
(p) ro✓ofs
(2) repair

Entries: Churches
Roofs. Repair

Roofs. Churches
Repair

Individual terms in the string can still be differenced if necessary, using allowed procedures. For example, the subject 'Repair of tiled roofs on churches' (which can hardly be expressed at all as an adjectival phrase), would be indexed as:

String: (1) chu✓rches
(p) ro✓ofs $21 tiled
(2) repair

Entries: Churches
Tiled roofs. Repair

Roofs. Churches
Tiled roofs. Repair

Tiled roofs. Churches
Repair

This rule also calls for the factoring of compound terms such as 'library management', 'book publishing' and 'forest conservation'. In each case the noun refers to an action ('management', 'publishing' and 'conservation'), and the difference refers to the object of the action ('library', 'book' and 'forest'). The following string and entries serve as a model for all three subjects:

String: (1) li✓braries
(2) ma✓nagement

Entries: Libraries
  Management

Management. Libraries

The *converse* of this rule can be stated as follows: *A term should be retained as a compound if the difference refers to a transitive action, and the focus refers to the object of the action.* Differencing codes can then be used, if necessary, to generate leads under selected parts of the term, as in the following examples:

Subject: Cultivated land

String: (1) land $21 cultivated

Entries: Land
  Cultivated land

Cultivated land

Subject: Hand-tooled bindings

String: (1) bindings $21 tooled $32 hand-

Entries: Bindings
  Hand-tooled bindings

Tooled bindings
  Hand-tooled bindings

Hand-tooled bindings

Rule 3. Do not difference an intransitive action by the entity which performs it.

Terms such as 'children's sleep' and 'bird migration' should therefore be factored into separate noun components, since their foci ('sleep' and 'migration') refer to intransitive actions, and the words that act as differences ('children's' and 'bird') identify the performers of the actions. Each component should therefore be written as a separate term in a string and preceded by its own operator:

Subject: Children's sleep

String: (1) children †
(2) sleep

---

† The order of terms in strings containing intransitive actions is explained in Chapter 8.

Entries: Children
  Sleep

Sleep. Children

Subject: Bird migration

String: (1) b✓irds
(2) m✓igration

Entries: Birds
  Migration

Migration. Birds

This rule is associated with the following converse condition: *A term should be retained as a compound if the difference refers to an intransitive action and the focus refers to its performer.* Each of the following terms can therefore be handled as a focus and difference:

Subject: Migrating birds

String: (1) bi✓rds $21 migrating

Entries: Birds
  Migrating birds

Migrating birds

Subject: Hibernating toads

String: (1) to✓ads $21 hibernating

Entries: Toads
  Hibernating toads

Hibernating toads

Terms of this kind cannot be factored without distorting the subject. The following string:

(1) to✓ads
(2) h✓ibernation

— is not invalid, but it does *not* express the subject 'hibernating toads'.

Rule 4. Do not difference a transitive action by its performer (i.e. its agent or instrument).

This means that compound terms such as 'wind damage' and 'computer teaching' should be factored:

Subject: Wind damage to trees

String: (1) trees
(2) damage $v by $w to
(3) wind

Entries: Trees
Damage by wind

Damage. Trees
By wind

† Wind
Damage to trees

Subject: Computer teaching

String: (2) teaching
(s) applications $v of $w in
(3) computer systems

Entries: Teaching
Applications of computer systems

† Computer systems
Applications in teaching

This rule is associated with a converse condition: *A performer can be differenced by the action in which it is (or was) engaged.* In many cases it will be found that this speciates a performer in terms of its purpose, as in the following example:

Subject: Polarizing microscopes

String: (1) microscopes $21 polarizing

Entries: Microscopes
Polarizing microscopes

Polarizing microscopes

Further notes on factoring

The 'Rules of differencing' were developed with two main objectives in mind:

(a) To avoid over-complex terms in strings and entries. As far as possible, every preferred term should refer to a single concept.

---

† The format of entries under performer terms is explained in Chapter 10.

(b) To raise the level of consistency, and hence predictability, in the indexing vocabulary by ensuring that different indexers, or the same indexer on different occasions, apply a common set of criteria when dealing with compound terms. Access to common standards should also reduce the chance of variations due to entirely subjective judgements.

These rules were first developed for PRECIS, but they can be applied to compound terms encountered in any controlled indexing language, whether pre- or post-coordinate, and regardless of subject field. Tests have shown that they are also applicable in different natural languages. The first three rules are incorporated into a British Standard on vocabulary control and thesaurus construction (1), and they also form part of the draft of the equivalent International Standard (2).

As noted earlier, Rules 2, 3 and 4 are regarded as strong recommendations rather than mandatory instructions. Some terms in common use may seem to be subject to these rules, but they should be retained as compounds if their expression as separate elements would distort the subject or hinder comprehension. This would apply to a term such as 'data processing', which should not be factored (invoking Rule 2) into 'processing' (a transitive action), and 'data' (the object of the action). The following classes of terms (listed in BS 5723 and the draft 2nd edition of ISO 2788), should also be retained in their unfactored forms:

1. *Proper names, including terms that incorporate proper names, e.g.*

   European Economic Community

   Freudian errors

2. *Terms in which the difference has lost its original meaning, e.g.*

   Trade winds

   Lawn tennis

3. *Terms containing a difference which suggests a resemblance, as a*

---

(1) British Standards Institution. Guidelines for the establishment and development of monolingual thesauri: BS 5723:1979. London, BSI, 1979

(2) International Organization for Standardization. Guidelines for the establishment and development of monolingual thesauri: ISO 2788. Draft 2nd edition [Published by Unesco as Document PGI-81/WS/15] 1981

simile, to an unrelated thing or event, e.g.

Butterfly valves

Tree structures

Wing nuts

4. *Terms containing syncategorematic nouns.* This covers a small proportion of compound terms that are not amenable to the kind of logical analysis considered so far. One of the elements appears to function as a difference, but it does not, as in earlier examples, specify a subclass of the focal concept; instead, it tends to *deny* membership of that class, to the extent that the terms —

Artificial limbs

Paper flowers

Fossil fishes

Model aircraft

Rubber ducks

— do not refer to species of 'limbs', 'flowers', 'fishes', etc. The noun in each of these cases is described as syncategorematic: it has significance *only* as part of the compound. These terms must therefore be treated at all times as single semantic units. Two special restrictions apply to the terms in this class:

(a) Their parts cannot be analysed as foci and differences. These terms should be input in natural language order, and their apparent foci should not be marked as leads. This will avoid an unsatisfactory sequence of display lines such as:

Ducks
— *Field guides*
Migration
Nesting
* Rubber ducks. Manufacture
etc.

(b) A concept of this kind should not be registered in the thesaurus as a member of the class identified by the apparent focus. For example, 'ducks' and 'rubber ducks' should not be coded as broader and narrower terms belonging to the same category. A reference between these terms may be justified in some cases, but it cannot be based on the hierarchical relationship (explained in Chapter 15).

Following differences

In English, as in other languages, compound concepts are sometimes expressed in the form of prepositional phrases, such as 'Management by objectives' or 'Games for children'. Each of these phrases, like the adjectival constructions considered so far in this chapter, can be analysed into a focus and difference, e.g.

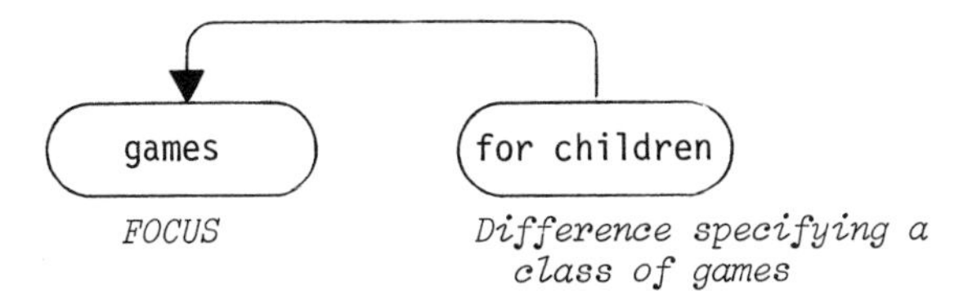

FOCUS — *Difference specifying a class of games*

In a limited number of cases the indexer can apply the techniques described above to terms containing these *following differences:*

Subject: Hospitals for children in London

String: (0) London
(1) children $21 hospitals for

Entries: London
Hospitals for children

Children. London
Hospitals for children

Hospitals for children. London

This must be done with caution, however, and only in special circumstances defined in relatively complex policy statements, intended to ensure that the noun which follows the preposition should not be selected as a lead (using the differencing procedures) *unless it can share the same context(s) as the focus in any circumstances.* This would avoid an analysis such as the following:

Subject: Documents on aircraft in public libraries

String: (1) public libraries
(p) stock
*(q) aircraft $21 documents on

Entries: Public libraries
Stock: Documents on aircraft

*Aircraft. Stock. Public libraries
Documents on aircraft

Documents on aircraft. Stock. Public libraries

For the sake of control and simplicity it is recommended that terms containing following differences should be input in natural language order, without using the differencing codes. Access from any significant word that follows the focus can then be provided through a *See also* reference extracted from the thesaurus, using techniques described in chapters 15 to 18. For example, a document on 'Games for children' would be indexed as follows:

String: (2) gámes for children
Entry: Games for children

— and this could be supported by a reference such as:

Children
See also
Games for children

Dates as differences

It is often necessary to indicate that a subject has been considered within the confines of a given period. Time expressed as a date span is then regarded as a difference on the grounds that it narrows the interpretation of the concept or concepts involved. Periods of time are preferably expressed numerically rather than verbally, i.e. '1800-1900' rather than 'nineteenth century'. Named periods, such as 'Roman' or 'Renaissance', frequently differ in meaning from country to country, and even from place to place within a country. References from named periods can be made, if necessary, using procedures described on p 224. In cases where no acceptable dates can be established, time spans may be expressed in words, e.g. 'Iron Age' or 'New Stone Age', but these should be regarded as exceptions.

****
$d = Date as a difference
****

Dates are introduced by the code $d. This code, followed immediately by the appropriate date, should usually be attached to the latest term in the string that the subject allows without risking a change in its meaning. The extent to which the meaning of an entry is likely to be affected by changing the position of the date can be judged from the following examples:

Subject: Restoration of Rotterdam's buildings after World War 2

String: (0) Rotterdam
(1) buildings
(2) restoration $d 1945-

Entries: Rotterdam
Buildings. Restoration, *1945-*

Buildings. Rotterdam
Restoration, *1945-*

Restoration. Buildings. Rotterdam
1945-

Subject: The restoration of pre-Revolutionary War farmhouses in New England

String: (0) New England
(1) houses $31 farm $d to 1775
(2) restoration

Entries: New England
Farmhouses, *to 1775*. Restoration

Houses. New England
Farmhouses, *to 1775*. Restoration

Farmhouses. New England
to 1775. Restoration

Restoration. Farmhouses, *to 1775*. New England

In the first of these subjects the act of restoration was carried out at a specified time on buildings of any prior date, while in the second topic the farmhouses of a known period were restored at some unspecified time. As seen in these examples, 'open' dates are frequently used, e.g. *1945-* or *to 1775*.

The entries above show the results of two special printing instructions associated with the code $d:

(1) When the term to which the date is attached appears in either the qualifier or display, the date is printed in italic, following a machine generated comma, immediately after the full form of the term.

(2) When the whole of the term to which the date is attached appears in the lead, the date is printed in italic without a preceding comma as the

first element in the display. A date introduced by $d never appears in the lead.

When the term to which a date is attached consists of a focus and one or more differences expressed as words, as in the second example above, the date should be written in the string *after* the verbal differences. This is seen again in the following example:

Subject: History of amphibious military vehicles since 1939

String: (1) vehicles $21 military $21 amphibious $d 1939-

Entries: Vehicles
Amphibious military vehicles, *1939-*

Military vehicles
Amphibious military vehicles, *1939-*

Amphibious vehicles
Amphibious military vehicles, *1939-*

When dates are present in a string such as this, the term 'history' becomes redundant.

A focal noun can sometimes be accompanied by various kinds of data, such as verbal differences, a date, and/or connectives ($v, $w). If all these elements are present at the same time they must be written in the order:

Focus - verbal difference(s) - $d (date) - $v - $w

The presence of a connective following a date can affect the position of the date in certain entries. This occurs in the following example:

Subject: Role of women in English politics, 1919-1939

String: (1) England
(2) politics
(s) role $d 1919-1939 $v of $w in
(3) women

Entries: England
Politics. Role of women, *1919-1939*

Politics. England
Role of women, *1919-1939*

Women. England
Role in politics, *1919-1939*

The meanings of these operators are explained in later chapters. Note that a date which precedes a connective ($v or $w) is transposed automatically to the end of any phrases based on that connective. For example, the first and second entries above contain the phrase 'Role of women, *1919-1939*', not 'Role, *1919-1939*, of women'.

A word of caution concerning dates is justified at this point. The code $d can be used to introduce specific dates down to a single year, e.g.

(0) England
(1) songs $21 popular $d 1913

It is doubtful, however, whether users' interests are really served by such a high level of specificity, remembering that strings which differ only in their dates will generate different display lines under common headings, causing a scatter of closely related materials. It is therefore recommended that commonsense policies concerning dates should be established. Dates should be stated only when they are significant, and the policies should favour the use of *block dates*, such as centuries or important political periods, as much as possible. A string containing a block date can then be used and re-used to index numbers of different documents on particular date spans falling within the block. For example, a block date such as '1919-1939' (the inter-war period) can be used to index several documents covering lesser parts of the span, such as '1920-1930', '1935-1939', etc. Policies of this kind, based on practical experience, have raised the efficiency of PRECIS in a number of agencies, using some of the management techniques described in a later chapter.

Place concepts, as well as time spans, can function as differences, and occur in compounds such as —

(1) coal $21 Welsh

(1) wines $21 Australian

The use of place names as differences is closely related to other roles they can assume, such as environments or key systems. These are therefor considered together in Chapter 9.

Parenthetical differences

In a very few cases, notably in the human sciences, a concept may lack a precise meaning until it has been related to the test or measure used during its observation. For example, a psychologist might regard a term such as 'intelligence' as relatively imprecise unless it has been qualified in some way, as in 'Intelligence *as measured by the Wechsler Scale*'. The noun 'intelligence' is clearly the focus in this phrase, and the words in italic function together as a difference, insofar as they logically narrow the meaning of the focus. However, a phrase of this kind is overlong for use as a lead, and the concept cannot reasonably be expressed in an adjectival form. In this situation, the salient part of the differencing phrase (e.g. 'Wechsler Scale') should be extracted and printed, between parentheses, after the focus. This is handled by the codes $n and $o.

****

$n = Non-lead parenthetical difference

$o = Lead parenthetical difference

****

The need for a lead parenthetical difference might occur in the following case:

Subject: Intelligence of infants as measured by the Wechsler Scale

String: (1) infants
(p) intelligence $o Wechsler Scale

Entries: Infants
Intelligence (Wechsler Scale)

Intelligence (Wechsler Scale). Infants

Wechsler Scale. Intelligence. Infants

The following features of these entries should be noted:

(a) The parentheses in the 1st and 2nd entries were generated automatically in response to the code $o. They were not written in the input string.

(b) The focal noun 'intelligence' is printed in the qualifier when the difference, without the parentheses, appears in the lead.

The code $o marked the parenthetical difference as a lead in the example above. If it had not been needed as a lead, it would have been prefixed by the code $n, e.g.

(p) intelligence $n Wechsler Scale

The 3rd entry above would then be dropped; the 1st and 2nd entries would remain unchanged.

If a parenthetical difference and one or more adjectival differences are used to modify the same focus, the adjectival difference(s) should be written in the string *before* the parenthetical difference:

Subject: Social maturity of children as measured by the Doll's Vineland scale

String: (1) children
(p) maturity $21 social $n Doll's Vineland scale

Entries: Children
Social maturity (Doll's Vineland scale)

Maturity. Children
Social maturity (Doll's Vineland scale)

Social maturity (Doll's Vineland scale). Children

Note that the parenthetical difference remains in the display until *all* other differences are present in the lead.

The measures named in the examples above were marked as differences to indicate their function in narrowing the meanings of their foci. A document on the *use* of one of these measures would call for a different approach, since the measure would then serve as a focus in its own right.

Subject: Use of the Stanford-Binet test in measuring infant intelligence

String: (1) infants
(p) intelligence $w of
(2) measurement $w of
(s) use $v of $w in
(3) Stanford-Binet test

Entries: Infants
Intelligence. Measurement. Use of Stanford-Binet test

Intelligence. Infants
  Measurement. Use of Stanford-Binet test

Stanford-Binet test
  Use in measurement of intelligence of infants

Operators such as 's' and '3', and the format of the final entry, are explained in later chapters.

Grounds for choosing between differences and references

In PRECIS, as in all language systems, the syntactical and categorial aspects overlap to a large extent. The manipulation of a string into entries appears to be a syntactical operation; nevertheless, whenever we deal with a compound term we are concerned with the categorial relations between its parts, notably between the focus (representing a broader concept) and the term as a whole (representing a narrower concept). A genus and its species can be seen as members of the same category, and these terms are frequently organised as a hierarchy in a thesaurus, e.g.

Mammals
  Rodents
    Mice
    Rats
     etc.

In the majority of cases the same kind of hierarchical relationship also holds between the focus of a compound term and the term as a whole. These terms could therefore be organized into equally logical hierarchies:

Milk
  Buttermilk
  Evaporated milk
  Full cream milk
  Powdered milk
  Skimmed milk
   etc.

Such a hierarchy could be assigned to the thesaurus and used as the source of *See also* references. The indexer therefore faces a choice when dealing with a compound term: it can either be handled by making a reference from the focus to the whole term, or it can be differenced. The former approach is recommended in the following circumstances:

1. *The compound term consists of a focus modified by a following difference.* These terms were considered earlier; see the example dealing with 'Games for children' on p 64.

2. *The term contains a syncategorematic noun* — this is defined and illustrated on p 62.

3. *Differencing would lead to an excessive number of display lines under a common heading.* If this reaches the point where the layout is likely to hinder rather than help the user, the indexer should examine the various displays and identify those that begin with a compound term whose focus is in the lead. These can be handled by references. The difference between these approaches is shown in the Table below:

Compounds handled by differencing	*References to compounds*
Boarding schools Administration Buildings Grammar schools Audio-visual aids Discipline Primary schools Activities: Dance Curriculum subjects Libraries Morning assembly Schools Administration Boarding schools. Administration Boarding schools. Buildings Catering services Grammar schools Grammar schools. Audio-visual aids Grammar schools. Discipline Primary schools Primary schools. Activities: Dance Primary schools. Curriculum subjects Primary schools. Libraries Primary schools. Morning assembly Streaming *etc.*	Boarding schools Administration Buildings Grammar schools Audio-visual aids Discipline Primary schools Activities: Dance Curriculum subjects Libraries Morning assembly Schools *See also* Boarding schools Grammar schools Primary schools Schools Administration Catering services Streaming *etc.*

Conclusions

This Chapter covers a number of points that fall within the area of indexing usually known as *vocabulary control*. This applies particularly to the 'Rules of differencing', and also the criteria for recognising terms that should be retained as compounds. Other aspects of vocabulary control occur in later Chapters; for example, Chapter 7 (p 104-106) deals with the choice of singulars *vs* plurals as indexing terms.

Readers familiar with the first edition of the *Manual* will have realised that the general differencing codes described above differ from those in the earlier version. Any of the older codes (based on lower case letters) can be matched by an equivalent in the number-based system, *but not the other way round:*

Old code	*New code*
$h	$01
$i	$21
$k	$02
$m	$22

The new system is more flexible and can be applied to compound terms beyond the scope of the earlier codes — for example, close-up differences, and differences beyond a second level. Other differencing codes, such as $d, $n and $o, remain unchanged. The general principles underlying the technique of differencing are also unaffected — in fact, they have been confirmed through contact with terms encountered in a range of different natural languages.

EXERCISES (For Answers, see Appendix 4, p 322)

Exercise 3

Write inputs for the following compound terms, marking foci as leads where necessary, and using codes to identify differences. Write the entries produced from your strings.

Example: *Term:* 16mm sound films

String: (1) films $21 sound $21 16mm

Entries: Films
16mm sound films

Sound films
16mm sound films

16mm films
16mm sound films

(a) gold coins

(b) English folk songs

(c) one-act plays

(d) pharmacogenetics (*Note:* a lead should be made on 'genetics')

(e) glass-fibre reinforced panels

(f) 17th century manor houses

Exercise 4

Check: (i) the *Rules of differencing* (p 55-61); (ii) the rule concerning terms containing syncategorematic nouns (p 62).
Mark the terms in the list below that should *NOT* be differenced. How should each term be indexed?

(a) decorated porcelain

(b) frog migration

(c) public libraries

(d) toy soldiers

(e) library buildings

5. Dependent elements

****

p = part or property

q = member of quasi-generic group

r = assembly

****

Introduction

We shall now consider how concepts represented by terms (whether simple or compound) should be organised into strings according to their roles as expressed by the operators. The present chapter deals with a group of operators known collectively as *dependent elements* (see the Schema in Appendix 1, p 307). A term introduced by one of these operators is said to 'depend' for its role upon some other term, to the extent that a concept cannot be labelled as a *part* (operator 'p') unless it has been related to another concept which stands as its *whole* and therefore serves as its context. The context-establishing term (e.g. the name of the whole) is always written *earlier* in the string. This means that a *dependent element operator cannot be assigned to the first term in a string* (or the first term in a theme if a string contains more than one theme). If this rule is ignored, the string will be rejected by the computer.

A term introduced by one of these operators, plus the term (or terms) on which it depends for its context, are together known as the *dependent element block*.

Example 1:

Subject: Career prospects of teachers in Indian schools

String: (0) India
(1) schools
(p) teachers
(p) career prospects — *Dependent element block*

Entries generated under terms in a dependent element block always conform to the *standard format* considered earlier. That is to say:

(a) When a term that precedes the block (e.g. 'India') appears in the lead, the terms in the block are printed in their input order in the display:

India
Schools. Teachers. Career prospects

(b) When a term that forms part of the block (e.g. 'teachers') appears in the lead, the earlier term(s) in the block (if any) are assigned to the qualifier, and the later term(s) in the block (if any) are printed in the display:

Schools. India
Teachers. Career prospects

Teachers. Schools. India
Career prospects

Career prospects. Teachers. Schools. India

This standard procedure is not affected by the primary operator assigned to the first term in the block (e.g. 'schools' in the example above). This should be borne in mind when other formats are described in later chapters.

****

Operator 'p' = Part or property

****

A need to distinguish between parts and wholes occurred in the previous chapter. According to the first of the *Rules of differencing*, a compound term (such as 'camera lenses') should be factored into separate noun components on the grounds that the focus (e.g. 'lenses') refers to a part, and the difference (e.g. 'camera') refers to its possessing whole. Each of these concepts should therefore be expressed as a noun, and the name of the part should be introduced by the operator 'p' following the name of its whole in the string.

Terms marked as parts or properties can refer to various kinds of concept:

Example 2: Physical part of a physical thing

Subject: Camera lenses

String: (1) cameras
(p) lenses

Entries: Cameras
Lenses

Lenses. Cameras

Example 3: Abstract property of a thing

Subject: Public accountability of industries

String: (1) industries
(p) public accountability

Entries: Industries
Public accountability

Public accountability. Industries

Example 4: Abstract part of an abstract concept

Subject: Christian mysticism

String: (1) Christianity
(p) mysticism

Entries: Christianity
Mysticism

Mysticism. Christianity

Example 5: Part of an action

Subject: Dental anaesthesia

String: (2) dentistry
(p) anaesthesia

Entries: Dentistry
Anaesthesia

Anaesthesia. Dentistry

Example 6: Property of an action

Subject: Costs of publishing newspapers

String: (1) newspapers
(2) publishing
(p) costs

Entries: Newspapers
Publishing. Costs

Publishing. Newspapers
Costs

Costs. Publishing. Newspapers

The string in Example 1 above ('Career prospects of teachers in schools') contained two consecutive terms introduced by the operator 'p'. This operator can be introduced into a string as often as necessary provided that a running sequence of whole/part relations is maintained, i.e. the work deals with a whole, which has a part or property, which in turn has a part or property, and so on. This condition occurs again in the following topic:

Example 7:

Subject: Strength of bolts in aircraft engines

String: (1) ✓aircraft ———— *whole*
(p) ✓engines ———— *part*
(p) ✓bolts ———— *part of part*
(p) strength ———— *property of part of part*

Entries: Aircraft
Engines. Bolts. Strength

Engines. Aircraft
Bolts. Strength

Bolts. Engines. Aircraft
Strength

When terms introduced by 'p' are written as sequences in this way, you need to ensure that the concepts are, in fact, related successively as part-to-part, etc. The subject 'Engines and wings of aircraft' should not be handled by the string:

*(1) aircraft
(p) engines
(p) wings

— which suggests that 'wings' are parts of 'engines'. The correct stringing of a topic of this kind is explained in the next chapter.

Wholes (identified by a primary operator), followed by parts or properties (identified by 'p') can occur at more than one position in a string. The operator pattern in the string shown below is not unusual:

Example 8:

Subject: Regulation of wheat prices in the Canadian prairie provinces

String: (0) Canada ——————— *whole (location)*
(p) prairie provinces — *part of location*
(1) wheat ——————— *whole (key system)*
(p) prices ——————— *part/property*
(2) regulation ————— *action*

Entries: Canada
Prairie provinces. Wheat. Prices. Regulation

Prairie provinces. Canada
Wheat. Prices. Regulation

Wheat. Prairie provinces. Canada
Prices. Regulation

Prices. Wheat. Prairie provinces. Canada
Regulation

Treatment of implied whole/part relations

The links between wholes and their parts or properties in the strings above represent what might be called *explicit whole/part relationships*. The name of the part or property does not imply the name of the whole according to usual expectations, so it was necessary to name both concepts in the string. For example, a term such as 'engines' does not automatically bring the concept 'aircraft' to mind, nor does 'lenses' imply only 'cameras'; these parts could occur in other contexts, such as 'tractors' and 'microscopes' respectively. In some cases, however, a term refers to a concept that does imply its containing whole, and this *implicit whole/part relationship* is valid in any context. For example, a discipline term such as 'zoology' carries an implied whole/part relationship with 'biology'; 'biology', in its turn, implies a larger area of discourse called 'science'. Similarly, the terms 'arteries' and 'veins' imply, as a containing whole, the concept 'vascular system'. Since these implied whole/part relations are context-independent there would be no point in writing a string such as:

*(2) science
(p) biology
(p) zoology

or

*(1) vascular system
(p) arteries

These relationships can be handled instead by once-for-all references:

Science
See also
Biology

Biology
See also
Zoology

Vascular system
See also
Arteries
Veins

The techniques for assigning these terms to the thesaurus and extracting the necessary references are explained in Chapters 15 to 18.

****
Operator 'q' = Member of quasi-generic group
****

The majority of implied or *a priori* relationships encountered in day-to-day practice involve concepts related as genus and species (broadly, *thing* and *kind*) rather than wholes and parts. This would apply to the link between, say, 'carrots' and 'vegetables' — a carrot may be cooked, frozen, fed to a rabbit or used as a table decoration, and it remains at all times an *a priori* member of a class called vegetables. A document on 'carrots' should therefore be indexed simply as:

(1) carrots

— and its relationship to the broader term should then be handled by a reference extracted from the thesaurus:

Vegetables
See also
Carrots

This reference handles what is called a *pure generic relationship*: one recognised so widely that it can be regarded as context-independent. The same applies to the links between broader and narrower terms such as 'birds/parrots', 'rodents/mice', 'vehicles/aircraft', and countless other genera and their species. Each of these relationships can be seen as a case of *class inclusion*, represented in the diagram:

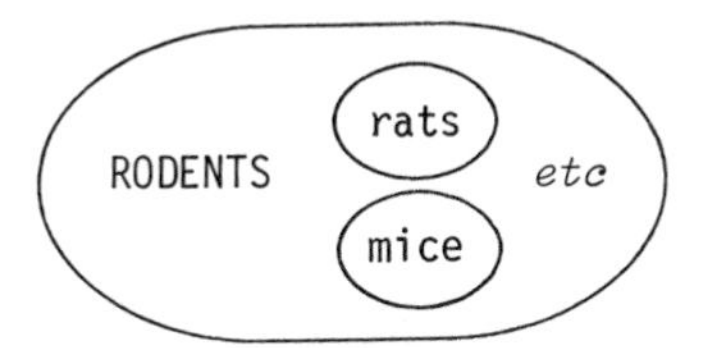

Any of these can be handled by a reference on a once-for-all basis, e.g.

Rodents
See also
Mice
Rats
etc

These pure generic relationships should now be seen in contrast to the link between, say, 'mice' and 'pests'. 'Mice' do not belong in an *a priori* sense to a class called 'pests'; some 'mice' are 'pets', some are 'laboratory animals', and so on. The relationship between 'mice' and each of these broader classes ('pests', 'pets', etc.), is called *quasi-generic*. It is valid only in certain contexts (which means that it is *context dependent*), and it represents a case of *class overlap* (not class inclusion):

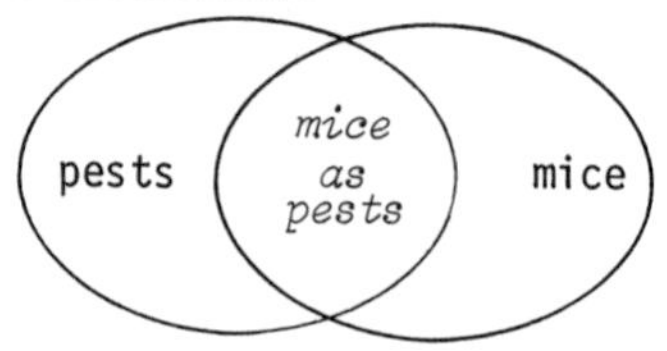

When this relationship occurs in indexing, the broader and narrower terms should both be written in the string, the name of the species following the name of its quasi-generic group. The species should then be identified by the operator 'q', e.g.

(1) pests
(q) mice

The indexer can apply a simple rule-of-thumb test, based on the concepts of 'all' and 'some', to determine whether a pair of terms are linked by a true generic relationship (handled by the thesaurus), or a quasi-generic relationship (expressed by the operator 'q' within the string). The former can be represented by the diagram:

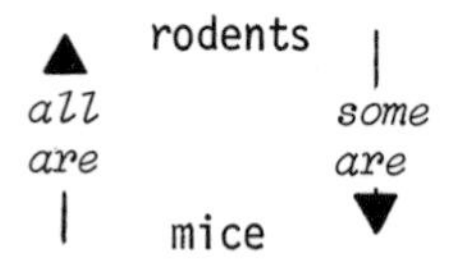

— which indicates that *some* rodents are mice, and *all* mice, regardless of context, are rodents. In contrast, the quasi-generic relationship cannot be expressed as 'all-and-some', but only as 'some-and-some':

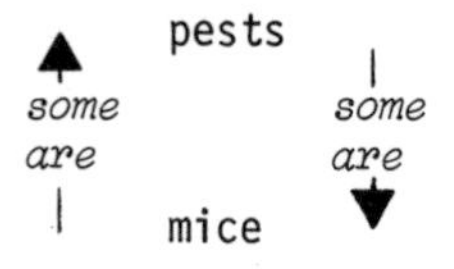

Since this relationship varies with context †, it is handled within the string, as seen in the following examples:

Example 9:

Subject: Control of ants as pests in Australia

String: (0) Australia
(1) pests
(q) ants
(2) control

Entries: Australia
Pests: Ants. Control

Pests. Australia
Ants. Control

Ants. Pests. Australia
Control

Control. Ants. Pests. Australia

Example 10:

Subject: Seaweed as a fertilizer for field crops in Scotland

String: (0) Scotland
(1) field crops
(3) fertilizers
(q) seaweed

Entries: Field crops. Scotland
Fertilizers: Seaweed

Fertilizers. Field crops. Scotland
Seaweed

Seaweed. Fertilizers. Field crops. Scotland

Certain points should be noted about the entries generated from these strings:

— they are all produced through shunting terms through the positions in the standard format considered earlier.

— when the term prefixed by the operator 'q' appears in the display, it is preceded by a colon *except* when it is the first term in the display. This punctuation mark, generated automatically in response to the operator 'q', carries its usual meaning, and indicates a 'kind of' — that

---

† This judgement can change with circumstances. Indexers working within a special field such as 'pest control', where *all* users would tend to regard mice as pests, should use the thesaurus to handle the link between these terms. This must be seen, however, as a special case.

is, 'seaweed' is seen as a *kind of* 'fertilizer' in the context established by the author.

Class names inserted deliberately into strings

It was noted above that the name of a class or genus should not be included in a string that deals with its species if these concepts are linked by the true generic relationship. This general rule is sometimes broken, however, if adding the name of a class can resolve an ambiguity or clarify an otherwise uncertain relationship. Some of the circumstances calling for this procedure are reviewed below.

Homographs (or *polysemes*) are terms that have the same spelling but more than one meaning. For example, 'cranes' can refer to 'birds' or 'lifting equipment'. The easiest way to indicate the intended meaning to the user is to include the name of the class in the string as a context-establishing term.

Example 11a:

Subject: The conservation of cranes in Florida

String: (0) Florida
(1) birds
(q) cranes
(2) conservation

Entries: Florida
Birds: Cranes. Conservation

Cranes. Birds. Florida
Conservation

Conservation. Cranes. Birds. Florida

Note that the class name 'birds' has not been marked as a lead. The link between the genus and the species should still be handled by a reference extracted from the thesaurus:

Birds
See also
Cranes. Birds

Example 11b:

Subject: Safety of cranes (as lifting equipment)

String: (l) lifting equipment
(q) cranes
(p) safety

Entries: Cranes. Lifting equipment
Safety

Safety. Cranes. Lifting equipment

Again, the broader term was not marked as a lead, and access from this concept would be provided by a reference:

Lifting equipment
See also
Cranes. Lifting equipment

Many strings contain the proper names of *classes-of-one*. These may refer to:

— persons, e.g. 'Albert Schweitzer';

— organizations, e.g. 'Canadian National Railway';

— unique but inanimate entities, e.g. 'Mona Lisa' or 'Halley's comet'.

It is not always necessary to context-establish these terms by naming a class within the string; Chapter 3 (p 41) contained a string for a biography of 'Elizabeth II, Queen of Great Britain' which did not include a preceding generic term. These broader terms are frequently included, however, for a number of reasons:

(a) to avoid the need for too many *See also* references to proper names extracted from the thesaurus;

(b) to improve collocation under the broader term. An example of this occurred in Chapter 3 (p 33) in a string dealing with 'Stonehenge';

(c) to avoid the potential ambiguities that could arise when a given class-of-one (e.g. a person) is associated with several subject fields or activities.

The third of these situations would be encountered if we were indexing a work on Schweitzer as a musician but not as a doctor or missionary. The distinction can be made quite simply by adding an appropriate quasi-generic term to the string:

Example 12:

Subject: Schweitzer: the musician

String: (1) musicians
(q) Schweitzer, Albert

Entries: Musicians
Schweitzer, Albert
Schweitzer, Albert. Musicians

In cases such as this the broader term *should* be marked as a lead, partly to offer a higher level of collocation (e.g. under 'musicians'), and also, as noted above, to avoid too many thesaural networks leading to proper names.

The same technique can be used to collocate entries under 'railway services' and 'Canada' when indexing a document on the 'Canadian National Railway', but this raises an additional minor problem. When the class-of-one term appears in the lead, its context-establishing terms are so clearly implied that both are strictly redundant. They should therefore be suppressed from the entry under the proper name, using the *blank substitute* procedure described in Chapter 3 (p 33).

Example 13:

Subject: The Canadian National Railway

String: (0) Canada
(1) railway services
(sub 2↑) (1)
(q) Canadian National Railway

Entries: Canada
Railway services: Canadian National Railway
Railway services. Canada
Canadian National Railway
Canadian National Railway

The name of a quasi-generic group is sometimes inserted deliberately into a string to avoid ambiguous entries, or to clarify the link between a pair of terms that would not be related in a self-evident way without the extra *explaining term*. Some terms are liable to more than one interpretation, yet they are not strictly homographs. This applies to the term 'architecture' in a topic such as 'Teaching architecture in universities'. An initial reaction might suggest the string:

*(1) universities
(p) architecture
(2) teaching

- which produces the following entry under the middle term:

*Architecture. Universities
Teaching

This could be misinterpreted as 'Teaching the architectural design of university buildings'. The correct relationship between 'architecture' and 'universities' can be 'explained' to the user by inserting an extra quasi-generic term, 'curriculum subjects', into the string:

Example 14:

Subject: Teaching architecture (the subject) in universities

String: (1) universities
(p) curriculum subjects
(q) architecture
(2) teaching

Entries: Universities
Curriculum subjects: Architecture. Teaching

Architecture. Curriculum subjects. Universities
Teaching

Teaching. Architecture. Curriculum subjects.
Universities

Once this procedure has been adopted, the name of the quasi-generic group should be inserted, for the sake of consistency, in any parallel situations. For example, 'curriculum subjects' should be used to context-establish terms such as 'mathematics', 'philosophy', etc..

An uncertain relationship could also arise when indexing, say, a survey of 'Soaps on sale in supermarkets'. A string such as the following:

*(1) supermarkets
(p) soaps

- would generate the entry:

*Soaps. Supermarkets

This is not entirely clear; it might refer to a kind of 'heavy-duty' soap intended for scrubbing out supermarkets. Again, we can 'explain' the intended meaning by choosing the name of an appropriate quasi-generic group and inserting this into the string:

Example 15:

Subject: Soaps on sale in supermarkets

String: (1) supermarkets ✓
(p) merchandise
(q) soaps ✓

Entries: Supermarkets
Merchandise: Soaps

Soaps. Merchandise. Supermarkets

Note: The term 'merchandise' has been chosen as a possibly neutral name. These terms can vary from country to country, and the same idea might be conveyed by 'goods' in Britain, but 'stock' in North America.

****

Operator 'r' = Assembly

****

This operator performs a double duty, and introduces two classes of concepts, each of which represents some kind of assembly:

— an *aggregate* refers to an assembly of *the concept named earlier in the string*. This covers terms such as 'herds', 'flocks', etc.

— *associates* refers to a collection of entities that are *independent of, but centred upon, the concept named earlier in the string*. This class is easier to recognise than to explain; it covers terms such as 'friends', 'associates', 'family', 'pupils', etc.

These two classes are explained and illustrated separately below.

Aggregates

An aggregate should be identified only when a document deals specifically with the features of a collection of the entities named earlier in the string; for example, the behaviour of 'wolf packs' rather than 'wolves' in general. An aggregate is classed as a dependent element on the grounds that its meaning (and frequently also its name) depends upon the entity named earlier. This applies particularly to *nouns of assembly*; these can vary considerably depending upon the class of assembled things, e.g. 'birds/*flocks*' but 'geese/*gaggles*', etc.

Example 16:

Subject: Flocks of birds

String: (1) birds
(r) flocks

Entries: Birds
Flocks

Flocks. Birds

The aggregate term was led in this example for the sake of demonstration, but nouns of assembly tend to vary to such an extent that they would not justify marking as leads in most cases.

An entry under a term that follows the name of an aggregate can frequently be improved by inserting a substitute to achieve collocation under the name of the entity (in its adjectival form) rather than the more variable name of the aggregate:

Example 17:

Subject: Behaviour of elephant herds

String: (1) elephants
(r) herds
(sub 2↑) (1) elephant herds
(2) behaviour

Entries: Elephants
Herds. Behaviour

Behaviour. Elephant herds

Associates

This term refers to a group of entities (often people) that is associated with, and context-dependent upon, a concept named earlier in the string, including his/her family, colleagues, circle of friends or pupils, etc.

Example 18:

Subject: Biographies of the wives of Henry VIII

String: (1) Henry VIII $f King of England
(r) wives
(6) biographies

Entries: Henry VIII, *King of England*
Wives — *Biographies*

Wives. Henry VIII, *King of England*
— *Biographies*

It should be noted that 'r' consistently introduces assemblies of associates, not individual members of a circle of associates. A particular wife of Henry VIII would be coded in her own right as a key system:

Example 19:

Subject: Biography of Catherine Parr

String: (1) Catherine Parr $f Queen, consort of Henry VIII, King of England
(6) biographies

Entry: Catherine Parr, *Queen, consort of Henry VIII, King of England*
— *Biographies*

A group of associates can be identified more specifically in some cases, but 'r' would still be used to introduce the term that refers to a general group or assembly:

Example 20:

Subject: The musician friends of Frederick the Great

String: (1) Frederick II $f King of Prussia
(r) friends $w of
(q) musicians

Entries: Frederick II, *King of Prussia*
Friends: Musicians

Musicians. Friends of Frederick II, *King of Prussia*

The proper names in the examples above are written in the forms required by *AACR2*. References from alternative access points (e.g. 'Parr, Catherine', or 'Frederick the Great') could be extracted from the thesaurus. The typographic code '$f' used in examples 18 to 20 was taken from the table on p 40.

The chapter on differencing referred to a special set of problems that can arise if the nouns within a prepositional phrase (such as 'Documents on aircraft' — see p 63) are capable of occupying different contexts. A similar problem can also occur if a group of *associates*, introduced by 'r', occupies one context, and the concept which serves to identify the group occupies a different context. This did not arise in any of the examples seen above; we can reasonably assume that Henry VIII and his wives (example 18) would occur in the same contexts; the same applies to Frederick the Great and his musician friends (example 20). The problem would occur, however, if a document deals with the influence of Bach's pupils on music in north Germany during the latter half of the 18th century — that is, at a time when Bach himself was not alive (he died in 1750). When indexing subjects of this kind, it may be necessary to treat the topic as though it consists of two or more separate themes:

— one theme relates to the set of associates (e.g. the pupils of Bach);

— another theme relates to the concept which is used to identify the associates (e.g. Bach).

These separate themes can then be handled by the theme codes 'x' and 'y' (see p 41-43), or by inserting a substitute, as in the example below:

Example 21:

Subject: Influence of the pupils of J. S. Bach on music in northern Germany during the second half of the 18th century

String:
(0) Germany $01 northern
(2) music $d 1750-1800 $w in
(s) influence $v of $w on
(sub 2↓) (3) pupils of Bach, Johann Sebastian
(1) Bach, Johann Sebastian
(r) pupils

Entries:

Germany
Northern Germany. Music, *1750-1800*. Influence of pupils of Bach, Johann Sebastian

Music. Northern Germany
1750-1800. Influence of pupils of Bach, Johann Sebastian

Bach, Johann Sebastian
Pupils. Influence on music in northern Germany, *1750-1800*

This problem does not arise when 'r' is used to introduce *aggregates*. We can, for example, safely assume that a herd of elephants must logically occupy all the same contexts as its individual members.

Operators 'p', 'q' and 'r' in combination

Some of the examples in this chapter have contained operators 'p', 'q' and 'r' assigned to consecutive terms (see examples 14, 15 and 20). These dependent elements can be mixed in any combination that might be necessary to express a topic, and the order of terms is then determined by the logical dependency that holds between them — it is not prescribed by the operators themselves. The following example contains all three dependent elements forming a sequence:

Example 22:

Subject: Undergraduate members of student committees in universities

String:
(1) universities
(p) students
(r) committees
(sub 2↑) (p) student committees
(p) members
(q) undergraduates

Entries:

Universities
Students. Committees. Members: Undergraduates

Students. Universities
Committees. Members: Undergraduates

Committees. Students. Universities
Members: Undergraduates

Undergraduates. Members. Student committees. Universities

EXERCISES (For Answers, see Appendix 4, p 323-324)

Exercise 5

Assign each of the pairs of terms listed below to one of two categories:

Category 1: Terms linked by *a priori* relationships that could be handled by a reference extracted from the thesaurus;

Category 2: Terms linked by context-dependent relationships such that both terms should be written in a string, the dependent term being introduced by the operator 'q'.

Assume that you are working in a non-specialist agency.

Example: *Term pairs:* Diamond/Carbon; Diamond/Gemstones

Assign to thesaurus Diamond/Carbon

Handle in string Diamond/Gemstones

Term pairs:

(a) Granite/Building materials; Granite/Rocks

(b) Molasses/Syrups; Molasses/Health foods

(c) Jewellery/Gifts; Jewellery/Ornaments

(d) Paintings/Investments; Paintings/Graphic arts

(e) Maps/Documents; Maps/Teaching aids

Exercise 6

Write strings and entries for the following subjects. When selecting primary operators, use (1) to prefix 'thing' concepts, (2) to prefix actions, and (0) to prefix locations.

(a) Leadership in hippie communes

(b) Decision making in management

(c) Prices of skimmed milk in developing countries

(d) Flammability of theatrical safety curtains

Exercise 7

What is wrong with the string shown below ?

```
*(1) bears $21 toy
 (p) eyes $21 glass
 (2) fastening
```

How should this topic be indexed ?

6. Coordinate concepts

****

Operator 'g' = 'Standard' coordinate concept

****

In Chapter 3 (p 41-44) we considered the use of the codes 'x' and 'y' to distinguish between the separate themes that can be embedded within a single string. These *coordinate themes* may share one or more concepts in common (indicated by the theme code 'z'), but the themes could have been written as separate strings, and the entries will appear, in fact, as though the themes had been input separately.

Another situation involving coordination occurs when a subject contains two or more coordinate concepts *within* a theme. This kind of coordination was mentioned in passing in the previous chapter (p 77), where it was explained that the topic 'Engines and wings of aircraft' should not be handled as a succession of parts introduced by the operator 'p'; 'engines' and 'wings' are equally related, in a one-to-one sense, to 'aircraft' as their common whole, but not to each other. Their independence can be shown by a diagram:

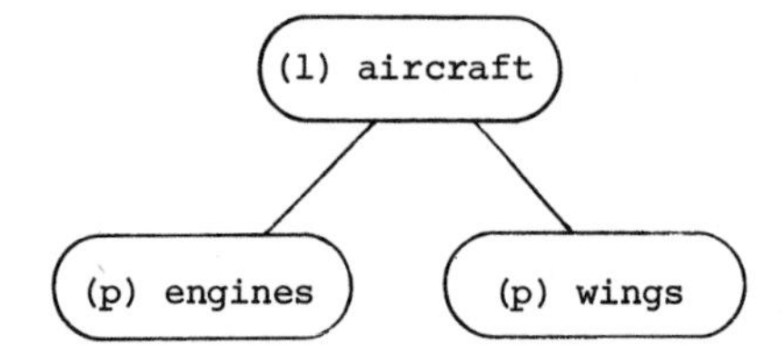

In a situation such as this, the grammatical role of one of the coordinate terms is indicated by a primary or dependent element operator. The other coordinate term should then be written as the next component in the string and preceded by the operator 'g'. In some special circumstances the operator 'f' should be used instead of 'g' — these are explained later (p 97).

Example 1:

Subject: Design of engines and wings of aircraft

String:
(1) aircraft
(p) engines $v &
(g) wings
(2) design

(p)–(g): *coordinate block*

Entries:

Aircraft
  Engines & wings. Design

Engines. Aircraft
  Design

Wings. Aircraft
  Design

Design. Engines & wings. Aircraft

The following points should be noted about the string and entries above:

(a) A connective code, $v, followed by an ampersand (&), is attached to 'engines' in the string. This code and adjunct should always be attached to the *penultimate* term in a coordinate block.

(b) When an entry is generated under a term that precedes the block (e.g. 'aircraft'), or under a term that follows the block (e.g. 'design'), the block as a whole is printed *in input order* as a pre-coordinated phrase, e.g. 'Engines & wings'.

(c) When a term *within* the block appears in the lead, the other term(s) comprising the block are *automatically suppressed from the entry.*

The analysis and coding of further subjects containing coordinate concepts are illustrated below. Note in particular how the terms in the block are organised as a phrase when a lead is made under a term outside the block, but the same terms are presented one at a time when an entry is made under a component of the block.

Example 2:

Subject: Training of cats and dogs (as pets)

String:
(1) pets
(q) cats $v &
(g) dogs
(2) training

Entries:

Pets
  Cats & dogs. Training

Cats. Pets
  Training

Dogs. Pets
  Training

Training. Cats & dogs. Pets

Example 3:

Subject: The durability, safety and strength of fibreglass canoes

String: (1) cánoes $21 fibreglass
(p) dúrability
(g) sáfety $v &
(g) śtrength

Entries: Canoes
  Fibreglass canoes. Durability, safety & strength

Fibreglass canoes
  Durability, safety & strength

Durability. Fibreglass canoes

Safety. Fibreglass canoes

Strength. Fibreglass canoes

Notes:
(a) Terms such as 'safety' etc. were marked as leads only for demonstration purposes.
(b) The display position of the first entry contains a three-term phrase. The comma that follows 'Durability' was inserted by the computer in response to the operator 'g'. This mark is automatically *replaced* by the ampersand before the final term in the phrase is printed.

Example 4:

Subject: Vaporization and solubility of crystals

String: (1) crýstals
(p) sólubility $v &
(g) vápórization

Entries: Crystals
  Solubility & vaporization

Solubility. Crystals

Vaporization. Crystals

Note: In this (unusual) case the coordinate terms do not possess the same grammatical role. 'Solubility' is a *property* of the crystals, whereas 'vaporization' is an *action*. The operator 'g' is not intended as an exact specification of the role of the term it introduces. It indicates only that terms in the block stand in a common one-to-one relationship with other terms in the string, without themselves being interrelated.

The example below shows that coordinate concepts can occur at more than one position in a string:

Example 5:

Subject: Staining and varnishing mahogany and teak

String: (1) mahogany $v &
(g) teak
(2) staining $v &
(g) varnishing

Entries: Mahogany
Staining & varnishing

Teak
Staining & varnishing

Staining. Mahogany & teak

Varnishing. Mahogany & teak

The extent to which this technique should be adopted is a matter for local policies. If documents on separate parts of the subject are likely to be encountered (e.g. 'Staining teak', 'Varnishing mahogany', etc.), it would be more economical to write separate (re-usable) strings for each part.

Order of terms in coordinate blocks

The coordinate terms in all the examples above were set down in alphabetical order, e.g. 'engines' before 'wings', and 'solubility' before 'vaporization', etc. For the sake of consistency among indexers this should be regarded as the standard order. When an adjectival compound occurs as a term in a coordinate block, it should be alphabetized under its first word, not under its focal noun.

Example 6:

Subject: Marketing of low-fat cream and unsalted butter

String: (1) cream $21 low-fat $v &
(g) butter $01 unsalted
(2) marketing

Entries: Cream
Low-fat cream. Marketing

Low-fat cream
Marketing

Butter
Unsalted butter. Marketing

Marketing. Low-fat cream & unsalted butter

Coordinate terms should be written in a different order (other than alphabetical) in the following circumstances:

(a) *Strict alphabetical order would lead to an ambiguous entry.* This would occur when indexing a subject such as 'Calorific values of peas and canned beans'. If the coordinate terms are organised alphabetically (i.e. 'canned beans & peas'), the position of the adjective is likely to suggest that both the 'beans' and the 'peas' were canned. This subject should therefore be indexed as follows:

Example 7:

Subject: Calorific value of peas and canned beans

String: (1) peas $v &
(g) beans $21 canned
(p) calorific value

Entries: Peas
Calorific value

Beans
Canned beans. Calorific value

Canned beans
Calorific value

Calorific value. Peas & canned beans

(b) *A 'canonical' order (one that is generally accepted as a kind of convention) exists and differs from alphabetical order.*

Example 8:

Subject: Plating of nuts and bolts

String: (1) nuts $v &
(g) bolts
(2) plating

Entries: Nuts
Plating

Bolts
Plating

Plating. Nuts & bolts

(c) *A set of coordinate actions can be organised as a logical, time-dependent sequence.*

Example 9:

Subject: Selection, acquisition and cataloguing of serials in national libraries

String: (1) libraries $21 national
(p) stock
(q) serials
(2) selection
(g) acquisition $v &
(g) cataloguing

Entries: Libraries
National libraries. Stock: Serials. Selection, acquisition & cataloguing

National libraries
Stock: Serials. Selection, acquisition & cataloguing

Serials. Stock. National libraries
Selection, acquisition & cataloguing

Cataloguing. Serials. Stock. National libraries

Note: The term 'stock' (or possibly 'collections') was inserted into this string to explain the relationship between 'national libraries' and 'serials'; these are not serials *about* national libraries. A parallel situation was encountered in the previous chapter — see Example 15 (p 86).

****

Operator 'f' = 'Bound' coordinate concept

****

When a term from a coordinate block appeared in the lead in the examples above, the other terms comprising the block were automatically suppressed from the entry. In some situations, however, it would be quite misleading to delete any term(s) from the block in this way. This occurs whenever a subject contains what is called a *binding concept*: that is, a concept that logically refers to the *whole* of the block, not simply to each of its individual components. We would encounter this situation when indexing subjects such as the following (the binding word is printed in italic in each case):

— *Joint* committees of students and teachers.

— *Comparative* studies of the protein content of fish and meat.

— *Mixed* flocks of ducks and geese in the Canadian arctic regions.

If we used the operator 'g' when indexing the third of the topics seen above:

```
*(O) Canada
 (p) arctic regions
 (1) ducks $v &
 (g) geese
 (r) mixed flocks
```

— the string would generate an entry such as:

```
*Geese.  Arctic regions. Canada
   Mixed flocks
```

This inevitably raises the question: "Mixed with what ?".

In any situation of this kind, the operator 'g' should be replaced by the coordinate concept operator 'f'. The rest of the string remains the same:

Example 10:

Subject: Mixed flocks of ducks and geese in the Canadian arctic regions

String:

```
(O) Canada
(p) arctic regions
(1) ducks $v &
(f) geese
(r) mixed flocks
```

Entries:

```
Canada
  Arctic regions. Ducks & geese. Mixed flocks

Arctic regions.  Canada
  Ducks & geese. Mixed flocks

Ducks.  Arctic regions. Canada
  Ducks & geese. Mixed flocks

Geese.  Arctic regions. Canada
  Ducks & geese. Mixed flocks
```

The first two entries are structurally similar to those seen earlier. When a term from the coordinate block appears in the lead, however, the *whole* of the block is printed as a phrase in the display.

An additional output routine is necessary when the second or subsequent concept in an 'f' block is represented by a compound term, and only part of this term appears in the lead:

Example 11:

Subject: Matching the patterns of soft furnishings and vinyl wallpapers

String: (1) furnishings $01 soft $v &
(f) wallpapers $21 vinyl
(p) patterns
(2) matching

If the usual differencing procedures were applied when the focal noun 'wallpapers' appears in the lead, the entry would be constructed in stages as follows:

— the noun 'wallpapers' would be assigned to the lead;

— the whole of the compound term, 'vinyl wallpapers', would then be printed as the first component of the display;

— finally, the remaining terms, including the block as a whole, would be assigned to their positions within the entry.

This would generate an entry such as:

*Wallpapers
Vinyl wallpapers. Soft furnishings & vinyl wallpapers.
Patterns. Matching

This may not be 'wrong', but the first term in the display is clearly redundant. *The second step above is therefore cancelled when this situation arises*, so that the string above would generate the entries:

Furnishings
Soft furnishings & vinyl wallpapers. Patterns. Matching

Wallpapers
Soft furnishings & vinyl wallpapers. Patterns. Matching

Vinyl wallpapers
Soft furnishings & vinyl wallpapers. Patterns. Matching

In all the examples above the binding concept was expressed by a term within the string. If PRECIS is used as an index to a classified file of citations (as in *BNB*), it will sometimes be found that the class number attached to a string can act as a binding concept, even though it falls *outside* the string. This will occur whenever a document deals with two or more concepts, and the classification schedules provide:

— a specific number for each of the separate concepts;

— a different number for works on the concepts in combination.

For example, the schedules of *DDC* (19th edition) contain the following places:

512 - Algebra

515 - Analysis (including calculus)

512.15 - Algebra & calculus (treated together).

A document on both concepts should therefore be indexed as follows:

Example 12:

Subject: Algebra & calculus

String: (2) ✓algebra $v &
(f) ✓calculus

DC number: 512.15

Entries: Algebra
Algebra & calculus 512.15

Calculus
Algebra & calculus 512.15

A word of warning is needed at this point. The operator 'f' should be used *only* when it is logically needed to handle a topic containing a binding concept. It should not be used to coordinate terms that are, in the indexer's opinion, usually thought of together (such as, say, 'Space & time'). Apart from the fact that users might not share this view, it could also lead to precedents in an authority file that are not easily taught or explained.

EXERCISES (For Answers, see Appendix 4, p 325)

Exercise 8

Write strings and entries for the following subjects. When selecting primary operators, use (1) to prefix things and (2) to prefix actions. Introduce dependent elements where necessary, using the procedures described in Chapter 5.

(a) Fatigue cracking of iron and cast bronze

(b) Basketry and weaving as occupational therapy

(c) Integration of normal students and handicapped students in primary schools

(d) Grinding & polishing of lenses for telescopes & binoculars

7. Basic concept types and fundamental relationships

Overview of the operators and codes

A check against the schema printed in two panels as Appendix 1 (p 307) will show that more than half the operators and codes have now been covered. We have dealt so far with the following:

Secondary operators

Coordinate concepts ('f' and 'g')

Dependent elements ('p', 'q' and 'r')

Primary codes

Theme interlinks ('x', 'y' and 'z')

Term codes ('a', 'c' and 'd')

Secondary codes

Connectives ('$v' and '$w')

Differences

Typographic codes

These operators and codes have been introduced before we get down to the business of subject analysis on the grounds that they can occur at almost any position within a string (although a secondary operator cannot be assigned to the first term in a string). Consequently, they can now be applied as needed in later examples without the need for further detailed explanations.

Some of the primary operators (printed in the right-hand panel of the schema) have also been used in earlier examples, but without attempting full descriptions. Before we examine these more closely in later chapters, we need to take a closer look at the schema as a whole. With the Appendix open, the following features should be noted:

1. Operators are distinguished from codes:

— The *operators* (in the right-hand panel) indicate *roles* of one kind or another. An operator always occupies the 3rd position in the *primary manipulation code* that precedes each term in an input string (this is explained in Chapter 14). They are divided into two groups:

(i) *Primary operators*, represented by numbers. These indicate grammatical roles (such as 'action', 'agent', etc.), and their numbers determine the order of basic concepts in an input string. They also regulate the format of an entry, the typography of terms, and their associated punctuation.

(ii) *Secondary operators*, represented by letters. These also indicate roles, but not always in the 'grammatical' sense expressed by the primary operators. For example, the operator 'p' (see Chapter 5) identifies a part or property, but does not specify the exact syntactical role of the term on which it depends (e.g. as an 'environment' or 'action').

— The *codes* (in the left-hand panel) do not indicate roles, and are more concerned with what might be called housekeeping functions. For example, the *connective codes* introduce adjuncts, such as prepositions. These codes are divided into three groups:

(i) *Primary codes*. These occupy fixed positions within a primary manipulation code (explained in Chapter 14);

(ii) *Secondary codes*. These *follow* terms (or foci) in an input string, and they indicate *parts of terms* (e.g. differences), or *adjuncts* (e.g. prepositions). These codes are identified as instructions, rather than data, by their special character prefixes.

(iii) *Typographic codes*, explained on p 40-41.

2. Note the lines drawn across the table of primary operators. These can be visualised as walls; an indexer is allowed to 'climb over' a wall when working *down* the schema, but cannot climb back once a wall has been crossed. For example, a string can begin with a term identified as a location (operator '0'), and this may be followed by a dependent element (see Example 8 on p 77-78). The indexer would then select an operator from the next set to indicate a core concept, but once this has been done, none of the later terms in the string (or in the theme, if the

string contains more than one theme) can be marked as a location. If the operator '0' is introduced after a core operator, the string will be rejected by the computer. Two further important validation checks are built into the schema:

— The first term in a string must be prefixed by one of three operators: '0' or '1' or '2'.

— Every string must contain a term prefixed by the operator '1' and/or '2'.

3. A horizontal line is printed across the width of the primary operators (between the operators '3' and '4'). This marks a boundary between concepts comprising the core of a subject and what might be called extra-core factors, such as the form of the document. This boundary is indicated to the reader of the index by a change of typeface to italic following a long dash in the display position. This occurs in some of the entries reproduced on p 20; see, for example, the display line under 'Contraction'. If a term preceded by one of the operators *below* the line (e.g. '4' or '6') is marked as a lead, its entry appears in a special format described in a later chapter.

Basic concept types, and forms of terms

The right-hand panel in the schema contains a total of 15 primary and secondary operators, each indicating a role of some kind. The concepts possessing these roles can be of various kinds — we have already seen terms such as 'cameras', 'pests' and 'railway services' marked as key systems (operator '1'). Despite this apparent diversity, each term in a PRECIS string is recognised, for practical purposes, as referring to one of only two basic types of concepts. Leaving aside adjuncts, such as prepositions, concepts are categorized as either *things* or *actions*. Linguists employ a similar dichotomy when they distinguish between nouns (or nominals) and verbs, but this analogy should not be pushed too far; all concepts, including actions, are expressed by nouns or noun phrases in PRECIS (as in other indexing languages). Terms that are marked as actions (for example, by the operator '2') refer to some kind of event or happening, including the effects of actions (e.g. 'diseases'), but these concepts cannot always be matched by verbs in a given natural language. It is an easy matter to detect the verbs that underlie action nouns such as 'management' and 'analysis', but we need to be aware that terms such as 'science', 'frost' and 'hockey' also refer to happenings, not things, and should therefore be marked as actions in PRECIS strings, even though they cannot be traced to verbs in English.

Recognizing a distinction between thing concepts and action con-concepts serves two practical purposes:

— Firstly, the choice of a primary operator is frequently limited by the kind of concept to which the term refers. For example, operators '0' and '1' can introduce things but not actions, whereas operator '2' can introduce actions but not things. The operator '3' can introduce concepts of either kind (we shall see examples of this later) but is mostly applied to things. The choice of some of the other operators is subject to similar restrictions; for example, operators 't' and 'u' can introduce actions but not things. The operator 's' is special, insofar as it identifies concepts that seem to function as things from some points of view but as actions from others. These distinctions are important when we remember that the choice of operator frequently affects the format of the entries in the printed index.

— Secondly, the class to which a concept belongs generally determines the form of its term in the index; in particular, its expression as a plural or singular noun. When choosing the appropriate form, we need to recognise further distinctions within the basic concept classes. These are set down as a Table on the facing page. Reference to this table will show that the choice of the noun form is based on the general rule that *count nouns* should be expressed as plurals, and *non-count nouns* as singulars. Count nouns can occur as answers to the question 'How many?' (e.g. 'How many penguins?'), but not 'How much?' — we are not likely to ask 'How much penguin?'. Non-count nouns can form part of an answer to the question 'How much?' (e.g. 'How much water?'), but not 'How many?'. This rule is not unique to PRECIS — many English-language indexes are based on these criteria, and they occur as recommendations in at least one national standard on the construction of monolingual

THING CONCEPTS

Class of concept	*Examples*	*Form of term*
Physical countable things	Penguins; Telephones	*Plural*
Physical non-countable things (materials)	Timber; Granite	*Singular* *(See Note 1)*
Abstract entities	Heat; Time	*Singular*
Systems of abstract entities	Christianity; Law	*Singular*
Systems of physical and abstract entities *(See Note 2)*	Primary schools; Anglican churches; Health services	*Plural*
Organs of the body	Nose; Lungs; Respiratory system	*Singular* if only one occurs in a fully-formed organism, otherwise *plural*
Classes-of-one *(See Note 3)*	Mona Lisa; Church of Ireland; Einstein, Albert	*Singular*

Notes:

(1) A material (or substance) may be expressed as a plural when this refers to a class (e.g. 'minerals'), and the index deals with documents on its species (e.g. 'quartz', 'mica').

(2) Since these systems are complexes of different types of concept, their parts (introduced by the operator 'p') can also be of quite different kinds, e.g.

(1) schools
(p) teachers —— *human component*

(1) schools
(p) buildings —— *hardware*

(1) schools
(p) curriculum —— *software*

(3) It is sometimes necessary to distinguish between animate and inanimate classes-of-one. The names of the former are generally determined by cataloguing rules, e.g. AACR2.

ACTION CONCEPTS

Express as singular nouns. Where possible, prefer a form other than the gerund (present participle)	*Examples:* 'analysis' and 'growth' rather than 'analysing' and 'growing', *but* 'baking', 'dredging', 'annealing', etc.

Types of concept and forms of nouns

thesauri (1). These rules, which clearly affect consistency, may seem to be somewhat pedantic. Nevertheless, they pass unnoticed when applied at an intuitive level in everyday language. Lewis Carroll, for example, talked ".. of many things — "

"... Of shoes — and ships — and sealing-wax —
Of cabbages — and kings —
And why the sea is boiling hot —
And whether pigs have wings" (2)

— where all the count nouns are expressed as plurals, and the non-count nouns ('sealing-wax' and 'sea') as singulars.

Action concepts can also be divided into sub-classes. A few of these take special operators (listed among the *secondary operators*), and are associated with special formats and output instructions described in later chapters.

Fundamental relationships

The various roles indicated by the operators (locations, parts, actions, etc.) can themselves be further reduced to a limited set of fundamental relations. An awareness of these can sometimes help to resolve problems or suggest alternative approaches when dealing with complex subjects, but the study of relationships, however interesting, tends to become somewhat abstract, and it should be stressed that a knowledge of these theoretical matters is *not* a necessary pre-requisite for the successful application of PRECIS. For indexers who are interested not only in 'How?' but also 'Why?', a brief account of these basic relations is offered in Appendix 3 (p 313).

---

(1) British Standards Institution. Guidelines for the establishment and development of monolingual thesauri: BS 5723. London, B.S.I., 1979

(2) Carroll, Lewis. Alice through the looking glass (Chapter 4 — any edition)

8. Things related to actions

****

Operator '1' = Key system

Thing concept when no action present.
Thing towards which an action is directed.

****

Operator '2' = Action/Effect

****

If the overall subject of a document can be summarised as a single word or phrase, such as 'Scotland' or 'apples' or 'nursing', it is sufficient to distinguish between thing concepts and action concepts, then write the appropriate operator as a prefix to the term, e.g.

(1) Scotland *or* (1) apples *or* (2) nursing.

Each of these strings passes the two validation checks printed on p 103: each contains a term prefixed by the operator '1' or '2', and they all begin with an operator in the range '0' to '2'. For obvious reasons at least one part of every single term string (the focus or difference) must be marked as a lead; otherwise the string should not have been written in the first place.

Thing concepts identified by the operator '1' can belong to any of the various classes set out as a table on p 105. When a single-term string represents an action, this term is always prefixed by the operator '2'. Some actions take other operators ('s', 't' and 'u'), but these are used only when other concepts are also present. The concepts introduced by the operator '2' belong to two main classes:

(a) *Actions*. These terms refer to some kind of event or happening. As noted earlier, they cannot always be traced to verbs in a particular natural language.

(b) *Effects*. This category includes terms, such as 'tuberculosis', 'hurricanes' and 'pain', which refer to the results of actions and cannot be classed as things.

Strings consisting of single terms (whether simple or compound), perhaps accompanied by extra-core terms (e.g. 'serials' or 'atlases'), are not uncommon when indexing monographs, but the majority of subjects deal with two or more interrelated concepts, e.g. 'Harvesting apples in Scotland'. In all the examples considered so far, concepts of this kind have been organised into sequences as follows:

(0) location (e.g. 'Scotland')
(1) thing = key system (e.g. 'apples')
(2) action (e.g. 'harvesting')

This operator pattern is common but not invariable. In some cases the name of a thing can *follow* the name of the action in which it is involved. When things and actions are interrelated, the order of concepts is determined in the first place by applying the general principle set down as part of the definition of the key system:

Key system: The thing *towards which an action is directed*.

As we shall see later, actions can be classed in various ways, and these different classes can be associated with concepts of several kinds. In every case, however, it will be found that the general principle stated above is the clue to identifying the key system †. This principle is applied below to two general classes of actions that are typically introduced by the operator '2', i.e. *transitives* and *intransitives*.

Transitive actions

These are defined as actions that are capable of taking objects (that is, they can be done *to* something). Before we consider the different kinds of transitive actions that can be coded '2', we need to dis-

---

† The concept identified in this way as the key system can be prefixed by the operator '1', or it may be marked as a dependent element ('p', 'q' or 'r') following a term coded '1'. This condition should be regarded as constant throughout the following explanations.

tinguish clearly between *grammatical objects/subjects* and *logical objects/performers*. The difference can be illustrated by analysing two natural language sentences, one active and the other passive:

– *The beagle chased the cat*, where 'The beagle' functions as the *grammatical subject* of the verb 'to chase', and 'the cat', embedded in the predicate, served as the *object* in this active voice sentence.

– *The cat was chased by the beagle*, where 'The cat' assumes the role of *grammatical subject*. This passive sentence has no object in the sense employed in traditional grammar.

Despite these surface differences, we can say that the transitive action 'chase' takes 'the cat' as its *logical object*, and 'the beagle' functions as its *performer*, in both versions of the sentence. Throughout all later explanations, terms such as 'object', 'performer', etc. will be used with these logical meanings unless a different meaning is specifically indicated.

The majority of transitive actions are performed, in a fairly self-evident way, upon some kind of thing †, in which case we can say that the key system, functioning as the logical object, is the thing *affected by the action*, to the extent that its condition is likely to be changed in some way. This would apply in the following cases:

Example 1:

Subject: Harvesting apples

String: (1) apples ——— *affected thing (key system)*
(2) harvesting — *transitive action*

Entries: **Apples**
Harvesting

Harvesting. Apples

Example 2:

Subject: Management of health centres

String: (1) health centres — *affected thing (key system)*
(2) management ——— *transitive action*

---

† We shall later see actions which take *other actions* as their objects. These 'second actions' are treated separately on p 116.

Entries: Health centres
  Management

Management. Health centres

Example 3:

Subject: Employment of unskilled personnel

String: (1) personnel $21 unskilled — *affected thing (key system)*
(2) employment ——————— *transitive action*

Entries: Personnel
  Unskilled personnel. Employment

Unskilled personnel
  Employment

Employment. Unskilled personnel

Some transitive actions can be applied to objects without actually 'affecting' them. For example, topics such as 'Classification of minerals' and 'Indexing of films' deal with things involved with actions, but nothing occurred which changed the state or condition of either the minerals or the films. The general principle still holds: we can logically say that these actions were *directed towards* the films and minerals as their objects. These objects should therefore be coded as key systems:

Example 4:

Subject: Classification of minerals

String: (1) minerals —— *object (key system)*
(2) classification — *transitive action*

Entries: Minerals
  Classification

Classification. Minerals

Example 5:

Subject: Indexing films

String: (1) films —— *object (key system)*
(2) indexing —— *transitive action*

Entries: Films
  Indexing

Indexing. Films

Direct and indirect objects

A limited number of actions are capable of taking two objects, identified as the *direct* and *indirect objects*. For example, a subject such as 'Donation of clothing to refugees' contains an action, 'donation', applied to a direct object, 'clothing', and also an indirect object, 'refugees'. We should again apply the general principle when choosing between the direct and indirect object as the key system. It is more reasonable to state that the donation of clothing was *directed towards* the refugees, rather than say that 'donations to refugees' was directed towards the clothing. Consequently, the indirect object (or *beneficiary*) should be coded as the key system:

Example 6:

Subject: Donation of clothing to refugees

String: (1) refugees ——— *indirect object (beneficiary)*
(3) clothing $w to ——— *direct object*
(2) donation ——— *transitive action*

Entries: **Refugees**
Clothing. Donation

Clothing. Refugees
Donation

Donation. Clothing to refugees

Note that the operator '3' was used to indicate the direct object. This choice of operators, which occurs again in later examples, is typical of subjects involving both direct and indirect objects.

Example 7:

Subject: Teaching mathematics to gifted students in secondary schools

String: (1) secondary schools
(p) gifted students ——— *indirect object (beneficiary)*
(3) curriculum subjects
(q) mathematics ——— *direct object*
(sub 3↑) (p) mathematics to gifted students
(2) teaching ——— *transitive action*

Entries: **Secondary schools**
Gifted students. Curriculum subjects: Mathematics.
Teaching

Gifted students. Secondary schools
Curriculum subjects: Mathematics. Teaching

Mathematics. Curriculum subjects. Gifted students.
Secondary schools
Teaching

Teaching. Mathematics to gifted students. Secondary schools

The following points should be noted about the string and entries shown as Example 7:

(a) We can again say that 'teaching mathematics' was *directed towards* the 'gifted students', but not that 'teaching gifted students' was directed towards 'mathematics'.

(b) In this case the terms 'gifted students' and 'mathematics' are both coded as dependent elements. We should remember that their syntactical roles are indicated by the core operators (numbers) assigned to their preceding terms (that is, '1' and '3' respectively).

(c) From the viewpoint of the 'gifted students', the concept 'mathematics' can be seen as a kind of intellectual *intake*. A check against the schema in Appendix 1 shows that intake terms are indicated by the operator '3'.

(d) The term 'curriculum subjects' was inserted into the string to achieve consistency with other topics where an 'explaining' term of this kind is necessary. A parallel situation occurred in Example 14 on p 85. Since this explanatory term becomes redundant when 'teaching' appears in the lead, it was suppressed by a substitute which effectively combines the direct and indirect objects into a single phrase.

Terms such as 'intake' and 'beneficiary' call for a liberal interpretation; from a logical point of view, the same relationship applies to concepts that can be described as 'losses' as well as 'gains'. This can be seen in the following example:

Example 8:

Subject: Unloading oil from supertankers

String:
(1) supertankers —— *indirect object (beneficiary)*
(3) cargoes —— *direct object (quasi-generic class)*
(q) oil —— *member of class*
(sub 3↑) (1) oil from supertankers
(2) unloading —— *transitive action*

Entries:

Supertankers
Cargoes: Oil. Unloading

Cargoes. Supertankers
Oil. Unloading

Oil. Cargoes. Supertankers
Unloading

Unloading. Oil from supertankers

An extra term, 'cargoes', has been inserted into this string to explain that the supertanker is not unloading its fuel oil; 'fuel' would have been coded 'p' (a part), not '3' (an intake in the broad sense indicated earlier). Exactly the same operator pattern would have been written for a document on '*Loading* oil *into* supertankers'.

Internal processes involving intakes

None of the subjects studied above dealt with the *performer* of an action. If a performer had been present (for example, when indexing a document on 'Donation of clothing to refugees *by children*'), the performer would have been recognised as an entity involved with, but *separate from*, the other concepts. Some action terms refer, however, to *internal processes* where a single entity possesses simultaneous roles as the recipient in a transaction and also its performer. This kind of concept occurs in a subject such as 'Digestion of cellulose by bacteria' — we can say that the 'bacteria' benefit from, and are also responsible for, the act of 'digestion'. 'Cellulose' can also be seen as having two roles: it is affected by the action, and it also fits the role of an intake. The choice of key system in these cases is based by analogy on the subjects studied earlier (examples 6 to 8). The *beneficiary* (doubling as the performer) should be identified as the key system, and the intake should again be prefixed by the operator '3'.

Example 9:

Subject: Digestion of cellulose by bacteria

String: (1) bacteria ——— *beneficiary/performer*
(2) digestion $v of $w by ——— *internal process*
(3) cellulose ——— *intake*

Entries: **Bacteria**
Digestion of cellulose

Digestion. Bacteria
Of cellulose

Cellulose
Digestion by bacteria

The special format generated under the term coded '3' ('cellulose') is explained in a later chapter. The same relational situation occurs in the following subject:

Example 10:

Subject: Breathing of oxygen-enriched atmosphere by premature babies

String: (1) babies $21 premature —— *beneficiary/performer*
(2) breathing $v of $w by —— *internal process*
(3) oxygen-enriched atmosphere — *intake*

Entries: Babies
Premature babies. Breathing of oxygen-enriched atmosphere

Premature babies
Breathing of oxygen-enriched atmosphere

Breathing. Premature babies
Of oxygen-enriched atmosphere

Oxygen-enriched atmosphere
Breathing by premature babies

It needs to be stressed that the pattern of concepts and operators shown above (where '3' marks things that were, in fact, physically changed by the transaction), is limited to subjects where *internal* (i.e. physiological) processes are applied to *intakes* (in the broad sense noted earlier). This kind of coding is not appropriate in other situations. For example, the subject 'Hunting of rodents by foxes' should be expressed by a relatively orthodox (and certainly commoner) sequence of roles:

(1) rodents ———————— *object*
(2) hunting $v by $w of —— *transitive action*
(3) foxes ————————— *performer*

- since 'hunting' is *not* an internal process.

Intransitive actions

These are actions which cannot take objects, to the extent that activities such as 'flight', 'sleep', 'flow', 'camping', 'hibernation', etc. cannot be done *to* anything (except, perhaps, in a reflexive sense). When indexing subjects based on these actions, the operator pattern follows the general model applied above to internal processes:

— the performer (again identified as the thing towards which the action is directed) is prefixed by the operator '1';

— the action is coded '2'.

Example 11:

Subject: Flight of birds

String: (1) birds — *performer*
(2) flight — *intransitive action*

Entries: Birds
Flight

Flight. Birds

Example 12:

Subject: Camping by boys

String: (1) boys — *performer*
(2) camping — *intransitive action*

Entries: Boys
Camping

Camping. Boys

Example 13:

Subject: Flow of fluidized particles

String: (1) particles $21 fluidized — *performer*
(2) flow ———— *intransitive action*

Entries: Particles
Fluidized particles. Flow

Fluidized particles
Flow

Flow. Fluidized particles

Example 14:

Subject: Growth rate of pines

String: (1) pines — *performer*
(2) growth — *intransitive action*
(p) rate — *property of action*

Entries: Pines
Growth. Rate

Growth. Pines
Rate

Only a small proportion of subjects encountered in day-to-day indexing contain terms that refer to internal processes and intransitive actions. The examples above nevertheless justify study, partly as models to be followed when similar topics are handled; also (and mainly) to demonstrate the working of the general principle on which their analyses are based, which calls for identification of the concept towards which the action is directed. This principle can then be applied more quickly, and with greater confidence, to the relatively simpler action concepts that occur more frequently in practice.

Second actions

Examples in previous chapters dealt with two relational situations where terms that represent actions can follow each other in a string:

(a) *Actions related as whole and part*

Example 15:

Subject: End games in chess

String: (2) chess
(p) end games

Entry: Chess
  End games

(b) *Actions forming a coordinate block*

Example 16:

Subject: Planting, cultivation and harvesting of potatoes

String: (1) potatoes
(2) planting
(g) cultivation $v & — *coordinate block forming a time-dependent sequence*
(g) harvesting

Entries: Potatoes
  Planting, cultivation & harvesting

Planting. Potatoes

Cultivation. Potatoes

Harvesting. Potatoes

We turn now to the different relational situation that arises when a string contains two actions, and the second takes the first (plus, usually, its associated concepts) as its *object*. This occurs in a subject such as the following:

Example 17:

Subject: Monitoring the flow of liquids

String: (1) liquids — *key system*
(2) flow $w of — *1st action (intrans.)*
(2) monitoring — *2nd action*

(lines (1)–(2) flow: *object of 2nd action*)

Entries: Liquids
Flow. Monitoring

Flow. Liquids
Monitoring

Monitoring. Flow of liquids

This class of *second actions* (e.g. 'monitoring' in the example above) contains a limited range of concept types. For obvious reasons, a second action must be transitive, since it takes other concepts as its object. It can also be recognised as belonging to one of the following three types or categories:

Type 'A'. Coming-into-being terms, i.e. terms that refer to the *origins or development* of the concept(s) named earlier in the string. This category includes terms such as 'evolution', 'development', 'variation', etc.

Example 18:

Subject: Development of industrialization in Taiwan

String: (0) Taiwan
(2) industrialization — *1st action*
(2) development — *2nd action*

Entries: Taiwan
Industrialization. Development

Industrialization. Taiwan
Development

Type 'B'. Information terms, i.e. terms that refer to the *gathering, processing or dissemination of information* concerning the concept(s) earlier in the string. This category includes terms such as 'research', 'evaluation', 'teaching', 'classification', 'tests', 'measurement', 'forecasting', etc.

Example 19:

Subject: Evaluation of teaching methods in primary schools

String: (1) primary schools
(2) teaching methods $w in — *1st action*
(2) evaluation — *2nd action*

Entries: Primary schools
Teaching methods. Evaluation

Teaching methods. Primary schools
Evaluation

Evaluation. Teaching methods in primary schools

Example 20:

Subject: Forecasting the costs of renovating country houses

String: (1) houses $21 country
(2) renovation $w of — *1st action*
(p) costs $w of
(2) forecasting — *2nd action*
[(1)–(p): *object of 2nd action*]

Entries: Houses
Country houses. Renovation. Costs. Forecasting

Country houses
Renovation. Costs. Forecasting

Forecasting. Costs of renovation of country houses

Type 'C'. 'Interference' terms, i.e. terms that refer to the *control or regulation* of the concept(s) named earlier in the string. This category includes terms such as 'management', 'planning', 'assistance', 'surgery', 'control', 'regulation', etc.

Example 21:

Subject: Behaviour therapy for obesity in children

String: (1) children
(2) obesity — *1st action (effect)*
(2) behaviour therapy — *2nd action*

Entries: Children
Obesity. Behaviour therapy

Obesity. Children
Behaviour therapy

Behaviour therapy. Obesity. Children

Example 22:

Subject: Planning the professional education of nurses

String: (1) nurses
(2) professional education $w of — *1st action*
(2) planning — *2nd action*

Entries: Nurses
Professional education. Planning

Professional education. Nurses
Planning

Planning. Professional education of nurses

There are sound (but somewhat abstract) reasons for assuming that all second action concepts must logically belong to one of the three categories noted above. This has practical implications: if a second action cannot be recognised as belonging to one of these three groups, the string as a whole should be checked for a possible fault in analysis.

A glance at the examples above shows that a second action is generally related to a set of earlier concepts, not simply the next preceding term. If a lead is generated under the second action, it is usually necessary to present the set to the user as a single semantic unit (the object of the second action). This can be achieved in either of two ways:

(a) using one or more connectives to link the terms comprising the set into a phrase (see examples 20 and 22);

(b) inserting a substitute. When substitutes were first explained (see p 29-30), they were illustrated by two examples, each of which contained a second action. Other examples occur in later chapters. It is likely that second actions account for the great majority of upward-reading substitutes in a typical authority file.

If sets of terms representing the objects of second actions are not organised into phrases, the entries produced under the second action terms are likely to be ambiguous. This can be simulated by dropping the '$w' connective from the string in Example 22, producing the entry:

*Planning. Professional education. Nurses

This could be misinterpreted as the subject of 'planning' included *as part of* the professional education of nurses.

Terms representing second actions can occur more than once in a string, as seen in the example below:

Example 23:

Subject: Financial assistance for research into the location of airports

String: (1) airports
(2) location $w of — *1st action*
(2) research $w into — *2nd action (Type 'B')*
(2) financial assistance — *2nd action (Type 'C')*

Entries: Airports
Location. Research. Financial assistance

Location. Airports
Research. Financial assistance

Financial assistance. Research into location of airports

When dealing with subjects containing two or more actions of this kind, the order in which the action terms should be cited is generally self-evident. It is not usually difficult to determine which of two actions (plus, perhaps, its associated concepts) functions as the *object* of the other. According to the general principle noted ealier, the object should then be written earlier in the string. This explains why the term 'research', in Example 23, follows its object 'location of air-ports', but precedes 'financial assistance'. If any doubts concerning this order should arise, another principle can be applied as a kind of diagnostic test. It has been observed that concepts in strings are generally organised into sequences which reflect the order in which they necessarily occur *as ideas*. This *time of conceptualization* does not correspond, except by coincidence, to real or historical time. The difference can be demonstrated by analysing a subject such as 'Planning the planting of vegetables' from both points of view. In terms of real time we can reasonably assume that an action such as 'planning' must precede whatever is being planned — indeed, from the planner's point of view, 'planting of vegetables' is a future event which might not happen at all. Similarly, 'planting' must antedate, in real time terms, the crop of 'vegetables'. Time of conceptualization calls for a reversal of this order. An idea such as 'planning' is unlikely to come to mind except when related to some kind of pre-conceived object; a remark such as 'I shall plan today' would make little sense unless it is related to *something* that calls for planning. Similarly, an action such as 'planting' necessarily assumes a pre-conceived object such as 'vegetables'. We can therefore say that the terms in the following string:

Example 24:

Subject: Planning the planting of vegetables

String: (1) vegetables
(2) planting
(2) planning

Entries: Vegetables
Planting. Planning

Planting. Vegetables
Planning

— have been written in the order in which they necessarily came to mind, not the order in which they occurred in a real time or historical sense.

Reference to this general principle is hardly needed in day-to-day practice — it represents the basis underlying context-dependency itself. An awareness of the principle can occasionally be useful, however, as a diagnostic test in difficult situations.

EXERCISE (For Answers, see Appendix 4, p 326)

Exercise 9

Write strings and entries for the following subjects:

(a) Crystallization of granite

(b) Case hardening of steel bearings for heavy-duty electric motors

(c) Volleying in lawn tennis

(d) Control of cross-infection of patients in hospitals

(e) Timing the delivery of ready-mixed concrete as a building material

9. Environment of the core concepts

****

Operator '0' = Location

****

Distinguishing between place as location and place as key system

At the beginning of Chapter 8 we saw that terms which refer to things (including places) are introduced by the operator '1' if no other core concepts are present. A work on, say, 'France' or 'Ontario' would therefore be input simply as:

(1) France *or* (1) Ontario

It follows that a concept cannot be marked as a location (operator '0') *except when another core concept also occurs in the string*. The validation rules printed on p 103 check this condition by stipulating that a string can begin with a term prefixed by '0' provided that it also contains a term prefixed by '1' and/or '2'.

When place names are accompanied by core concepts they are not prefixed by '0' as a matter of course. The operator assigned to the locality depends upon the role it assumes *vis-a-vis* the other concepts in the subject. This chapter deals with locations coded '0' or '1', or else treated as differences, but we shall later see examples of subjects where place names are introduced by other operators, e.g. '3' or '5'.

The basic difference between place as key system and place as environment is illustrated by the two examples below:

Example 1:

Subject: Exploration of Greenland

String: (1) Greenland
(2) exploration

Entries: Greenland
  Exploration

Exploration. Greenland

Example 2:

Subject: Camping in Greenland

String: (0) Greenland
(2) camping

Entries: Greenland
  Camping

Camping. Greenland

Assigning the operator '1' to 'Greenland' in Example 1 simply continues the kind of analysis studied in the previous chapter; 'Greenland' represents the *object* of the transitive action 'exploration'. This should be seen in contrast to the looser relationship between 'Greenland' and 'camping' in Example 2; 'Greenland' specifies only the *location* where the action, 'camping', happened to occur. Two points emerge from these examples:

(a) Identifying a place name either as an environment (operator '0') or as a key system (operator '1') depends upon the *other* concept(s) present in the subject. In the explanations that follow, we shall refer to this as the *second concept*;

(b) A locality is identified as an environment when it indicates *only the spatial boundaries within which the other core concept(s) occurred*, without involving any direct interaction between the place and the second concept(s).

It is not especially difficult to distinguish between *place as key system* and *place as environment* when indexing subjects such as those seen above. In some cases, however, the choice of operator is less obvious, as seen in the following examples:

Example 3:

Subject: Rivers of Mexico

String: (1) Mexico
(p) rivers

Entries: Mexico
  Rivers

Rivers. Mexico

Example 4:

Subject: Canals in Mexico

String: (0) Mexico
(1) canals

Entries: Mexico
Canals

Canals. Mexico

When choosing operators in cases such as these, we need to distinguish between two ways in which place can be viewed as a concept: as a *geographical entity* or as a *social entity.*

(1) *Place is interpreted as a geographical entity* when the second concept refers to physical things or phenomena, e.g. 'rivers', 'bridges', 'mountains', 'schools', etc. In these cases:

(a) *The place should be coded as the key system* if the second concept refers to physical features which do not imply a use by human beings (that is, they consist entirely of natural features). This accounts for the choice of operator '1' in Example 3 above; the concept 'rivers' does not, of its own accord, imply any use by man. It also explains the choice of operators in the following example:

Example 5:

Subject: Lakes of the Algonquin Provincial Park in Ontario

String: (1) Ontario
(p) Algonquin Provincial Park
(p) lakes

Entries: Ontario
Algonquin Provincial Park. Lakes

Algonquin Provincial Park. Ontario
Lakes

Lakes. Algonquin Provincial Park. Ontario

(b) *The place should be coded as an environment* if the second concept represents a class of physical things with implied or overt use by human beings. This accounts for the choice of operator '0' in Example 4 above, and also in the following cases:

Example 6:

Subject: The freeways of Michigan

String: (0) Michigan
(1) freeways

Entries: Michigan
Freeways

Freeways. Michigan

Example 7:

Subject: The schools of South Island, New Zealand

String: (0) New Zealand
(p) South Island
(1) schools

Entries: New Zealand
South Island. Schools

South Island. New Zealand
Schools

Schools. South Island. New Zealand

(2) *Place is interpreted as a social system* when the second concept refers to a population rather than physical features. When we speak, for example, of 'Economic conditions in Sweden', we mean the people of Sweden, not its rivers, forests, etc. Within this context, a given place can be seen from various viewpoints: *social, economic* and *legal/political*. Each of these is covered by one or more examples below.

(a) *The place should be identified as the key system* when the second concept refers to, or can be applied to, the *whole* of the population.

Example 8 (place as social system):

Subject: Growth of the population of South-East Asia

String: (1) Asia $21 South-East
(p) population
(2) growth

Entries: Asia
South-East Asia. Population. Growth

South-East Asia
Population. Growth

Population. South-East Asia
Growth

Example 9 (place as social system):

Subject: Social life in England in the 18th century

String: (1) England
(2) social life $d 1700-1800

Entry: England
Social life, *1700-1800*

Example 10 (place as economic system):

Subject: Economic conditions in Zimbabwe

String: (1) Zimbabwe
(2) economic conditions

Entries: Zimbabwe
Economic conditions

Economic conditions. Zimbabwe

Example 11 (place as legal/political system):

Subject: The Constitution of the United States

String: (1) United States
(p) constitution

Entries: United States
Constitution

Constitution. United States

Example 12 (place as legal/political system):

Subject: Law of the Federal Republic of Germany

String: (1) Germany $i (Federal Republic)
(p) law

Entries: Germany *(Federal Republic)*
Law

Law. Germany *(Federal Republic)*

Note: The typographic instruction '$i' is explained on p 40.

Example 13 (place as legal/political system):

Subject: Chinese foreign relations

String: (1) China
(2) foreign relations

Entries: China
Foreign relations

Foreign relations. China

The list below shows terms which, when they occur as 2nd concepts, call for places to be coded as key systems. This list is not exhaustive.

(2) emigration
(2) environment planning
(2) exploration
(2) government
(2) immigration (*but not* 'immigrants'; see Example 14)
(p) imports
(2) settlement
(2) social change
(2) social customs
(2) social life
(2) social planning
(2) social reform
(2) wars (including civil wars, revolutions, etc.)

(b) *The place should be identified as an environment (operator '0')* when the second concept refers to, or implies, only a *subset* of the total population.

Example 14:

Subject: Social life of immigrants in New York City in the 1920's

String: (0) New York $i (City)
(1) immigrants
(p) social life $d 1920-1930

Entries: New York *(City)*
Immigrants. Social life, *1920-1930*

Immigrants. New York *(City)*
Social life, *1920-1930*

Social life. Immigrants. New York *(City)*
1920-1930

Example 15:

Subject: Law of education in Scotland

String: (0) Scotland
(2) education
(3) law

Entry: Education. Scotland
Law

Note: The concept 'education' implies only part of the total population, i.e. those being educated.

Reasons for distinguishing between place as location and place as key system

The formats of the entries seen in the examples above are not affected by the operator ('0' or '1') assigned to their locality terms. The entries appeared in the standard format in all cases. There are sound practical reasons, nevertheless, for distinguishing between these two conceptions of place. The operator assigned to the locality name offers a logical basis for indexing policies related to the choice of leads. Most indexing agencies cannot afford to generate entries under heavily-used terms, and it is doubtful whether users are genuinely served by long runs of display lines under common headings. Two kinds of term, in particular, call for caution:

(a) *The name of the 'local' country.* It is unlikely that a Canadian indexer would seriously wish to generate an entry under 'Canada' whenever this term occurred in a string — almost certainly, this would become the most heavily-used term in the system. The choice of leads can then be determined by a policy which states that the name of the local country (and other selected countries, if they occur often enough) should be marked as a lead *only* when coded '1, but *not* when coded '0'.

(b) *Other heavily-used terms*, such as 'social life', etc. These can be marked as leads when related to particular social groups (the locality being coded '0'; see Example 14), but not when they refer to localities coded '1' (as in Example 9).

Environments other than geographical/political regions

In all the examples above, the localities could be described as either geographical or political regions. These are the kinds of environment term encountered most often in practice, mainly because the bulk of literature deals with human affairs or activities in one way or another. Nevertheless, these terms reflect a strictly homo-centred viewpoint. It should be remembered that the coding of a concept as key system or environment is determined by the *second concept* in the subject. Occasionally a second concept belongs naturally within an environment more restricted in scope than those considered so far.

Example 16:

Subject: Blind fish living in caves

String: (0) ✓caves
(1) ✓fish $21 blind

Entries: Caves
Blind fish

Fish. Caves
Blind fish

Blind fish. Caves

Some students have difficulty following this coding, and would prefer a string such as the following:

*(1) caves
(p) fish $21 blind

This wrongly indicates, however, that the fish (living organisms) are *parts* of caves (inanimate geographical features).

Place as a difference

The name of a location, re-expressed if necessary in its adjectival form, can be used as a difference to indicate the source or origin of the concept it qualifies, provided that the focal concept is a strictly *exportable* entity — i.e. one that is likely to occur in a different environment. If this condition is satisfied, the use of location terms as differences allows the indexer to distinguish clearly between subjects where concepts of the same basic types occupy quite different roles.

Example 17:

Subject: Prices of Californian wines

String: (1) wines $21 Californian
(p) prices

Entries: **Wines**
Californian wines. Prices

Californian wines
Prices

Prices. Californian wines

The string above deals with the prices of Californian wines wherever they are sold. This should be seen in contrast to the following:

Example 18:

Subject: Prices of wines in Europe

String: (0) Europe
(1) wines
(p) prices

Entries: **Wines.** Europe
Prices

Prices. Wines. Europe

— which deals with the prices of wines in Europe (*not* the same as European wines) regardless of their countries of origin. These concepts can now be brought together:

Example 19:

Subject: Prices of Californian wines in Europe

String: (0) Europe
(1) wines $21 Californian
(p) prices

Entries: **Wines.** Europe
Californian wines. Prices

Californian wines. Europe
  Prices

Prices. Californian wines. Europe

It is again stressed that place names should be used as differences only when they qualify 'exportable' concepts. We can therefore apply this technique to subjects such as 'Spanish armour', 'English furniture', etc., but *not* to 'English cathedrals' or 'Spanish holiday resorts'.

EXERCISES (For Answers, see Appendix 4, p 327)

Exercise 10

Write strings and entries for the following subjects:

(a) The jungles of Kampuchea

(b) Buddhist temples in Kampuchea

(c) Buddhist temples in the jungles of Kampuchea

(d) Italian balance of payments

(e) Commercial television in the European Economic Community countries

10. Agents of transitive actions, and the predicate transformation

****
Operator '3' = Performer of transitive action
(*Agent, Factor*)
****

One kind of performer was considered in Chapter 8 — the agents of intransitive actions, introduced by the operator '1'. The same chapter dealt with 'intake' concepts, introduced by the operator '3'. The present chapter deals mainly with another kind of performer — the agents of transitive actions, also introduced by the operator '3'. Terms assuming this role are interesting, insofar as they frequently call for a special format when they appear as leads. Entries in this format have occurred in earlier examples (e.g. the entry under 'Industries' on p 38), but the procedures used to produce them, known collectively as the *predicate transformation*, have not yet been explained. Entries in this format are generated under agent terms (operator '3') in the following examples:

Example 1 (previously shown on p 114):

Subject: Hunting of rodents by foxes

String: (1) ✓rodents
(2) ✓hunting $v by $w of
(3) ✓foxes

Entries: Rodents
  Hunting by foxes

Hunting. Rodents
  By foxes

Foxes
  Hunting of rodents

Example 2:

Subject: Training of apprentices by foremen in the aerospace industries

String: (1) aerospace industries
(p) apprentices
(2) training $v by $w of
(3) foremen

Entries: Aerospace industries
Apprentices. Training by foremen

Apprentices. Aerospace industries
Training by foremen

Training. Apprentices. Aerospace industries
By foremen

Foremen. Aerospace industries
Training of apprentices

Entries under concepts with roles as performers (such as 'foxes' and 'foremen' in the examples above), are generated in stages as follows:

Stage 1: The performer term is assigned to the lead.

Stage 2: Since a performer term is prefixed by the operator '3', the computer then automatically reads the operator assigned to the next *preceding* term, checking for the presence of an action. Action concepts are identified by one of four operators: '2' (considered here); 'u' (introduced later in this chapter); 's' and 't' (described in later chapters).

Stage 3: If an action term is present, it is assigned to the *display*, e.g.

Foxes	Foremen
Hunting	Training

Stage 4: If the action is also accompanied by an upward-reading connective ('$w'), the computer continues producing the phrase in the display, e.g.

Foxes	Foremen
Hunting of rodents	Training of apprentices

This step is repeated if the last term added to the phrase is also accompanied by a $w connective.

Stage 5: When the string contains no further candidates for the phrase in the display (i.e. terms accompanied by $w), the remaining terms in the string (if any) are assigned to their standard format positions:

Foremen. Aerospace industries
  Training of apprentices

To understand why this set of procedures is called the *predicate transformation*, we should relate the terms in Example 1 to the roles of words in the equivalent sentence, 'Foxes hunt rodents', where 'foxes' serves as the grammatical *subject*, and the verb phrase 'hunts rodents' functions as its *predicate*. Assigning the indexing equivalent of the predicate (the phrase 'Hunting of rodents') to the display represents a departure from the shunting procedures used to generate entries in the standard format (see p 14-15). Straightforward shunting, applied to the strings above, would have produced the following entries under their performer terms:

*Foxes. Hunting of rodents

*Foremen. Training of apprentices. Aerospace industries

— where the 'predicate' appears in the qualifier, not the display. Asterisks have been added to mark these entries as 'unacceptable', but strictly speaking there is nothing logically wrong with them — they convey their subjects as clearly as the versions shown in examples 1 and 2. Nevertheless, entries produced by the predicate transformation offer advantages not only for the index user but also the index producer. These entries frequently bring together terms that are logically linked by one-to-one relations but are necessarily separated in the input string. This occurs in Example 2 above, where the concept 'apprentices' is coded as *part* of the 'aerospace industries', and 'foremen' is coded, equally logically, as the *agent* of 'training'. A moment's reflection will show, however, that the 'foremen' are also *part* of these industries. A document on a limited aspect of 'foremen', e.g. their 'remuneration', would be indexed as follows:

Example 3:

Subject: Remuneration of foremen in the aerospace industries

String: (1) aerospace industries
(p) foremen
(2) remuneration

Entries: Aerospace industries
  Foremen. Remuneration

Foremen. Aerospace industries
  Remuneration

Remuneration. Foremen. Aerospace industries

It can be seen that the heading (lead + qualifier) in the entry under 'foremen' in Example 2 (generated by the predicate transformation), exactly matches the heading in the second entry above (produced in the standard format). Since common headings are automatically cancelled, these outputs will be filed together:

Foremen. Aerospace industries
  Remuneration
  Training of apprentices

This represents an advantage for the user, since it reduces the scatter of entries relating to agent terms (such as 'foremen'), and brings their various attributes together as a sequence of displays that covers not only their properties and the actions directed towards them but also the actions they perform. This is also advantageous from the index producer's point of view, since it generates shorter headings, and also allows a more economical stacking of displays under common headings.

When anticipating the entries that will be produced under performer terms, we need to remember that the predicate transformation will not operate unless the term coded '3' *immediately* follows an action concept. Strings can contain terms coded '3' *without* immediately preceding actions, e.g.

Example 4:

Subject: Labelling containers for skimmed milk

String: (1) milk $21 skimmed
(3) containers $w for
(2) labelling

Entries: Milk
  Skimmed milk. Containers. Labelling

Skimmed milk
  Containers. Labelling

Containers. Skimmed milk
  Labelling

Labelling. Containers for skimmed milk

The term 'containers' in the string above has rightly been coded as a performer, but it implies an action ('containing') so clearly that there is no need to state this concept overtly in the string. Consequently, all the entries are produced in the standard format.

Further examples of subjects involving the predicate transformation, selected to show particular features of performer terms and their entries, are analysed below:

Example 5:

Subject: Frost damage to buildings

String: (1) buildings
(2) damage $v by $w to
(3) frost

Entries: Buildings
Damage by frost

Damage. Buildings
By frost

Frost
Damage to buildings

Note: The majority of terms coded as agents refer to animate entities (such as 'foxes' and 'foremen' in examples 1 and 2), but this role is occasionally assumed by inanimate concepts, including actions or effects (as in the example above). It might be noted in passing that most inanimate things coded as performers have roles as *instruments* (considered in the next chapter) rather than *agents*.

Example 6:

Subject: Pollution of rivers by industrial chemicals

String: (1) rivers
(2) pollution $v by $w of
(3) chemicals $21 industrial

Entries: Rivers
Pollution by industrial chemicals

Pollution. Rivers
By industrial chemicals

Chemicals
Industrial chemicals. Pollution of rivers

Industrial chemicals
Pollution of rivers

Note: If a concept with the role of performer is expressed as a compound term consisting of a focus and difference(s), the differencing procedures are always applied *before* the predicate transformation when entries are produced under part(s) of the performer term.

This accounts for the structure of the entry under 'chemicals', where the full form of the agent term, 'industrial chemicals', precedes the predicate, 'pollution of rivers', in the display.

Example 7:

Subject: Research into tropical diseases by Scottish universities

String: (2) diseases $21 tropical
(2) research $v by $w into
(sub 2↓) (3) Scottish universities
(0) Scotland
(1) universities
— *Substitute block* [(0) and (1)]

Entries: Diseases
Tropical diseases. Research by Scottish universities

Tropical diseases
Research by Scottish universities

Universities. Scotland
Research into tropical diseases

Note: This resembles, in some respects, a string used earlier (p 31) to illustrate the downward-reading substitute. From the viewpoint of the action, 'research', the term 'Scottish universities' represents a *single* agentive concept — this is expressed by the substitute. This concept is amenable, however, to analysis into simpler components, each assuming its own role — these are conveyed by the terms and operators following the substitute. Straightforward shunting, determined by the '0-1' pattern of operators, is applied to the terms within the downward-reading substitute block. This ensures consistency, when 'universities' comes into the lead, with entries generated from simpler strings such as:

(0) Scotland
(1) universities

Agents and actions without objects

Most of the examples in this chapter have dealt with concepts related as object, transitive action and performer. Terms with these roles have been organised into strings matching the general model:

(1) *object*
(2) *action*
(3) *performer*

For the sake of consistency in authority files (leading to simpler explanations) this model should be taken as the standard when indexing subjects that deal with actions and performers *without* referring to objects (except, of course, by implication). This is seen in the two examples below:

Example 8:

Subject: Reading by children

String: (2) réading $v by
(3) children

Entries: Reading
By children

Children
Reading

Example 9 (derived from Example 5, with the object term deleted)

Subject: Frost damage

String: (2) damage $v by
(3) frost

Entries: Damage
By frost

Frost
Damage

The entries generated under the agent terms ('children' and 'frost') in the examples above resemble, in terms of layout, those that are typically generated from strings containing actions related to objects (rather than agents), where the object term appears in the lead and the action in the display, e.g.

Buildings
Damage

In the examples above, this structural resemblence does not give rise to problems, since the roles of concepts (as actions and agents) are self-revealing; 'children' are not subject to 'reading', and 'frost' is immune to 'damage'. In some cases, however, ambiguous entries will be produced if the object is not clearly identified. This would occur if we dropped the term 'rodents' from Example 1, leaving the more general topic, 'Hunting by foxes'. Expressing this subject by the string:

*(2) hunting $v by
(3) foxes

- would lead to the following entry under the agent term:

*Foxes
Hunting

This suggests a valid and quite common topic, 'fox hunting', but not the subject intended by the indexer †. In cases such as this, it is necessary to select a term to express the general class of objects to which the action refers (e.g. 'animals'), and introduce this into the string:

Example 10:

Subject: Hunting by foxes

String: (1) animals
(2) hunting $v by $w of
(3) foxes

Entries: Animals
Hunting by foxes

Hunting. Animals
By foxes

Foxes
Hunting of animals

Blank field inserts

As noted earlier, some agent terms so clearly imply the actions with which they are usually associated that these actions can safely be left unstated in strings (see, for example, the string dealing with 'containers' on p 134). Occasionally, however, a term of this kind (coded '3' as an agent), follows the name of an action (coded '2') for which it is *not* responsible. This would occur in the following string:

*(1) women
(2) employment $w of
(3) law

Since a '2-3' pattern of operators automatically triggers the predicate transformation when the term coded '3' appears in the lead, this string would generate the following entry under 'law':

*Law
Employment of women

---

† There is evidence to suggest that users of PRECIS indexes become accustomed to the appearance of *done-to* terms in the heading and *done-by* terms in the display. This is offered as a reason (among others) for regarding consistency as important, and for care in constructing phrases when leads are made under performer terms.

This could be misinterpreted as 'Employment of women in the legal services' (see the Footnote on p 138). A more appropriate output can be achieved, without changing the operators assigned to terms, by inserting a *blank field*, coded '2', into the string:

Example 11:

Subject: Law of employment of women

String: (1) women
(2) employment $w of
(2) — *blank field insert*
(3) law

Entries: Women
Employment. Law

Employment. Women
Law

Law. Employment of women

Inserting a blank field in this way does not prevent the functioning of the predicate transformation, but the computer, following instructions, assigns the *empty* field to the display position. The rest of the terms in the example above were then assigned to their standard format positions in accordance with Stage 5 of the procedures described earlier (see p 132-133).

In effect, the blank field in the example above identifies the space that would have been occupied by the implied action for which 'law' is responsible — this might be expressed by a phrase such as 'social regulation and control'. This string therefore contains an implied *second action*: one which clearly belongs to Type 'C' (see p 116).

Terms expressing 'factors'

Many topics call for reference to concepts with roles that can be grouped conveniently under the general label 'factors', as in '*Safety factors* in the design of electrical equipment in mines'. A study of typical terms belonging to this category shows that they consistently refer to some kind of external influence (a sort of 'pressure'), directed towards the other concepts comprising the core of the subject. To that extent they represent performers, in much the same way that the concept 'law' was recognised as a performer in Example 11 above. Their treatment in strings also resembles the earlier treatment of 'law':

— the 'factors' term should be prefixed by the operator '3';

— if this term is marked as a lead, and if it also follows an action concept in the string (e.g. a term coded '2'), the factors term should be preceded by a *blank field insert.*

Both conditions apply to the first and second examples below.

Example 12:

Subject: Safety factors in the design of electrical equipment in mines

String:
(1) ✓mines
(p) ✓electrical equipment
(2) design $w of
(2)
(3) ✓safety factors

Entries:
Mines
Electrical equipment. Design. Safety factors

Electrical equipment. Mines
Design. Safety factors

Safety factors. Design of electrical equipment. Mines

Example 13:

Subject: Psychological factors in human cardiovascular diseases

String:
(1) man
(p) ✓cardiovascular system
(2) ✓diseases
(2)
(3) ✓psychological factors

Entries:
Cardiovascular system. Man
Diseases. Psychological factors

Diseases. Cardiovascular system. Man
Psychological factors

Psychological factors. Diseases. Cardiovascular system. Man

Example 14:

Subject: Genetic factors in seed dormancy of flowering plants in deserts

String: (0) deserts
(1) plants $21 flowering
(p) seeds
(p) dormancy
(3) genetic factors

Entries: Deserts
Flowering plants. Seeds. Dormancy. Genetic factors

Plants. Deserts
Flowering plants. Seeds. Dormancy. Genetic factors

Flowering plants. Deserts
Seeds. Dormancy. Genetic factors

Seeds. Flowering plants. Deserts
Dormancy. Genetic factors

Dormancy. Seeds. Flowering plants. Deserts
Genetic factors

Genetic factors. Dormancy. Seeds. Flowering plants. Deserts

Note: A blank field insert is not needed in this case since the string does not contain a term coded '2', 's' or 't' which would otherwise trigger the predicate transformation.

The performatory role of a 'factors' concept is conveyed by the meaning embedded within its focal noun: a *factor* is defined in Webster's as an *agent* or *doer* (1). This concept is separated by an unstated second action from the rest of the concepts comprising the core of the subject †. Due to this separation, a 'factors' term indicates a shift in the author's focus of attention that can be significant enough to affect the user's assessment of a document as relevant or non-relevant. Usually, therefore, it should be included in a string if it clearly comprises the major part of a subject.

Many subjects deal with the indirect effects of one concept upon another where the role of the affecting concept is *not* clearly implied

---

(1) Webster's Third new international dictionary. Springfield, Mass., G & C Merriam, 1971

† It is not difficult to relate these implied concepts to the classes of second actions considered earlier (p 109-110). Terms such as 'safety factors' and 'psychological factors' suggest some kind of *interference*; 'genetic factors' implies a *coming-into-being*. Some blank field inserts can be seen as traces of these unstated second actions.

by its name. Its role as a performer should then be made explicit, using procedures based on the operator 's' described in Chapter 11.

Concepts involved in two-way interactions

****
Operator 'u' = Two-way interaction
****

Almost all the subjects containing actions considered so far have dealt with relationships that can be described as *one-way*. That is to say, one of the concepts could be identified as the object, and another as the performer, with no suggestion that these roles could be shared or reversed except by changing the subject. A number of actions belong, however, to a special category of concepts which entail reciprocal or *two-way* interactions. If, for example, we say that 'A is married to B', we can then infer the reciprocal statement, 'B is married to A'. Actions belonging to this category can be recognised by certain features when indexing:

— they always involve at least two other concepts, one on either side of the interaction;
— these interrelated concepts serve simultaneously as object and performer of the *same action*.

When indexing subjects containing these concepts, a special operator, 'u', is used to indicate the two-way interaction. The interrelated concepts also form special operator patterns, as seen in the example below:

Example 15:

Subject: Foreign relations between Brazil and Portugal

String: (1) ✓d Brazil
(u) ✓ foreign relations $v with $w with
(1) ✓d Portugal

Entries: Brazil
Foreign relations with Portugal

Foreign relations. Brazil
With Portugal

Foreign relations. Portugal
With Brazil

Portugal
Foreign relations with Brazil

The following points should be noted in the string and entries above:

(a) The terms on either side of the action coded 'u' are prefixed by the same operator, i.e. '1' †. This coding marks the concepts 'Brazil' and 'Portugal' as sharing the role of key system and also the role of performer. For the sake of consistency in these cases, terms should be set down alphabetically, e.g. 'Brazil' before 'Portugal'.

(b) The operator 'u' which precedes 'foreign relations' marks it as a *two-way interaction*. A clue to this two-wayness is given by the prepositions attached to the action term; the same word occurs as both the upward- and downward-reading connective (such as 'with' above).

(c) Since the term coded 'u' was marked as a lead it automatically generated *two* entries:

(i) one produced by standard shunting, where the earlier term, 'Brazil', appears in the qualifier, and the following term, 'Portugal', is printed in the display;

(ii) one produced in a special format, where the term that *follows* the action in the string is *assigned to the qualifier*, and the earlier term in the string *appears in the display*.

(d) When 'Portugal' appears in the lead it is treated as a performer (this role is embedded in the meaning of 'u'), and the entry is generated by the predicate transformation, so that the phrase 'Foreign relations with Brazil' is assigned to the display.

A two-way interaction can link concepts at almost any position within the core of a subject. A reciprocal action linking *parts* occurs in the following example:

---

† This is one of only three circumstances in which the operator '1' can logically be assigned to more than one term in a theme. This coding could also occur in the following cases:
— a substitute is coded '1';
— the operator '1' is assigned to the concept immediately following an *author-attributed association* (operator 't', described in Chapter 12).

Example 16:

Subject: Interpersonal relations between nurses and patients in hospitals

String:
(1) hospitals
(p) nurses
(u) interpersonal relations $v with $w with
(p) patients

Entries:

Hospitals
Nurses. Interpersonal relations with patients

Nurses. Hospitals
Interpersonal relations with patients

Interpersonal relations. Nurses. Hospitals
With patients

Interpersonal relations. Patients. Hospitals
With nurses

Patients. Hospitals
Interpersonal relations with nurses

Note that the operator 'p' assigned to 'patients' indicates that this concept shares, with 'nurses', a whole-part relationship to 'hospitals' — it does *not* indicate part of the two-way interaction. In fact, *terms identified by the operator 'u' cannot have dependent elements*. They can, however, be differenced, and they can be linked, as coordinate concepts, to other two-way interactions. These two conditions occur in the following subjects:

Example 17:

Subject: Economic cooperation between Hungary and the Soviet Union

String:
(1) Hungary
(u) cooperation $21 economic $v with $w with
(1) Soviet Union

Entries:

Hungary
Economic cooperation with Soviet Union

Cooperation. Hungary
Economic cooperation with Soviet Union

Economic cooperation. Hungary
With Soviet Union

Cooperation. Soviet Union
Economic cooperation with Hungary

Economic cooperation. Soviet Union
With Hungary

Soviet Union
Economic cooperation with Hungary

Example 18:

Subject: Chinese cultural & economic relations with Canada

String: (1) Canada
(u) cultural relations $v &
(g) economic relations $v with $w with
(1) China

Entries: Canada
Cultural relations & economic relations with China

Cultural relations. Canada
With China

Cultural relations. China
With Canada

Economic relations. Canada
With China

Economic relations. China
With Canada

China
Cultural relations & economic relations with Canada

Faced by the amount of output generated from the relatively simple 3- and 4-term strings shown as examples 17 and 18, the use of a computer to handle the clerical side of index production becomes an attractive, and clearly economical, proposition.

The list below, which is not exhaustive, shows terms that are typically coded 'u':

Contracts	Ecumenical relations
Cooperation	Foreign relations
Cultural relations	Interpersonal relationships
Economic relations	Negotiations

Further notes on the operator 'u'

Agencies using PRECIS as an index to a classified file cannot use 'u' if the concepts which precede and follow the two-way interaction are associated with different class numbers. This would occur if the subject shown as Example 15 were to be matched by numbers taken from the Dewey Decimal Classification:

— the first and second entries should lead to one class number, i.e.

Brazil
  Foreign relations with Portugal 327.810469

Foreign relations. Brazil
  With Portugal 327.810469

— the second and third entries should lead to a different number, i.e.

Portugal
  Foreign relations with Brazil 327.469081

Foreign relations. Portugal
  With Brazil 327.469081

This should be handled by writing two strings, each associated with its own class mark, e.g.

String 1	*String 2*
(1) Brazil	(1) Portugal
(2) foreign relations $v with	(2) foreign relations $v with
(3) Portugal	(3) Brazil
Class mark: 327.810469	*Class mark:* 327.469081

These will generate exactly the same entries as those shown on p 142-143.

EXERCISES (For Answers, see Appendix 4, p 327)

Exercise 11

Write strings and entries for the following subjects:

(a) Hijacking of aircraft by terrorists

(b) Assimilation of ammonium by plants

(c) Financial assistance for the preservation of steam locomotives

(d) Singing by male voice choirs

(e) Local authority care of mentally handicapped persons

(f) Painting by numbers

(g) Research into dreaming by children

(h) Environmental factors in the location of oil refineries

11. Role definers and directional properties

****

Operator 's' = Role definer, Directional property

****

Role definers

As noted earlier (p 141), the performing role of a concept such as 'safety factors' is conveyed by the meaning usually attached to the focal noun, i.e. 'factors'. This would also apply in the following case, where the presence of a focal noun, 'models', in the term coded '3', sufficiently implies its role as the performer of an unstated second action (i.e. 'modelling' or 'simulation').

Example 1:

Subject: Mathematical models of the diffusion of innovations

String:
(1) innovations
(2) diffusion $w of
(2)
(3) mathematical models

Entries:
Innovations
  Diffusion. Mathematical models

Mathematical models. Diffusion of innovations

Note: It is worth noting, in passing, the misleading entry that would have been generated under the term coded '3' if neither a blank field nor a connective had been inserted into the string:

*Mathematical models. Innovations
  Diffusion

Concepts in many subjects can be identified as performers of actions a step 'removed' from the other concepts in the string (similar to 'mathematical models' in the example above), but their performatory roles are not suggested by their names. This can be illustrated by contrasting the following pair of subjects:

(i) Care of babies by fathers

(ii) Role of fathers in the care of babies

The concepts in the first of these topics are directly interrelated, with roles that are similar to those seen in many earlier examples:

Example 2:

Subject: Care of babies by fathers

String: (1) babies
(2) care $v by $w of
(3) fathers

Entries: Babies
Care by fathers

Fathers
Care of babies

The role of 'fathers' is not quite so definite in the second subject. We can say that they have some kind of indirect performatory role, but they cannot be identified as agents directly responsible for the action 'care of babies'. In these situations, we need to insert an explaining term into the string to indicate the role of a concept such as 'fathers' as an *indirect performer*. These *role defining terms* are identified by the operator 's'.

Example 3:

Subject: Role of fathers in the care of babies

String: (1) babies
(2) care $w of
(s) role $v of $w in
(3) fathers

Entries: Babies
Care. Role of fathers

Fathers
Role in care of babies

Note that terms prefixed by 's' are classed as actions, so that the predicate transformation operates when an entry is generated under a concept coded '3' which immediately follows a concept coded 's'.

The inserted phrase 'role-of-in' represents the loosest kind of relationship between an indirect performer and the concepts named earlier in the string. In some cases the roles of these performers can be indicated more specifically; for example, as *participators*, *influencers*, *instruments*, *tools*, etc. Many of these roles can be assumed by concepts of various kinds, both things and actions. These features occur in the following examples:

Example 4:

Subject: *Participation* of clergy in Italian resistance movements, 1940-1945

String:
(0) Italy
(1) resistance movements $d 1940-1945
(s) participation $v of $w in
(3) clergy

Entries:

Italy
Resistance movements, *1940-1945*. Participation of clergy

Resistance movements. Italy
1940-1945. Participation of clergy

Clergy. Italy
Participation in resistance movements, *1940-1945*

Example 5:

Subject: Canada's *influence* on American foreign relations with Iran

String:
(1) Iran
(u) foreign relations $v with $w with
(1) United States
(sub 3↑) (2) foreign relations between Iran and United States
(s) influence $v of $w on
(3) Canada

Entries:

Iran
Foreign relations with United States. Influence of Canada

Foreign relations. Iran
With United States. Influence of Canada

Foreign relations. United States
With Iran. Influence of Canada

United States
Foreign relations with Iran. Influence of Canada

Canada
Influence on foreign relations between Iran and United States

Note: As in some previous examples, a substitute is needed when a string contains a second action (e.g. 'influence'), and a later term (e.g. 'Canada') appears in the lead.

Example 6:

Subject: *Effect* of taxation on the living standards of pensioners

String: (1) pensioners
(p) living standards $w of
(s) effects $v of $w on
(3) taxation

Entries: Pensioners
Living standards. Effects of taxation

Living standards. Pensioners
Effects of taxation

Taxation
Effects on living standards of pensioners

Note: The term 'effects' is more appropriate than 'influence' when the *influencer* is an inanimate concept, such as 'taxation' in the example above. In other circumstances, 'taxation' would have been coded as an action, operator '2'.

Example 7:

Subject: *Use* of psychotropic drugs in behaviour modification in animals

String: (1) animals
(2) behaviour $w in
(2) modification $w of
(s) use $v of $w in
(3) drugs $21 psychotropic

Entries: Animals
Behaviour. Modification. Use of psychotropic drugs

Behaviour. Animals
Modification. Use of psychotropic drugs

Drugs
Psychotropic drugs. Use in modification of behaviour in animals

Psychotropic drugs
Use in modification of behaviour in animals

Note: When the term coded '3' consists of a focus and difference(s), the differencing procedures are (again) completed *before* the predicate transformation is applied if the lead contains only part of the compound term (e.g. 'drugs').

Example 8:

Subject: Software packages for microcomputer systems *applied* to school administration

String: (1) schools
(2) administration $w of
(s) applications $v of $w in
(3) computer systems $31 micro
(p) software packages

Entries: Schools
Administration. Applications of microcomputer systems. Software packages

Administration. Schools
Applications of microcomputer systems. Software packages

Computer systems
Microcomputer systems. Software packages. Applications in adminstration of schools

Microcomputer systems
Software packages. Applications in administration of schools

Software packages. Microcomputer systems
Applications in administration of schools

Notes:

(a) In this example, the performer is not only expressed by a compound term (as in Example 7), but is also followed by a dependent element. The components of the display line in the entry under 'computer systems' were then selected in the following order:
(i) the full form of the term, 'microcomputer systems';
(ii) its dependent element, 'software packages';
(iii) the action term earlier in the string, 'applications', plus its connective, 'in', then the rest of the phrase.
This means that the predicate transformation was given a lower priority than the differencing codes and dependent element when the display was assembled. An explanation of this choice of order is suggested in Appendix 3 (p 313).

(b) *Instruments* and *tools* are typically indicated (as in examples 7 and 8) by the phrases 'applications-of-in' and 'use-of-in'. The choice of 'use' rather than 'applications' is more appropriate when the performer is an inanimate concept with no suggestion of a human component, e.g. 'drugs' in Example 7. The concept 'computer systems' in the subject above represents a complex system, including human operators, etc. (see Note 2 on p 105).

English allows distinctions that cannot be made in all other languages — for example, between 'influence' and 'effects', or between 'use' and 'applications'. Even so, this role defining function is regularly handled by a limited repertory of standard terms and connectives:

role-of-in

participation-of-in

influence-of-on

effects-of-on

use-of-in

applications-of-in.

Directional properties

The terms listed above ('role', etc.) are sometimes used to distinguish between *direct agents* (Example 2), and *indirect performers* (examples 3 to 8). They were all inserted into strings to 'explain' the functions of their following terms. None of them was marked as a lead, and a special operator to cope with this role defining function hardly seems to be justified. All these concepts behave as actions (they trigger the predicate transformation when their following terms, coded '3', appear as leads), and they could have been indicated by the operator '2'. A need to regard these terms as members of a special class called *directional properties* becomes apparent, however, as soon as we consider one of them as a candidate for the lead. This reveals the need for a new format, which calls, in its turn, for a special operator with its own output instructions.

A term such as 'role' would sometimes acquire sufficient importance to justify a lead when it refers to the social role of a particular class of persons, as in 'Role of women in English politics in the 19th century'. A string coded as follows:

(1) England
(2) politics
*(2) role $d 1800-1900 $v of $w in
(3) women

— will generate the following entries:

England
Politics. Role of women, *1800-1900*

Politics. England
Role of women, *1800-1900*

*Role. Politics. England
Of women, *1800-1900*

Women. England
Role in politics, *1800-1900*

These outputs appear generally acceptable with the exception of the entry under 'role', where the order of terms is not particularly helpful. Sociologists tend to associate roles with their *possessors* (e.g. 'women') rather than the areas of social activity in which they are exercised (e.g. 'politics'). A diagnosis along these lines points to two important characteristics of the concepts belonging to this special class:

(a) They behave somewhat like actions, to the extent that they are *directed towards* other concepts (such as 'politics' in the example above). We can hardly conceive of a role that is not directed in this way. This 'target' concept cannot be rated as an object in the grammatical sense considered on p 109, but we can usefully refer to it as a *quasi-object*, and recognise, again, the working of the general principle which underlies the order of terms in any PRECIS string containing an action and its object, which calls for the concept towards which the action is directed to be cited before the action itself.

(b) At the same time, these concepts belong in a whole-part or thing-property sense to the concept which *follows* them in the string. We might even refer to a person's role as a kind of 'software component'. This means that the order of whole and part terms in the string shown above differs from the standard order seen in earlier examples, where the names of wholes were consistently cited *before* their parts or properties. For example, a general work on the role of women would be indexed as follows:

Example 9:

Subject: The role of women

String: (1) women
(p) role

Entries: **Women**
Role

Role. Women

For the sake of consistency in outputs, we need to take the entries from this simple string as our models if 'role' is selected as a lead in the more complex subject considered earlier †. That is to say, when the name of the part or property ('role') appears in the lead, the name of the whole ('women') should be printed in the qualifier. This is, in fact, the format generated whenever a term coded 's' appears in the lead, as seen in the following examples.

---

† For obvious reasons, we cannot take complex subjects as paradigms when analysing simpler subjects.

Example 10:

Subject: Role of women in English politics in the 19th century

String:
(1) England — /d
(2) politics ——— *Quasi-object*
(s) role $d 1800-1900 $v of $w in —— *Directional property*
(3) women ——— *Possessor/Performer*

Entries:

England
Politics. Role of women, *1800-1900*

Politics. England
Role of women, *1800-1900*

Role. Women. England
In politics, *1800-1900*

Women. England
Role in politics, *1800-1900*

The entries produced under 'England' and 'politics' are in the standard format. The entry under 'women' is a further example of the predicate transformation. The structure of the entry under 'role' differs from most of those seen in earlier examples, insofar as its later term (i.e. 'women', coded '3') was assigned to the *qualifier*, and its earlier term (embedded within the phrase 'In politics') appeared in the *display* †.

A concept such as 'attitudes' demonstrates all the salient features of this class of directional properties, and illustrates particularly well their Janus-like characters. From one point of view an attitude can be perceived as a part or property of the person holding it — we refer to someone as *having* (rather than 'doing') an attitude, just as we say that a person has a role. At the same time, the concept 'attitudes' has some characteristics of an action; it must be *directed towards* some other concept, in much the same way that a transitive action is directed towards its object (whether stated or implied). A term such as 'attitudes' cannot be traced to a verb in English; nevertheless, we cannot conceive of an attitude except when related to some kind of 'target' concept (its quasi-object). The concept 'attitudes' therefore qualifies on two essential counts as a directional property, and should be coded 's' in a topic such as the following:

---

† A similar structure has, in fact, been seen before. It is characteristic of the second of the two entries generated under a two-way interaction (operator 'u') — see the examples on p 144.

Example 11:

Subject: Students' attitudes to homework

String: (2) homework
(s) attitudes $v of $w to
(3) students

Entries: Homework
Attitudes of students

Attitudes. Students
To homework

Students
Attitudes to homework

Note: The structures of the second and third entries offer a basis for collocating various entries on students' attitudes, whether or not their quasi-objects are also present, e.g.

Attitudes. Students
To homework
To parents
etc.

Students
Attitudes
Attitudes to homework
Attitudes to parents
etc.

Further concepts that are typically coded 's' are included in the examples below:

Example 12:

Subject: Israeli government policies on control of inflation

String: (1) Israel
(2) inflation
(2) control $w of
(s) policies $v of $w on
(3) government

Entries: Israel
Inflation. Control. Policies of government

Inflation. Israel
Control. Policies of government

Policies. Government. Israel
On control of inflation

Government. Israel
Policies on control of inflation

Example 13:

Subject: Marx's theories of religion

String: (2) religion
(s) theories $v of $w of
(3) Marx, Karl

Entries: Religion
Theories of Marx, Karl

Theories. Marx, Karl
Of religion

Marx, Karl
Theories of religion

Note: The term 'theories' was led only for the sake of demonstration.

Directional properties coded 's' are also expressed by terms such as 'implications', 'accountability', 'responsibility', etc. The extent to which these terms justify marking as leads tends to vary according to subject field, and should be determined by local policies.

As we might expect, directional properties occur far less often in practice than the more usual actions coded '2'. Distinguishing between these different classes of action, and therefore choosing the appropriate operator, is not difficult in most cases. Even in the act of writing the string, an indexer tends to visualise the entry that will be generated under each lead, and so would anticipate the 'wrong' entry produced by a directional property coded '2' (see the example under 'role' on p 152). In cases of doubt, two tests for directional properties can be applied:

1. Some kind of possessive relationship should link a directional property with the term coded '3' which follows it in the string. This is illustrated by examples 9 and 10 (p 153-154) — we can say that women *have* roles, not that they *do* them.

2. As a further test, the indexer should mentally visualise a substitute phrase which begins with the name of the action or directional property, and also includes the adjacent earlier and later terms in the string. This is the kind of substitute that would be needed if the string were extended by a second action (e.g. 'research') marked as a lead. It will then be found that substitutes based on directional properties tend to differ, in terms of their structure, from those beginning

with the more usual '2-type' actions:

Example 14 (string containing an action coded '2')

Subject: Research into atmospheric pollution by industries

String: (1) atmosphere
(2) pollution $v by $w of
(3) industries
(sub 3↑) (2) pollution of atmosphere by industries
(2) research

Entries: Atmosphere
Pollution by industries. Research

Pollution. Atmosphere
By industries. Research

Industries
Pollution of atmosphere. Research

Research. Pollution of atmosphere by industries

In substitutes based upon 2-type actions, the components of the phrase are consistently set down in the order:

Action-$w-object-$v-performer

Changing the order of the object and performer terms, as in *'Pollution by industries of atmosphere', produces an awkward, non-idiomatic phrase. This should be seen in contrast to the following analysis of a subject containing a directional property:

Example 15 (string containing a directional property coded 's')

Subject: Research into accountability of industries for pollution

String: (2) pollution
(s) accountability $v of $w for
(3) industries
(sub 3↑) (2) accountability of industries for pollution
(2) research

Entries: Pollution
Accountability of industries. Research

Accountability. Industries
For pollution. Research

Industries
Accountability for pollution. Research

Research. Accountability of industries for pollution

In cases such as this, the components of the substitute are set down in the order:

Directional property-$v-possessor-$w-quasi-object

Again, reversing the order of the second and third noun components produces an unidiomatic (and even ambiguous) expression, e.g. *'Accountability for pollution of industries'. Research has shown that this test can also be applied successfully in other non-inflected languages, both European and non-European. A possible explanation is suggested in Appendix 3 (p 313). In some unusual cases, concepts seem to give satisfactory outputs whether the terms in the substitute are ordered one way or the other. If this occurs, the term should be coded '2' rather than 's'.

EXERCISES (For Answers, see Appendix 4, p 329)

Exercise 12

Write strings and entries for the following subjects:

(a) Effects of inflation on civil servants' pensions in France

(b) Participation of employees in the management of small firms

(c) Investment by Swiss banks in multinational companies

(d) The use of artificial satellites in prospecting for mineral resources

(e) Public accountability of local authority officers

(f) Effects of advertising on the sales of Japanese cars in West Germany

(g) Trade union attitudes to automation in the printing industries

12. Author-attributed associations

****
Operator 't' = Author-attributed association
****

All the actions considered so far could be described as 'system initiated'. This simply means that the performer, if stated explicitly as part of the subject, would be identified as a core concept or the dependent element of a core concept. Two main classes of actions have been noted:

— *Intransitives*, where the performer is coded as the key system (operator '1') or one of its dependent elements.

— *Transitives*, where the performer is usually coded '3'. These can be further distinguished as:

(i) *one-way actions*, such as 'classification' and 'harvesting', where the roles of the object and performer cannot be reversed;

(ii) *two-way interactions*, such as 'foreign relations', where a given concept functions simultaneously as both agent and object.

This summary is offered as a contrast to the final class of actions recognised in PRECIS — those identified by the operator 't'. Actions belonging to this class differ from those considered earlier insofar as they are not performed by any of the concepts present within the core of the subject (whether stated or implied), but by an unstated entity outside the core — that is, the author. Three actions of this type have been recognised in practice; these are considered separately below.

'A' compared with 'B'

This refers to an act of comparison in a subject such as 'Home care of mentally handicapped persons *compared with* their hospitalization'. Although we can say that the action expressed by 'compared' was directed equally towards both kinds of 'care' (which means that it can be classed as a two-way interaction), neither of the concepts being compared was in any sense responsible for the performance of the action. This kind of *author-attributed association* is introduced by the operator 't':

Example 1:

Subject: Mentally handicapped persons: home care compared with hospitalization

String:
(1) mentally handicapped persons
(2) home care
(t) compared with — *Author-attributed block*
(2) hospitalization

Entries:
Mentally handicapped persons
Home care *compared with* hospitalization

Home care. Mentally handicapped persons *compared with* hospitalization

Hospitalization. Mentally handicapped persons *compared with* home care

The string and entries seen above differ in some important respects from examples studied earlier:

(a) The term following 'compared with' in the string (i.e. 'hospitalization') is prefixed by the operator '2'. This does not, as in previous examples, indicate an action directed towards the preceding concept (i.e. 'compared'). In fact, the concepts which precede and follow the author-attributed association in this example logically share the same context, as shown in the diagram:

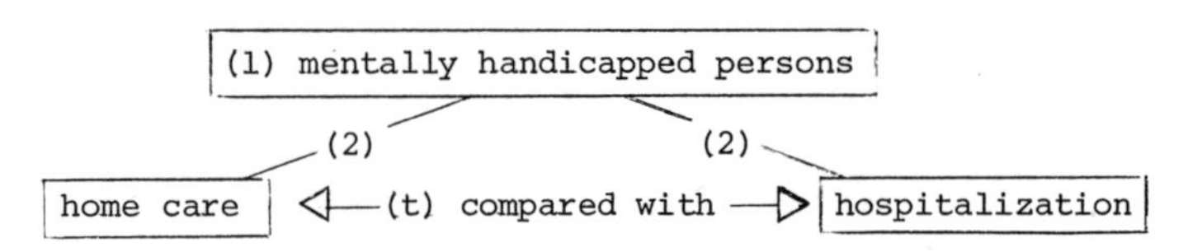

This diagram also indicates why:

— a term coded 't' can function only as a 'pivot' between the concepts associated by the author. It cannot possess its own dependent element(s), nor can it stand in its own right as the object of an action.

— a 't-term' must be accompanied by both an earlier and later concept; these together comprise the *author-attributed block*.

(b) The action 'compared' is expressed by a past participle; the same applies to some of the other 't-terms' studied later. These are the only cases in PRECIS where actions are not expressed as nouns.

(c) No attempt was made to generate a lead under the term coded 't'. In fact, the output program does not provide for a lead under one of these terms — it is even difficult to imagine how such an entry should be formatted.

(d) The term coded 't' appears in italic with a lower-case initial at all positions in the entry †. The term which follows the 't-term' in an entry (e.g. 'hospitalization' in the 1st and 2nd entries, and 'home care' in the 3rd) is also printed with a lower-case initial. These output conventions ensure that the terms comprising the author-attributed block are offered to the user as an unbroken sequence wherever they occur. Since this sequence is generated automatically in response to the operator 't', there is no need to write a connective code to mark, as a separate element, any preposition which might be attached to the 't-term' (e.g. 'with' in the example above).

(e) The predicate transformation is automatically triggered if the concept which follows the 't-term' in the string (e.g. 'hospitalization') is also marked as a lead. This, too, is determined by the operator 't'; it is not affected by the operator assigned to the following term.

The author-attributed block will also be printed as a single phrase if a later term, such as a second action, is added to a string and marked as a lead. If, for example, the string in Example 1 is extended by the term 'research' (led for demonstration purposes):

(1) mentally handicapped persons
(2) home care
(t) compared with
(2) hospitalization
(2) research

— the computer will generate the further entry:

---

† It is worth noting, in passing, that italic is frequently used as a de-emphasising device in indexes based on the Latin alphabet.

† Research. Hospitalization *compared with* home care. Mentally handicapped persons

In effect, the computer has then constructed the substitute which is sometimes needed when a later term is marked as a lead. This works, however, only when the 't-term' links relatively simple concepts. The indexer would still need to write a substitute in some of the more complex situations considered below.

In the example above the author compared a pair of concepts sharing a common context. A higher proportion of subjects involving 't-terms' deal with a given concept or set of concepts (e.g. 'economic development') reviewed in different contexts (e.g. 'Belgium *compared with* France'). This calls for a slightly more complex input, but the general procedures remain the same:

Example 2:

Subject: Economic development in Belgium compared with economic development in France

String:
(1) Belgium ✓d
(2) economic development $w in ✓
(t) compared with
(sub 2↓) (2) economic development in France
(1) France ✓d
(2) economic development ✓

Entries:

Belgium
Economic development *compared with* economic development in France

Economic development. Belgium
compared with economic development in France

France.
Economic development *compared with* economic development in Belgium

Economic development. France
compared with economic development in Belgium

---

† Some versions of the PRECIS programs arrange the terms in this phrase in their input or 'downward-reading' order, i.e.

Home care *compared with* hospitalization.

This does not affect the meaning or comprehensibility of the entry.

As shown in Example 2, a subject based on an author-attributed association can be seen as a pair of interrelated sub-themes:

Economic development in Belgium — *Sub-theme 1*
compared with
Economic development in France —— *Sub-theme 2*

Each theme is capable of standing as a topic in its own right. In many cases it is also amenable to further analysis, but for the sake of comprehensibility the sub-theme which *follows* the 't-term' in an entry should be presented to the user as a coherent whole. This was achieved in the example above by using two standard procedures:

(a) 'economic development' was linked to 'Belgium' by a $w connective, giving the phrase 'economic development in Belgium' in the 3rd and 4th entries;

(b) the phrase 'economic development in France' in the 1st and 2nd entries was handled by a downward-reading substitute.

The same procedures are used again in the following example, although the subject field, and some of the operators, are quite different.

Example 3:

Subject: Costs of coal-fired power stations compared with the costs of nuclear power stations

String:
(1) pǒwer stations $21 coal-fired
(p) cǒsts $w of
(t) compared with
(sub 2↓) (1) costs of nuclear power stations
(1) pǒwer stations $21 nuclear
(p) cǒsts

Entries:

Power stations
Coal-fired power stations. Costs *compared with* costs of nuclear power stations

Coal-fired power stations
Costs *compared with* costs of nuclear power stations

Costs. Coal-fired power stations
compared with costs of nuclear power stations

Power stations
Nuclear power stations. Costs *compared with* costs of coal-fired power stations

Nuclear power stations
Costs *compared with* costs of coal-fired power stations

Costs. Nuclear power stations
compared with costs of coal-fired power stations

'A' related to 'B'

Concepts introduced by the operator 's', used as a role definer, sometimes imply an element of causality: this certainly applies to terms such as 'effects' and 'influence' (see p 141-143). In certain fields, notably in the social sciences, making an implication of this kind could sometimes be seen as overstating a case — an author might claim that he studied a possible link between, say, 'inflation' and 'unemployment', without being prepared to identify one of these concepts as the cause of the other. Causality is likely, in any case, to be vaguely reciprocal in these situations. This vagueness is conveyed to the user by the weakest of the author-attributed associations, i.e. 'related to'.

Example 4:

Subject: Unemployment in the United States related to inflation

String:
(0) United States
(2) inflation
(t) related to
(2) unemployment

Entries:
United States
  Inflation *related to* unemployment

Inflation. United States
  related to unemployment

Unemployment. United States
  related to inflation

When the concepts on either side of an association term are logically equal in this way, they should, for the sake of consistency, be input in alphabetical order, e.g. 'inflation' before 'unemployment'.

'A' expounded by 'B'

In structural terms, the string and entries above resemble those seen in Example 1; 'compared with' and 'related to' can both be classed as *two-way* attributions. Only a single *one-way action* introduced by 't' has been encountered in practice. This occurs when an author uses the concepts belonging to one field as tools for explaining ideas usually associated with a different field, as in the following example:

Example 5:

Subject: Meaning expounded by information theory

String: (1) meaning
(t) $v expounded by $w expounding
(3) information theory

Entries: Meaning
expounded by information theory

Information theory
expounding meaning

The relative roles of the core concepts are expressed in the string by their operators: the object of exposition is coded '1', and the tool is coded '3'. These roles are made explicit in the entries by the difference between the phrases 'expounded by' and 'expounding' †. Selection of the phrase appropriate for each entry is regulated by the connective codes $v and $w, used in this case to identify complete connecting phrases, not simply prepositions.

Limitations on the use of 't'

This operator is useful provided that a subject can be analysed as a *pair* of sub-themes (whether simple or complex) associated by an author in one of the three ways considered above. Many topics consist, however, of *three or more* interrelated sub-themes — for example, a 'Comparative study of higher education in France, Switzerland and West Germany' (or even in Western Europe as a whole). Complexity at this level exceeds the intended scope of 't', and calls for the use of one of the operators ('4', '5' and '6') described in the next chapter. For example, the act of comparison in the subject above could be indicated by a term introduced by the operator '6' (form of document):

(0) France
(f) Switzerland $v &
(f) West Germany
(2) higher education
(6) comparative studies

---

† Some indexing agencies, particularly in North America (where 'exposition' seems to possess a stuffy connotation), prefer the input:

(t) $v explained by $w explaining

Since 'comparative' (embedded in the name of the form) functions as a *binding concept* in the string above, the coordinate concepts are coded 'f' rather than 'g' (see p 97-99). The entries produced from strings containing terms prefixed by '4', '5' and '6' are explained in the next chapter.

EXERCISES (For Answers, see Appendix 4, p 331)

Exercise 13

Write strings and entries for the following subjects:

(a) Social status of engineers in Japan compared with their self-image

(b) Christian doctrine expounded by the psychoanalytical theories of C. G. Jung

(c) Academic achievement related to motivation in university students

(d) Relationship between growth rate in plants and soil humidity

13. Extra-core factors: operators 4, 5 and 6

The operators in this final set introduce concepts which generally fall outside the core of a subject, i.e.

— the author's viewpoint: *operator 4*.

— a selected instance, used as a model when explaining the topic expressed in the core: *operator 5*.

— the form of the document and/or its target user: *operator 6*.

Most documents, at least in theory, could be characterized in terms of these various factors. We could, for example, identify a textbook on the structure of inorganic compounds as written from a chemist's viewpoint (operator 4); we could trace and name the compounds used as examples (operator 5); we could even identify the document as a narrative text (operator 6). In normal practice, of course, none of these extra-core factors would be stated in the index; they are all sufficiently present by implication. It follows that a term introduced by one of these operators should be added to a string only when it indicates an unusual combination of circumstances. These operators are intended primarily to introduce what might be called *negative discrimination factors* — that is, terms which are likely to contradict a user's expectations to such an extent that they could serve as grounds for rejecting the entry, even though the subject expressed as the core appears to be relevant. For example, a reader might register a 'hit' when tracing an entry generated from the following string:

(1) birds ✓
(2) migration ✓

— but would still reject the document if the entry goes on to name a form other than a narrative:

Birds
  Migration — *Bibliographies*

The entry above shows that a term introduced by one of these operators (plus its dependent elements, if any) is printed in italic; again, this typeface is used as a de-emphasising device. When a term prefixed by '4', '5' or '6' is printed in the display it is also preceded by a long dash; this marks the boundary between the core of the subject and the extra-core factors considered in this chapter. If one of these extra-core terms is marked as a lead, the entry appears in a special format (the *inverted format*) illustrated in later examples.

Agencies using PRECIS to produce an index to citations arranged by class marks (such as the *British National Bibliography* and *Australian National Bibliography*) find that a term introduced by one of these operators often calls for a change to the class number, and can lead to a document being assigned to a different main class. For example, a work indicated by the entry shown above would be classed in the Dewey Decimal Classification (19th edition) with subject bibliographies at 016.5982525, not with works on bird migration at 598.2525.

Only one term in a string can be introduced by the operator '4'. Operators '5' and '6' can be repeated if necessary. If a string contains more than one of these operators, they must be written in the order *4, then 5, then 6*. They are introduced separately in this order below.

Aspects, viewpoints, perspectives

****
Operator '4' = Viewpoint-as-form
****

The expression 'viewpoint-as-form' is intended to highlight a difference between the extra-core factors introduced by '4' and those 'viewpoint' concepts (represented by terms such as 'attitudes', 'public opinion', etc.) which can occur as part of the core. Terms coded '4' consist of adjectival phrases, and can be separated into three groups distinguished by their focal nouns:

— terms ending in 'viewpoints', preceded by words that refer to *classes of people*, e.g. 'Christian viewpoints', 'Trade union viewpoints', etc.

— terms ending in 'perspectives', where the differencing words identify *disciplines*, as in 'sociological perspectives', 'philosophical perspectives', etc.

— terms ending in 'aspects'. In these cases the differencing words do not refer (except indirectly) to the holders of viewpoints, but instead identify *facets of the core* that were subjected to special study or emphasis, as in 'economic aspects', 'social aspects', etc.

The choice of one of these focal nouns rather than another is largely a matter of convention — they all convey the same general idea. It follows that an index should not contain two or more of these nouns preceded by the same adjective(s); for example, it should not contain 'psychological perspectives' and also 'psychological aspects'. None of the nouns listed above ('viewpoints', etc.) calls for a lead in its own right, although an entry is sometimes made under the whole of a '4-term'. The three classes of term noted above, and the special format associated with operators '4', '5' and '6', are illustrated in the examples below.

Example 1:

Subject: Christian viewpoints on marriage

String: (2) marriage
(4) Christian viewpoints

Entries: Marriage
— *Christian viewpoints*

Christian viewpoints
Marriage

Example 2:

Subject: Sociological perspectives on public transport services in urban regions

String: (0) urban regions
(1) transport services $21 public
(4) sociological perspectives

Entries: Urban regions
Public transport services — *Sociological perspectives*

Transport services. Urban regions
Public transport services — *Sociological perspectives*

Public transport services. Urban regions
— *Sociological perspectives*

Sociological perspectives
Urban regions. Public transport services

Example 3:

Subject: Economic aspects of nuclear power

String: (2) nuclear power
(4) economic aspects

Entries: Nuclear power
— *Economic aspects*

Economic aspects
Nuclear power

Certain characteristics of the entries above should be noted:

(a) The term coded '4' is printed in italic following a long dash whenever it occurs in the display. The long dash is also retained when the 'viewpoint' term appears as the *first* component of the display. This differs from entries seen earlier, where machine-generated punctuation marks were suppressed from the first position in the display. Retaining the dash in this position affects the filing of display lines under a common heading. Since punctuation marks (including the long dash) usually file ahead of alpha-numeric characters, retaining the dash leads to a set of interfiled entries such as:

Public transport services
— *Sociological perspectives*
Fares. Increases

— rather than:

*Public transport services
Fares. Increases
— *Sociological perspectives*

This means that extra-core factors which relate only to concepts in the heading are presented to the user *before* the core itself is extended by further concepts, such as parts, properties, actions, etc.

(b) The term coded '4' is printed in bold when it appears in the lead. The entry is then produced in the *inverted format*: the display consists of terms selected from the string in their *input order* (this can be seen clearly in the entry under 'Sociological perspectives' in Example 2).

(c) In all the examples above, the term coded '4' was dropped from the display when it appeared in the lead. It would have been repeated in the display in any of the following circumstances:

(i) if the lead did not contain the *whole* of the term (for example, if only the focus had been marked as a lead);

(ii) if the string contained a *later* term (coded '5' or '6');

(iii) if the term formed part of a block (seen in later examples), and *the whole of the block was not present in the heading* (i.e. the lead + qualifier). This applies particularly to terms coded '5', which always occur as the first components of blocks.

The effects of these conditions are shown in later examples.

It is again emphasised that a term coded '4' should be added to a string *only* when an explicit reference to the author's viewpoint might affect the user's perception of relevance. If one of these terms is used, the holder of the viewpoint should not be specified beyond a level that will serve this intended purpose. In particular, names of specific organizations should not be used as differences on 'viewpoints' terms; the viewpoint should be generalised as much as possible †. For example, a work on 'whaling' issued by an organization such as Greenpeace should be indexed as:

(2) whaling
(4) conservationist viewpoints

- not as:

*(2) whaling
(4) Greenpeace viewpoints

The more general string is then available for re-use if a later work on the same subject is issued by, say, Friends of the Earth. This policy of deliberate generalization is unlikely to affect the retrieval of documents containing the viewpoints of specific organizations. If a work has any kind of official standing, the name of the organization can usually be traced through another field in the document record (e.g. the author or publisher field).

---

† This applies mainly to general indexes. A different policy might be needed in an index to a special field or a limited range of materials.

Selected instance

****

Operator '5' = Selected instance

****

This operator was introduced to deal with those 'awkward' situations where an author sets out to present a relatively general subject, then consistently cites a particular instance as a model or source of evidence. For example, a general study of 'Personnel management in industry' might be illustrated throughout by cases (real or imaginary) encountered in the 'aerospace industries'. This topic would be indexed as follows:

Example 4:

Subject: Industrial personnel management (illustrated by cases in the aerospace industries)

String:
(1) industries
(2) personnel management
(5) study examples
(q) aerospace industries
} — *'5-block'*

Entries:

Industries
Personnel management — *Study examples: Aerospace industries*

Personnel management. Industries
— *Study examples: Aerospace industries*

Aerospace industries. *Study examples*
Industries. Personnel management

Some typical features of strings and entries containing '5-terms' can be seen in the example above:

(a) The term coded '5' ('study examples') has only an explanatory function. The same applies to the other '5-terms' considered later. None of these terms would normally be marked as a lead.

(b) Since the name of the selected instance ('aerospace industries') was prefixed by the operator 'q', this term was preceded by a colon in the display. It was also printed in italic in this position — remember that typography is controlled by the *numbered* operators.

(c) When the name of the instance appeared in the lead:

(i) the '5-term', in italic, was assigned to the qualifier. This is a further example of the standard format associated with all dependent elements (see p 75);

(ii) the terms comprising the 5-block were not repeated in the display, since the heading then contained the whole of the block, and the string did not contain a later term (see the conditions listed as *c(i)* to *c(iii)* on p 171);

(iii) the display again consisted of terms set down in their input order.

This operator is needed in only a limited number of situations, represented by the following repertory of standard '5-terms':

(a) *study examples*

(b) *study regions*

(c) *sample populations*

(d) *sources of evidence*

When one of the terms listed as (a) to (c) above is used to explain the role of a selected instance, the instance itself (e.g. 'aerospace industries' in Example 1) should represent either a *kind* or *part* of a concept that is present (or at least strongly implied) in the core (e.g. 'industries'). This condition does not apply to 'sources of evidence'. The standard terms listed as (b) to (d) above are illustrated in the following examples:

Example 5:

Subject: A Christian view of leisure in the United States, based on studies in California and New England

String:
(0) United States
(2) leisure
(4) Christian viewpoints
(5) study regions
(q) California $v &
(g) New England

(5) to (g): *5-block*

Entries:
Leisure. United States
— *Christian viewpoints — Study regions: California & New England*

Christian viewpoints
United States. Leisure — *Christian viewpoints — Study regions: California & New England*

California. *Study regions*
United States. Leisure — *Christian viewpoints — Study regions: California & New England*

New England. *Study regions*
United States. Leisure — *Christian viewpoints — Study regions: California & New England*

Note: In this example, all the terms in the string are repeated in the display lines of the 2nd, 3rd and 4th entries:

— 'Christian viewpoints' is repeated in the 2nd entry, since it is not the final term in the string;

— 'California' and 'New England' are both repeated in the 3rd and 4th entries, since neither of these headings contains the whole of the 5-block.

Example 6:

Subject: Literacy of young persons in Denmark, based on a study of adolescent girls in Copenhagen

String:
(0) Denmark
(1) young persons
(p) literacy
(5) sample populations
(q) girls $21 adolescent
(5) study regions
(q) Copenhagen

Entries:

Denmark
Young persons. Literacy — *Sample populations: Adolescent girls — Study regions: Copenhagen*

Young persons. Denmark
Literacy — *Sample populations: Adolescent girls — Study regions: Copenhagen*

Literacy. Young persons. Denmark
Sample populations: Adolescent girls — Study regions: Copenhagen

Girls. *Sample populations*
Denmark. Young persons. Literacy — *Sample populations: Adolescent girls — Study regions: Copenhagen*

Adolescent girls. *Sample populations*
Denmark. Young persons. Literacy — *Sample populations: Adolescent girls — Study regions: Copenhagen*

Copenhagen. *Study regions*
Denmark. Young persons. Literacy — *Sample populations: Adolescent girls*

Notes:

(a) When the focal noun 'girls' appears in the lead, the compound term 'adolescent girls' is not printed as the 1st component of the display. The whole of the term is printed instead in its input position.

(b) The compound term 'adolescent girls' is also repeated in the display of the 5th entry, since it is not the final term in the string.

(c) When more than one 5-block occurs in a string, as in the example above, the block beginning 'study regions' is usually cited last.

Example 7:

Subject: Unidentified flying objects: the Old Testament evidence

String: (1) ✓unidentified flying objects
(5) sources of evidence
(q) ✓Bible. O.T.

Entries: Unidentified flying objects
— *Sources of evidence: Bible. O.T.*

Bible. O.T. *Sources of evidence*
Unidentified flying objects

Notes:

(a) 'Sources of evidence' can also occur in the core of a subject such as 'How to use parish registers in genealogy'. This would be indexed as:

String: (2) ✓genealogy
(2)
(3) sources of evidence
(q) ✓parish registers

Entries: Genealogy
Sources of evidence: Parish registers

Parish registers. Sources of evidence. Genealogy

(b) It is necessary to distinguish between:

(i) references to records etc. associated with one field as *evidence* of phenomena in a possibly different field (as in Example 7 above);

(ii) using the concepts derived from one field as tools for *expounding* ideas in a different field.

The latter calls for the use of operator 't' (see p 164-165). In cases of doubt, strings should be based on '5' rather than 't'.

Subjects containing selected instances were earlier described as 'awkward'. This refers particularly to a problem that arises in agencies using PRECIS to produce indexes to classified files of citations. For practical reasons considered later, each PRECIS string should be matched by only one class mark from a given scheme. Consequently, the classifier has to choose either the core concept(s) or the instance as the primary factor when determining where the document should be classed. For example, the following subject:

Example 8:

Subject: Ergonomic factors in designing public institution buildings, based on trends in public library design

String:
(1) public institutions
(p) buildings
(2) design $w of
(2)
(3) ergonomic factors
(5) study examples
(q) public libraries

Entries:
Public institutions
Buildings. Design. Ergonomic factors — *Study examples: Public libraries*

Buildings. Public institutions
Design. Ergonomic factors — *Study examples: Public libraries*

Ergonomic factors. Design of buildings. Public institutions
— *Study examples: Public libraries*

Public libraries. *Study examples*
Public institutions. Buildings. Design. Ergonomic factors

— could be assigned to either of two places in the Dewey Decimal Classification:

— Public building design: 725

— Public library design: 727.8.

The choice of one place rather than the other is essentially a matter of local policy. It can be reported, however, that the majority of classifiers prefer to class consistently at the instance (i.e. 727.8 in the example above), on the grounds that although this might not fully capture the author's intention, it "cannot be wrong".

Like the other operators covered in this chapter, '5' should be used with caution, and only in the following circumstances:

(a) When the author states quite explicitly (usually in the Introduction) that the work is intended as a general study which happens to use a particular instance as a model or source of evidence.

(b) When the name of the instance can also be rated as a useful retrieval term.

If either of these conditions does not hold, or if a work refers to so many instances that they cannot all be specified, the work should be indexed more generally, without naming the instances, by adding a form term, 'case studies', introduced by the operator '6'.

Forms and targets

****

Operator '6' = Form of document and/or target user

****

Two kinds of concept are introduced by this operator:

(a) The physical or intellectual form of a document, expressed by terms such as 'tables', 'serials', 'atlases', 'biographies', etc.

(b) The class of users for whom a work is particularly intended, conveyed by phrases such as 'for children', 'for nursing', 'for librarianship', etc.

Forms

In line with the general recommendations concerning the operators described in this chapter, the name of a form should be added to a string only when it indicates such an unusual physical form or intellectual treatment that the user might have grounds for rejecting the entry. A term such as 'books', for example, would not normally be used to indicate a form in an index to a general library, although it might serve a useful purpose in a special environment, such as the index to a music collection where most of the documents consist of scores.

Experience has shown that the names of forms should be selected with care, based on guidelines such as the following:

(a) Forms should be expressed as generally as possible, bearing in mind the intended use of the terms covered in this chapter — that is, as negative discrimination factors. For example, it would normally be sufficient to indicate 'journals', 'newspapers', 'annuals', etc. by the single term 'serials'.

Example 9:

Subject: Pop music: a weekly review

String: (2) pop music
(6) serials

Entry: Pop music
— *Serials*

(b) In agencies that deal with more than one medium (including, say, films and recordings as well as printed materials) the name of a form should not 'favour' a given medium if a more general term is available. For example, preference should be given to a term such as 'visitors' guides' rather than 'guidebooks' — the former can be applied to audio presentations as well as printed guides.

Example 10:

Subject: Visitors' guide to the Tower of London

String: (0) London (NU)
(1) Tower of London
(6) visitors' guides

Entries: London
Tower of London — *Visitors' guides*

Tower of London
— *Visitors' guides*

This recommendation holds equally for networks of agencies which handle different media but share common authority files. This increases the chance (within commonsense limits) that a given agency can re-use a string first constructed by a different agency, using procedures described in a later chapter.

A string can contain more than one form term, e.g.

Example 11:

Subject: Weekly directory of vacation accommodation in the Scottish Highlands

String: (0) Scotland
(p) Highlands
(1) vacation accommodation
(6) directories
(6) serials

Entries: Highlands. Scotland
Vacation accommodation — *Directories* — *Serials*

Vacation accommodation. Highlands. Scotland
— *Directories* — *Serials*

Forms should then be cited in a context-dependent order.

Names of forms are rarely selected as leads, although entries under terms such as 'atlases' and 'bibliographies' can be justified in some circumstances:

— in a general library index, as a means of access, via the subject index, to materials that are frequently stored together;

— in an index to current publications, to allow a scan of certain forms for stock selection purposes, e.g.

Bibliographies
Children. Diseases — *For nursing*
Spain. Political events, *1850-1937*
Videotex systems

Other potential leads are considered at the end of this chapter.

Targets

Naming the target user frequently serves as a warning to the reader when the topic expressed as the core otherwise seems relevant:

Example 12:

Subject: A sixth form introduction to elementary particle collisions

String: (1) elementary particles
(2) collisions
(6) schools $01 for

Entries: Elementary particles
Collisions — *For schools*

Collisions. Elementary particles
— *For schools*

Schools
Elementary particles. Collisions — *For schools*

In this example no attempt was made to specify the target group beyond a level that will serve its intended purpose. A target term such as 'for schools' would then be applied to works intended for, say, primary schools, secondary schools, etc. †. Targets are typically expressed as compound terms beginning with 'for', as in the example above. This term was then repeated in the display of the final entry, since the lead did not contain the whole of the compound term (see Condition *c(i)*, p 171).

An indexer can sometimes use a target term to distinguish between two quite different kinds of subject involving the same concepts. A work on 'navigation mathematics' would be indexed as follows:

Example 13:

Subject: Mathematics of navigation

String: (2) ňavigation
(p) ňathematics

Entries: Navigation
Mathematics

Mathematics. Navigation

This should be seen in contrast to the following:

Example 14:

Subject: Mathematics for navigators

String: (2) ňathematics
(6) ňavigation $01 for

Entries: Mathematics
— *For navigation*

Navigation
Mathematics — *For navigation*

The difference between these topics consists of more than a subtle change of title, and would usually be revealed by a study of their contents listings. We would expect the work indexed in Example 13 to be organised by navigational problems leading to mathematical solutions, with few if any concessions to applications outside this field. The chapters of a work indexed by the string in Example 14 are likely to deal, however, with general mathematical problems, using navigational examples. This might not be the ideal choice for, say, a biology student needing an introduction to practical mathematics, but it would probably serve at a pinch. Note that the target term in Example 14 was expressed as an activity, 'navigation', rather than a group of

---

† This policy might be modified, of course, in a specialist index.

persons, e.g. 'navigators'. This leads to a more useful collocation in the index, and represents standard practice wherever a choice exists. Consequently, targets should be expressed by terms such as 'for nursing', 'for teaching' or 'for librarianship', rather than 'for nurses', 'for teachers' or 'for librarians'.

Summary of forms and targets

A string can contain both a form and a target term, e.g.

Example 15:

Subject: Sex roles in family life — an animated film for adolescents

String:
(2) family life
(p) sex roles
(6) adolescents $01 for
(6) animated films

Entries:

Family life
Sex roles — *For adolescents — Animated films*

Sex roles. Family life
— *For adolescents — Animated films*

Adolescents
Family life. Sex roles — *For adolescents — Animated films*

Animated films
Family life. Sex roles — *For adolescents*

Other things being equal, targets should usually be cited before forms.

We saw earlier that the name of a form can sometimes be used to suggest a concept or relationship which would otherwise call for expression within the core. For example, the term 'comparative studies' was used (p 165) to suggest an act of comparison that would have been handled in other circumstances by the operator 't'. The same applies to a small group of terms which convey both forms and targets. For example, 'climbers' guides' suggests a particular kind of systematic treatment ('guides') and also a group of users linked by a common activity ('climbers'). Compound terms of this kind are particularly useful when indexing works intended for groups of persons engaged in a common activity (e.g. 'collectors' or 'climbers'), where the activity concepts do not logically belong to the core.

Example 16:

Subject: Walkers' guide to the Snowdonia National Park

String: (0) Gwynedd (NU)
(1) Snowdonia National Park
(6) walkers' guides

Entries: Gwynedd
Snowdonia National Park — *Walkers' guides*

Snowdonia National Park
— *Walkers' guides*

Walkers' guides
Gwynedd. Snowdonia National Park

A lead under the name of the form is justified in these cases if it offers the only route into the index through the activity concept. The 3rd entry above could be supported by a reference such as:

Walking. Recreations
See also
Walkers' guides

Further readings

A collection of the form terms used in the British Library has been published as:

PRECIS: categories of forms

These terms are organised as a systematic thesaurus supported by an alphabetical index. The principles used when selecting and organising terms are set out in the Introduction. Details of the current edition can be obtained from:

The British Library, Bibliographic Services Division
Marketing and Support Group
2 Sheraton Street
London W1V 4BH

EXERCISES (For Answers, see Appendix 4, p 333)

Exercise 14

Write strings and entries for the following subjects:

(a) Role of women in industrial management: a feminist view

(b) Collectors' guide to 20th century wood engravings

(c) Measuring lead pollution of the atmosphere in cities, based on a study in Chicago

(d) Dictionary of electronics

(e) Semantics for librarians — a programmed instruction

14. Manipulation coding

This final chapter on syntax deals with the translation of a string containing instructions expressed by standard conventions, e.g.

(0) tropical regions
(1) buildings $21 timber
(2) damage $v by $w to
(3) insects

— into an equivalent machine-readable *manipulation string* †:

$z 0 103 0$d tropical regions
$z 1 103 0$a buildings $21 timber
$z 2 103 0$a damage $v by $w to
$z 3 103 0$a insects

As noted earlier (p 22), two kinds of code can occur in a machine-readable string:

- *primary codes*. These consist of nine characters, e.g. $z 0 103 0$d in the example above. One of these codes must precede each term in an input string. Some of the instructions embedded in this code relate to the term as a whole; others refer only to the focus.

- *secondary codes*, such as $21 and $v in the example above. These optional codes identify non-focal components, such as differences and connectives.

Machine-readable secondary codes have been used consistently in examples throughout this *Manual*, which means that we are now concerned only with the primary manipulation codes.

---

† The string above has been set down in list form for the sake of easier explanations. It would, of course, be input as an unbroken sequence of codes, terms and adjuncts, e.g.

$z01030$dtropical regions$z11030$abuildings$21timber$z21030$adam
agevbywto$z31030$ainsects #

A few basic points should be borne in mind when learning the primary coding system:

(a) The result of each decision by an indexer (e.g. the choice of a focus as 'lead' or 'non-lead') is recorded at a *fixed position* within the code. For example, the role operator is always, and only, written in the 3rd position.

(b) Only a limited range of characters (letters or numbers) is allowed in each position. The 4th position, for example, can hold either '0' or '1'; if any other character is written in this position, the string will be rejected at a validation stage.

(c) *All* positions in a primary code must be occupied by valid characters. Consequently, we can no longer use some of the short cuts allowed by the earlier conventions. Non-lead terms were previously left unmarked, and common nouns (as opposed to proper names of persons, places, etc.) were not specifically identified, but these 'preferred options' must now be indicated, in the form of codes, to the computer.

(d) One of the set of characters associated with a given position sometimes identifies a 'normal' response by the computer. This should be input as standard except when the indexer deliberately selects a non-standard procedure, such as suppressing a term from certain entries (previously indicated by conventions such as (NU), etc.).

Three positions in the primary code (1, 7 and 8) hold predetermined characters which play no part in entry generation:

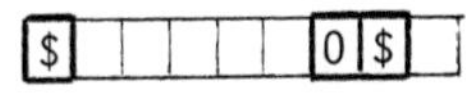

Position *1 2 3 4 5 6 7 8 9*

These consist of:

— two standard symbols, held at positions 1 and 8, which mark the following character(s) as instructions, not data. This function has been handled by $ signs throughout the *Manual*, but see the Footnote printed below the schema of operators in Appendix 1.

— a zero in position 7. This is a 'spare' position which has been used occasionally in experiments.

If indexers write their strings on standard input forms, these three characters should be pre-printed. They can also be displayed on a screen, as part of a grid, if strings are input online. Some of the other characters considered below (those that represent 'standard' responses) are also pre-printed on input forms in some agencies, and are overwritten if a non-standard procedure is required.

The functions of the characters in the remaining six positions are introduced below in an order which allows the previous conventions to be replaced, one at a time, by their equivalent manipulation codes. These codes not only regulate the contents and formats of entries, but also offer a basis for checking the logic of some indexing decisions. Certain combinations of codes will cause a string to be rejected. This validation function is noted, where appropriate, in the following explanations.

Position 3: Role operator

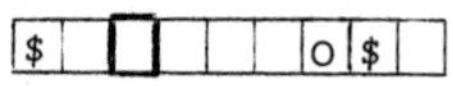

Position 1 2 3 4 5 6 7 8 9

This position holds the characters listed as *primary operators* and *secondary operators* in Appendix 1 (that is, any of the operators previously written between parentheses).

Example 1:

Subject: Frost damage to buildings

String:

1	2	3	4	5	6	7	8	9	
$		1				o	$		buildings
$		2				o	$		damage &v by $w to
$		3				o	$		frost

Entries:

Buildings
  Damage by frost

Damage. Buildings
  By frost

Frost
  Damage to buildings

Two standard validation checks, noted in previous chapters, are carried out on the characters in this position:

1. The first operator in the string must consist of a number in the

range '0' to '2'.

2. The string must also contain the operator '1' and/or '2'.

Position 4: Focus as lead or non-lead

Position	1	2	3	4	5	6	7	8	9
	$			☐			0	$	

One of only two characters can be written in this position:

0 = non-lead focus

1 = lead focus

Example 2:

Subject: Tests for dyslexia in children *(assuming that 'tests' is not required as a lead).*

String:

1	2	3	4	5	6	7	8	9	
$		1	1			0	$		children
$		2	1			0	$		dyslexia
$		2	0			0	$		tests

Entries: Children
Dyslexia. Tests

Dyslexia. Children
Tests

The number in this position controls the production of a lead *only under the focus*. The selection of a difference as the first component in a lead is determined by the secondary differencing codes.

Position 6: Appearance or non-appearance of a term in selected entries

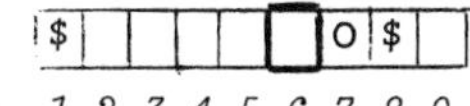

Position 1 2 3 4 5 6 7 8 9

The character in this position regulates the appearance/non-appearance of the term-as-a-whole in entries generated under *other* components of the string. It consists of a number in the range '0' to '3', most of which can be matched exactly by earlier conventions:

0 = (LO)

1 = (NU)

2 = (ND)

3 = no previous convention; represents the 'standard' case.

0 = Suppress this term from the entry when either an earlier or later term appears in the lead.

This instruction, previously indicated by the convention (LO), was illustrated on p 25 by the example:

(1) man
(p) eyes (LO)
(2) glaucoma

The same instruction would be conveyed by the following codes:

Example 3:

Subject: Human glaucoma

String:

$		1	1			0	$		man
$		p	1		0	0	$		eyes
$		2	1			0	$		glaucoma

Entries: Man
Glaucoma
Eyes. Man
Glaucoma
Glaucoma. Man

In the example above, the term 'eyes' is prefixed by '0' in the sixth position and '1' in the fourth position. A term can be prefixed by '0' in both positions *provided that it contains at least one preceding difference marked as a lead* †. However, the following string:

	$		1	1			0	$		hospitals
*	$		2	0		0	0	$		management

— would fail the validation tests at input (see routine F4, p 386). We can reasonably infer, on reading this string, that 'management' should not have been written at all — its focus will not appear in the lead (this is controlled by the '0' in position 4), the term does not contain a preceding lead difference, and the whole of the term will be suppressed from entries generated under earlier or later terms (controlled by the '0' in position 6).

1 = Suppress this term from the entry when a later term appears in the lead.

This instruction, previously expressed by the convention (NU), was

† A special routine in the program deals with 'Differences on lead-only terms'. This is described and illustrated in Algorithm 4, p 347.

illustrated (on p 26) by the example:

(1) man
(p) eyes (NU)
(2) glaucoma
(2) therapy

The same instructions would be conveyed by the following primary codes:

Example 4:

Subject: Human glaucoma therapy

String:

$		1	1			0	$		man
$		p	1		1	0	$		eyes
$		2	1			0	$		glaucoma
$		2	1			0	$		therapy

Note: For the sake of demonstration, different codes were applied to 'eyes' in Examples 3 and 4. Both versions should not occur in the same authority file.

Entries: Man
Eyes. Glaucoma. Therapy

Eyes. Man
Glaucoma. Therapy

Glaucoma. Man
Therapy

Therapy. Glaucoma. Man

2 = Suppress this term from the entry when an earlier term appears in the lead.

This instruction, indicated in earlier examples by the convention (ND), occurs most often with upward-reading substitutes. It is demonstrated later when the substitute codes are explained.

3 = This term can appear in any entry under an earlier or later term.

This code would be applied to all the terms in previous examples *not* marked by one of the special suppression instructions considered above.

Example 5:

Subject: Applications of microcomputer systems in office management

String:

$		1	1		3	0	$		offices
$		2	1		3	0	$		management
$		s	0		3	0	$		applications $v of $w in
$		3	1		3	0	$		microcomputer systems

Entries: Offices
Management. Applications of microcomputer systems

Management. Offices
Applications of microcomputer systems

Microcomputer systems. Offices
Applications in management

Writing the figure '3' in this position should be regarded as the standard response *except* when an indexer deliberately chooses to delete a term from certain entries. It should therefore be applied to a single term string such as the following:

String: | $ | | 2 | 1 | | **3** | 0 | $ | | management

Entry: Management

— even though the term 'management' cannot appear in an entry under an earlier or later term (there are none). The same output could be achieved by the following string:

| $ | | 2 | 1 | | **0** | 0 | $ | | management

— where 'management' is coded 'Lead only'. This string has not been marked as invalid; nevertheless, it is not recommended, for the following reasons:

(a) It is easier for an indexer to remember '3' as the normal response in any standard situation;

(b) It is also faster for the computer; '3' identifies a relatively straightforward route through the program, and the machine does not waste time on the special routines associated with the other codes.

Position 5: Substitute

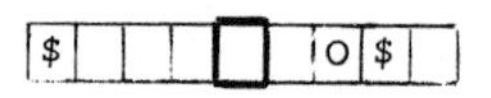

Position 1 2 3 4 5 6 7 8 9

A number in this position, within the range '0' to '9', indicates whether or not the term functions as a substitute:

0 = This term is *not* a substitute

1 to 9 = This term is a substitute. It replaces the stated number of

terms. This corresponds to the number seen in earlier conventions such as (sub *3*↑) and (sub *2*↓).

The direction of the substitute, conveyed by an arrow in the earlier conventions, is indicated by the number in the 6th position of the code (explained above):

$					1	0	$	

= *Downward-reading substitute.* As noted earlier, a figure '1' in this position suppresses the term from entries generated under later terms. In effect, the substitute is 'invisible' when the string is read in a later-to-earlier direction.

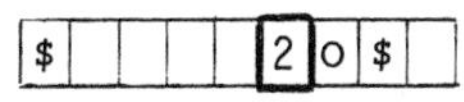

= *Upward-reading substitute.* This number suppresses the term from entries generated under earlier terms.

Both kinds of substitute occur in the following example:

Example 6:

Subject: Research by American universities into the life cycle of desert locusts in North Africa

String:

$		0	1	0	3	0	$		North Africa
$		1	1	0	3	0	$		desert locusts
$		2	1	0	3	0	$		life cycle
$		2	0	3	2	0	$		life cycle of desert locusts in
$						0	$		North Africa
$		2	0	0	3	0	$		research $v by $w into
$		3	0	2	1	0	$		American universities
$		0	0	0	3	0	$		United States
$		1	1	0	3	0	$		universities

Entries:

North Africa
Desert locusts. Life cycle. Research by American universities

Desert locusts. North Africa
Life cycle. Research by American universities

Life cycle. Desert locusts. North Africa
Research by American universities

Universities. United States
Research into life cycle of desert locusts in North Africa

Since substitutes are never marked as leads, they are easily recognised by standard patterns of manipulation codes in the 4th, 5th and 6th positions:

0	*n*	2	= Upward-reading substitute

0	*n*	1	= Downward-reading substitute

— where '*n*' is a figure in the range 1 to 9 indicating how many terms should be replaced by the substitute.

Position 9: Type of term

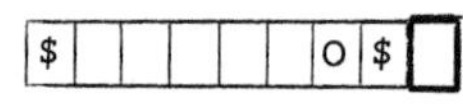

Position *1 2 3 4 5 6 7 8 9*

Only two types of term, i.e. proper names and place names, have been indicated by special characters in previous examples. The majority of terms, consisting of common nouns, were left unmarked. In a full manipulation string, all terms must be coded according to their types, using the symbols:

a = common noun
c = proper name (other than places)
d = place name.

All three codes occur in the following example:

Example 7:

Subject: Forestry Commission policies on landscape design in North Wales

String:

1	2	3	4	5	6	7	8	9	
$		0	1	0	3	0	$	d	Wales $21 North
$		2	1	0	3	0	$	a	landscape design $w in
$		s	0	0	3	0	$	a	policies $v of $w on
$		3	1	0	3	0	$	c	Great Britain $h Forestry Commission

Entries: Wales
North Wales. Landscape design. Policies of Great Britain. *Forestry Commission*

North Wales
  Landscape design. Policies of Great Britain. *Forestry Commission*

Landscape design. North Wales
  Policies of Great Britain. *Forestry Commission*

Great Britain. *Forestry Commission*
  Policies on landscape design in North Wales

In this example the proper name of the Forestry Commission has been set down in the standard form required by a cataloguing code. The correct punctuation and typography are achieved by the code $h, taken from the Table on p 40.

Since the majority of terms in strings consist of common nouns, a letter 'a' is often pre-printed in this position on input forms, then overwritten as 'c' or 'd' when proper names are indexed.

Position 2: Theme interlinks

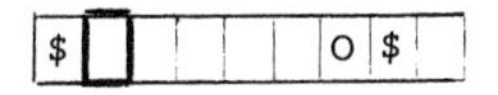

Position 1 2 3 4 5 6 7 8 9

x = First element in a coordinate theme
y = Second or subsequent element in a coordinate theme
z = Element common to all themes

These codes, first described in Chapter 3 (p 41-44), have been used in examples only when strings contained two or more themes which needed to be distinguished by the codes 'x' and 'y'. Since all the terms in a single-theme string rate as common elements, the great majority of terms are prefixed by 'z' in this position. The string offered above as Example 7 would therefore be written as follows in its fully-coded version.

Example 7, fully coded (Entries shown above)

String:

1	2	3	4	5	6	7	8	9	Term
$	z	0	1	0	3	0	$	d	Wales $21 North
$	z	2	1	0	3	0	$	a	landscape design $w in
$	z	s	0	0	3	0	$	a	policies $v of $w on
$	z	3	1	0	3	0	$	c	Great Britain $h Forestry Commission

A two-theme string, including common elements, would be coded as follows:

Example 8 (first shown on p 43)

Subject: The costs of beekeeping, and the costs of marketing honey, in Nova Scotia

String:

$	z	0	1	0	3	0	$	d	Nova Scotia
$	x	2	1	0	3	0	$	a	beekeeping
$	x	1	1	0	3	0	$	a	honey
$	y	2	1	0	3	0	$	a	marketing
$	z	p	1	0	3	0	$	a	costs

Entries: Nova Scotia
Beekeeping. Costs

Beekeeping. Nova Scotia
Costs

Costs. Beekeeping. Nova Scotia

Nova Scotia
Honey. Marketing. Costs

Honey. Nova Scotia
Marketing. Costs

Marketing. Honey. Nova Scotia
Costs

Costs. Marketing. Honey. Nova Scotia

In a number of agencies, a letter 'z' is pre-printed in this position on their standard input forms, and is overwritten (by 'x' or 'y') when a multi-theme string is needed. Certain validation routines are carried out on the characters in this position:

(a) If one of the terms in a string is prefixed by 'x' in the second position, then at least one other term must also be prefixed by 'x'. This simply means that a string marked as 'multi-theme' must actually contain more than one theme.

(b) A term cannot be prefixed by 'y' unless the string contains an earlier term coded 'x'.

Summary of manipulation coding

The meanings attached to the various positions in the primary code are displayed (some as questions) in the diagram below:

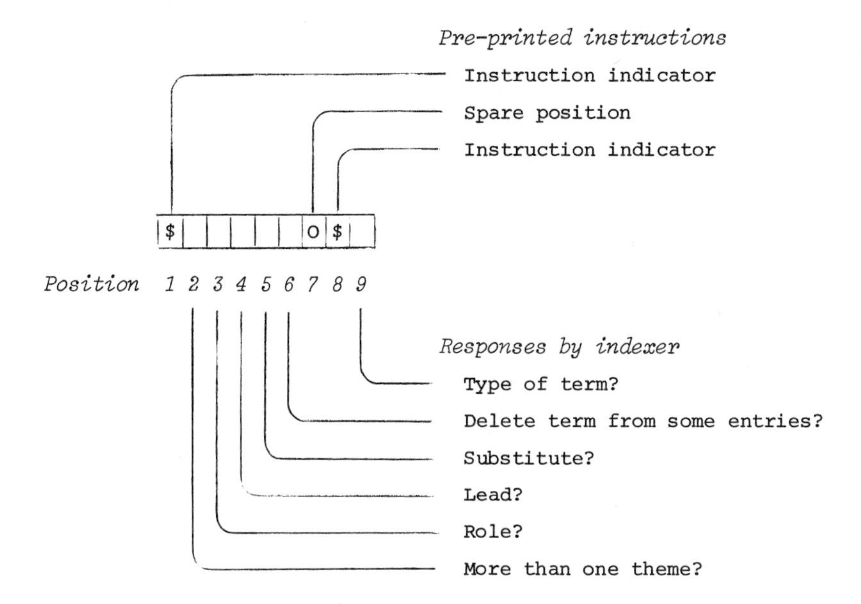

This coding system appears more complex than the shorter conventions used throughout the rest of the *Manual*, but these machine-readable characters also acquire the status of conventions when used on a day-to-day basis. Indexers tend to refer to a 'One hundred term' (previously a 'Lead only' term), meaning the characteristic pattern of codes in the 4th, 5th and 6th positions, e.g.

| $ | z | 1 | 1 | 0 | 0 | o | $ | a |

The computer routines for generating entries, based on the primary and secondary manipulation codes, are set down in the form of algorithms in Appendix 5 (p 340). This also includes a summary of the validation checks applied to strings at the input stage.

For Exercises, see p 196

EXERCISES (For Answers, See Appendix 4, p 334)

Exercise 15

Rewrite the following strings (based on the earlier conventions) in their machine-readable versions. Show the entries that would be generated.

Example

Subject: Sponsorship of sport by multinational companies

String as given (using conventions):

(2) sport
(2) sponsorship $v by $w of
(3) companies $21 multinational

Manipulation string:

$z21030$a sport
$z21030$a sponsorship $v by $w of
$z31030$a companies $21 multinational

Entries: **Sport**
Sponsorship by multinational companies

Sponsorship. Sport
By multinational companies

Companies
Multinational companies. Sponsorship of sport

Multinational companies
Sponsorship of sport

(a) *Subject:* Nutritional value of soy protein as a food additive

String: (1) food
(p) additives $w to
(q) protein $21 soy
(p) nutritional value

(b) *Subject:* Disappearance of the crew of the 'Mary Celeste' — a dramatization on videotape

String: (1) sailing ships (NU)
(q) Mary Celeste $i (Ship)
(p) crew
(2) disappearance
(6) dramatizations
(6) videotape recordings

Note: The term 'Mary Celeste' is: (a) context-established by 'sailing ships' (see recommendation on p 83); (b) set down in the form required by AACR2 and marked as a proper name.

(c) *Subject:* Effects of economic development on the social role of women in the rural regions of South-east Asia

String: (1) Asia $21 South-east
(p) rural regions
(p) society
(s) role $v of $w in
(3) women
(sub 3↑) (2) role of women in society
(s) effects $v of $w on
(3) economic development

Exercise 16

Write the entries generated from the following strings:

(a) $z21030$a weather
$z21030$a forecasting
$z20220$a weather forecasting
$zs0030$a use $v of $w in
$z31030$a satellites $21 artificial

(b) $z11030$a schools
$zp1030$a students
$z31030$a records $01 confidential
$zp0120$a confidential records on students
$z20030$a access $w to
$zs0030$a rights $v of $w of
$z31030$a parents

(c) $z01030$d developing countries
$z21030$a welfare work $w in
$zt0030$a compared with
$z20210$a welfare work in developed countries
$z01030$d developed countries
$z21030$a welfare work

15. Thesaurus construction: basic relationships

Earlier chapters showed evidence of a close relationship that can exist betwen entries generated from strings, and references extracted from the thesaurus. A choice of one procedure rather than the other is sometimes possible — the Table on p 71 showed how access to the focal part of a compound term, such as 'grammar schools', can be provided either by using the differencing procedures:

Schools
  Grammar schools

— or by providing a reference:

Schools
  See also
    Grammar schools

Some of the rules associated with string writing can clearly affect the contents and structure of the thesaurus. A general rule on p 17 states that "Two terms should not be written as adjacent elements in a string if the first serves only to indicate the class of which the second is usually regarded as a member". It was recommended that the link between these broader and narrower terms should be provided by a reference such as:

Education
  See also
    Training

The four 'Rules of differencing' introduced on p 55-62 not only determine the structure of the terms admitted into the thesaurus, but also affect the categories it contains. According to Rule 1 (p 55), an adjectival compound such as 'Aircraft engines' should be factored into two noun components. Each of these should then be assigned to its own category: 'aircraft' would be recorded as a member of a class called 'vehicles', while 'engines' belongs to the class 'prime movers'.

The thesaurus can be described as adding a second dimension to the indexing language, as shown in the diagram below:

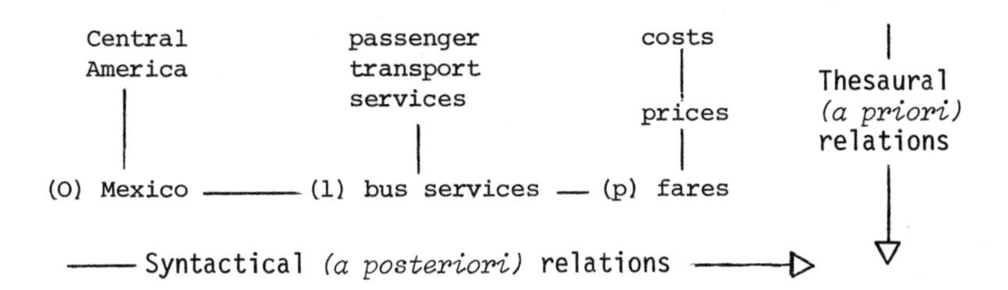

This diagram draws a distinction between two kinds of relationships in PRECIS (and in other indexing languages):

(a) *syntactical relations* (shown horizontally) link the terms that comprise a string. These are also known as *a posteriori* relationships, since we cannot assume that concepts such as 'Mexico' and 'bus services' are semantically related until they occur together as part of a subject. To that extent these relations are document dependent.

(b) *thesaural relations* (shown vertically) are also known as *a priori* or document independent relationships. These link lead terms in strings with other terms that might occur to a user who would regard this document as relevant, but the extra terms were excluded from entries on the grounds that they are not essential to a summary statement of the subject, being sufficiently present by implication.

The diagram also illustrates one of the principal functions of a thesaurus: it allows the use of shorter and simpler strings without a loss of access points. Terms that are clearly present in a topic by implication (to the extent that we imply some kind of 'prices' whenever we speak of 'fares') can usually be excluded from strings and entries, and handled instead by once-for-all references such as:

Prices
  See also
    Fares

The procedures used in the PRECIS thesaurus are squarely based upon techniques and relationships described in national and international standards on monolingual thesauri (1; 2). Some of the examples and explanations offered below are 'borrowed', in fact, from these standards. The standards deal at some length with two aspects of thesaurus construction:

(a) *Vocabulary control.* This has been covered in earlier chapters of the *Manual*, e.g.

— criteria for recognizing compound terms that should be factored or retained in their compound forms were described in Chapter 4;

— the choice of singulars or plurals was covered in Chapter 7.

(b) *Basic thesaural relationships.* The standards recognise three classes of basic relationships linking the terms assigned to a thesaurus:

— *the equivalence relationship;*

— *the hierarchical relationship;*

— *the associative relationship.*

Each of these can be divided further into subclasses, with special names noted below.

The equivalence relationship

This relationship links terms that are regarded, for indexing purposes, as referring to the same concept, so that they form an *equivalence set.* A distinction must then be made between:

— the *preferred term*: that is, the term that is used consistently to express this concept in strings and entries;

— one or more *non-preferred terms*: these are not used in entries, but

---

(1) British Standards Institution. Guidelines for the establishment and development of monolingual thesauri: BS 5723:1979. London, B.S.I., 1979

(2) International Organization for Standardization. Guidelines for the establishment and development of monolingual thesauri: ISO 2788. Draft 2nd edition (provisional text by Derek Austin), published by Unesco, Paris, as Document PGI-81/WS/15, 1981

are provided as source terms in *See* references directing the user to the preferred equivalent, e.g.

Staff *See* Personnel

The equivalence relationship covers two classes of terms, known as 'synonyms' and 'quasi-synonyms'.

Synonyms are terms whose meanings can be regarded as the same in a wide range of contexts, so that they are virtually interchangeable. Synonym sets occur more commonly in a controlled indexing language than in natural language, mainly because indexers and linguists use different criteria when recognising synonymity. A linguist would rate a pair of terms as synonyms only if they are interchangeable in almost any sentence, whereas an indexer would tend to judge terms as synonyms if it appears that a user interested in one of the terms should, *as a matter of course*, retrieve and examine all documents indexed by the other. Within that context, various kinds of synonym are likely to be encountered in practice. The following list indicates some common classes, but is by no means exhaustive.

(a) *Terms of different linguistic origin*, e.g.

Polyglot dictionaries; Multilingual dictionaries

(b) *Popular names and scientific names*, e.g.

Penguins; Sphenisciformes
Allergy; Hypersensitivity

(c) *Common names and trade names*

Vacuum flasks; Thermos™ flasks
Ball point pens; Biros™

Preference should be given to common names

(d) *Variant names for newly-emerging concepts*, e.g.

Supertankers; Very large crude carriers; VLCCs

These may require a change of preferred term as soon as general usage has settled down, using the correction procedures described in Chapter 18 (p 249).

(e) *Current or favoured terms versus outdated or deprecated terms*, e.g.

Chairpersons; Chairmen
San; Bushmen
Radio; Wireless

(f) *Variant spellings, including stem variants and irregular plurals:*

Chad; Tchad
Geese; Goose
Thought; Thinking
Paediatrics; Pediatrics

(g) *Terms originating from different cultures, e.g.*

Flats; Apartments
Mobile libraries; Bookmobiles

(h) *'Standard' names versus slang, e.g.*

Association football; Soccer

Preference should be given to the standard name, and a reference should be provided from its slang equivalent only if the slang term is likely to be sought by users.

(i) *Abbreviations versus full names, e.g.*

C.B.I. { Committee on Biological Information
Cumulative Book Index

Since a given abbreviation can frequently stand for a number of different concepts, the full form of the name should be preferred unless the abbreviation (usually an acronym) is well-established and unlikely to represent more than one concept, e.g. Unesco.

(j) *The factored and unfactored forms of a compound term, e.g.*

Schools + Libraries; School libraries

This situation will arise if one of the Rules of differencing calls for a term to be factored, and it is considered that users are likely to seek the term in its unfactored form. The unfactored version should then be treated as a non-preferred equivalent and offered as the source term in a *See* reference, e.g.

School libraries *See* Libraries. Schools

The typography and spacing seen in the target term above are achieved by special instruction codes described in the next chapter.

As a general rule, preferred terms should be selected with the needs of the majority of users in mind. For example, 'Penguins' should be treated as the preferred term in a general or non-zoological index, but 'Sphenisciformes' might be more appropriate in a specialist index in the field of zoology. Once a criterion for choosing preferred terms has been established (e.g. common nouns rather than scientific names), it should be applied consistently for the sake of predictability.

Quasi-synonyms are terms whose meanings are generally recognised as different in common usage, yet they are treated as synonyms for indexing purposes (bearing in mind the indexer's criterion for recognising synonyms noted above). These terms usually represent points on a continuum, e.g.

Wetness; Dryness
Hardness; Softness.

The extent to which terms can be treated as quasi-synonyms depends upon the subject field(s) covered by the index. An agency dealing with documents within a limited field, such as 'Washing equipment', might decide that either 'Wetness' or 'Dryness' should serve as the preferred term, the other being treated as its non-preferred quasi-synonym, if it seems clear that specialists studying one of these concepts need to examine all documents on the other. This might not apply in a different subject field, such as 'Climatology', and quasi-synonyms are least likely to be encountered in an index covering several disciplines.

The hierarchical relationship

This is the basic relationship which most distinguishes a systematic thesaurus from an unstructured list of terms, such as a glossary or dictionary. It is based upon the notions of superordination and subordination, where the superordinate term represents a class or whole, and the subordinate term refers to its member or part. This general relationship covers three subclasses:

- *the generic relationship*
- *the hierarchical whole-part relationship*
- *the instance relationship.*

Each of these leads to hierarchies of terms which can be tested for logical fitness (at least in part) through reference to the basic concept types shown as a Table on p 105. It can be stated as a general rule that *every subordinate term must refer to the same basic kind of concept as its superordinate term*. Consequently:

- 'Documents' and 'Books' can be hierarchically related (as genus and species) since both terms refer to kinds of physical things.

— 'Books' (a class of things), and 'Binding' (an action) refer to different kinds of concept and cannot be related hierarchically (although they might be linked by the associative relationship considered later).

The *generic relationship* links a genus and its species. It represents the basis of scientific taxonomic systems, and it can be applied with equal effect to concepts of any kind. In addition to the test for validity noted above, this relationship is also subject to the logical 'all-and-some' test described on p 80, where it was used to distinguish between the true generic relationship (handled by the thesaurus), and the quasi-generic relationship (handled in strings by the operator 'q'). As noted in a footnote on p 81, the conclusion drawn for the all-and-some test can vary, in exceptional circumstances, according to the subject field covered by the index.

The *hierarchical whole-part relationship* covers a limited range of situations where the name of a part implies the name of its whole *in any context*, allowing the terms to be organised as a hierarchy. The name of the whole then functions as the superordinate term, and the part as the subordinate term. This applies to four principal classes of concepts:

(a) *Systems and organs of the body*, e.g.

Circulatory system
  Cardio-vascular system
    Vascular system
      Arteries
      Veins

(b) *Geographical locations*, e.g.

Australia
  New South Wales
    Sydney
    Wollongong

(c) *Disciplines or fields of discourse*, e.g.

Science
  Biology
    Botany
    Zoology

(d) *Hierarchical social structures*, e.g.

Armies
  Corps
    Divisions
      Battalions
      Regiments

The examples of hierarchies shown above are all based upon generally recognised whole-part relations that could be established through reference to standard works such as dictionaries and gazetteers. Other classes of terms can also be organised into hierarchies on the basis of their whole-part relations in indexes to special subject fields. For example, a thesaurus of terms limited to the field of 'Turbine engineering' might contain a hierarchy such as:

Turbines
  Compressors
    Blades

— on the understanding that users of this index would regard 'Blades' as parts of 'Turbines' as a matter of course. This should not be attempted, however, outside the limited field where the name of the whole is clearly implied by the name of the part. In a general index, for example, a term such as 'Blades' can be related, as a part, to a number of different concepts, such as 'Knives', 'Harvesters', etc., in which case both terms should be written in the string, and the part should be identified by the operator 'p'.

One of the examples above shows a sequence of place names organised as a hierarchy based on their whole-part relationships. This must be seen in contrast to some of the examples seen in earlier chapters, where place names were coded as wholes and parts within strings, e.g.

(0) France
(p) Paris
(1) students

Both approaches are logically sound, and the choice of one procedure rather than the other should be determined by local policies; it is not prescribed by the indexing system *per se*. Large geographical areas are usually handled by references, e.g.

Australia
See also
New South Wales †

Smaller regions (e.g. below state or county, depending on country) are usually handled within strings, e.g.

(l) Vermont (p) St. Albans	*or*	(l) Hertfordshire (p) St. Albans

This helps to identify smaller places that may not be familiar to readers, and it allows the indexer to distinguish between towns, etc. that have the same names but occur in different regions.

The *instance relationship* links a general class of things or actions, expressed by a common noun, with a particular instance of that class (a class-of-one) expressed by a proper name, e.g.

Mountain regions ——— *general class*
Alps
Himalayas } ——— *specific instances*

Although 'Alps' and 'Himalayas' are assigned to subordinate positions within this hierarchy, they are neither kinds nor parts of 'Mountain regions' — in fact, they *are* mountain regions. As noted on p 83, the name of a specific instance is usually context-established by the name of its class within the string, the instance being identified by the operator 'q'. This is the preferred procedure, since it avoids overloading the thesaurus with hierarchies leading to proper names. If, however, a record of this relationship is also required in the thesaurus (not necessarily as a source of references, but perhaps for the sake of completeness), the class-of-one term should be identified by one of the special term codes described in the next chapter (p 218-219).

Polyhierarchical relationships

Some concepts belong, on equally logical grounds, to more than one class at a time. They are then said to possess *polyhierarchical relat-*

---

† This relationship could also be handled by one of the 'blanket references' described on p 264-267.

ionships, e.g.

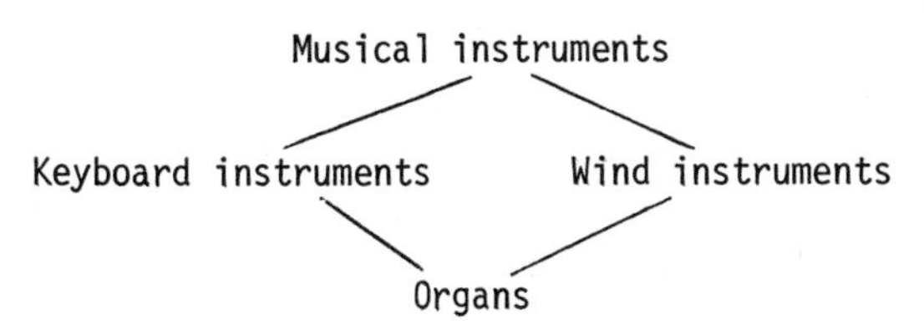

The concept 'Organs' in the example above is assigned to subordinate positions on the basis of its common generic relationship to each of two broader concepts. Polyhierarchical links can also be based upon logically different relationships. In the following example:

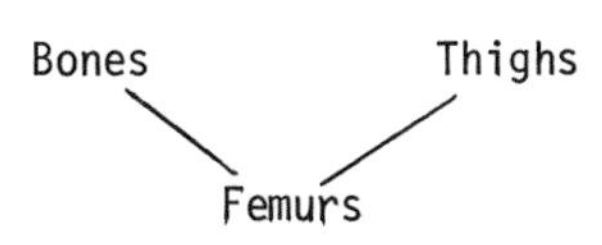

— the concept 'Femurs' is generically related to 'Bones' (a femur is a *kind* of bone), but its link with 'Thighs' is based upon the hierarchical whole-part relationship (a femur, by definition, is *part* of the thigh).

The associative relationship

It is difficult to describe this loosest of the basic relations in terms of positive rather than negative characteristics. It covers the link between a pair of terms that are not members of an equivalence set, nor can they be organised as a hierarchy where one of the terms is subordinated to the other, yet they are mentally associated to such an extent that we can reasonably assume that a user searching the index under one of the terms would be helped by a reference to entries containing the other. As it stands, this definition would explain the link between a pair of terms such as 'Birds' and 'Ornithology', but it could also be cited as evidence by an agoraphobic indexer who proposes a reference from 'Fear' when indexing a document on 'Open spaces'. To avoid this kind of subjectivity, a special condition is attached to the definition above. It is stipulated that a pair of terms should not be linked by the associative relationship *unless one of the concepts forms an essential component in any explanation or definition of the other* †. This explanatory role need not be reciprocal; 'Ornithology' cannot be defined except by reference to 'Birds' or one of its synonyms, but a definition of 'Birds' does not require a reference to 'Ornithology'. This extra condition allows an associative link between a pair of terms such as 'Plants' and 'Herbicides', but not between 'Fear' and its possible causes, such as 'Open spaces', 'Spiders', etc. Two kinds of concept can be linked by the associative relationship:

- those belonging to the same category;
- those belonging to different categories.

These are considered separately below.

The class of *terms belonging to the same category* covers siblings with overlapping meanings, such as 'Ships' and 'Boats', or 'Carpets' and 'Rugs'. Each of the terms in these pairs has its own particular meaning (so that the pairs do not form equivalence sets), but the boundary between them is often confused in common usage, to the extent that a user checking one of them in the index should be informed of documents indicated by the other. It is not necessary to link all sibling terms in this way. For example, there is no need to generate references between terms such as 'Horses' and 'Donkeys' (sibling members of the class 'Equines'), since their meanings do not overlap.

Concepts linked by a familial or derivational relationship (one of the concepts being derived from the other)) can also be regarded as belonging to this group. This would apply, for example, to names of crossbreeds such as 'Mules' and 'Hinnies', each of which can be associated with its parent species, 'Horses' and 'Donkeys'. In this case, all four terms share a common subordinate relationship to 'Equines'.

Terms belonging to different categories (which therefore refer to different conceptual types) can be associated on a number of different

---

† The standards listed in the footnote on p 200 have not gone this far, and state only that "... It will often be found that one of the terms is a necessary component of any definition or explanation of the other". In trying to be cautious, the standards may have been careless.

bases while satisfying the requirement that one of the terms should function as a component in explanations of the other. The following types of association are likely to be encountered in practice, but the list is not exhaustive:

(a) *A discipline or field of study and the objects or phenomena studied*, e.g.

Birds; Ornithology
Landforms; Geomorphology

(b) *An action and the product of the action*, e.g.

Weaving; Cloth
Welding; Welds

(c) *An operation or process and its agent or instrument*, e.g.

Typing; Typewriters
Data processing; Computer systems

(d) *An action and its patient*, e.g.

Harvesting; Crops
Imprisonment; Prisoners

(e) *Concepts related to their properties*, e.g.

Poisons; Toxicity
Perception; Acuity

(f) *Concepts related to their origins*, e.g.

Americans; United States

(g) *Concepts linked by causal dependence*, e.g.

Bereavement; Death
Diseases; Pathogens

(h) *Concepts and their counter operations or agents*, e.g.

Pain; Analgesia; Analgesics
Aircraft; Anti-aircraft weapons

(i) *Phrases containing syncategorematic nouns and their apparent foci*, e.g.

Ships; Model ships
Plants; Fossil plants

This class of terms was first encountered on p 62, where it was stated that they should not be factored, nor should they be input to the thesaurus as narrower terms subordinated to their apparent foci.

Basic relations and the direction of references in printed indexes

A reference between a pair of terms linked by the *equivalence relationship* can be printed only in one direction, i.e. from the non-preferred term to its preferred synonym or quasi-synonym, e.g.

Sphenisciformes *See* Penguins

Hierarchically-related concepts can be linked, at least in theory, by references in each of two directions:

— *downward-reading references* from broader to narrower concepts, e.g.

Birds
See also
Penguins

— *upward-reading references* from narrower to broader concepts, e.g.

Penguins
See also
Birds

In practice, only downward-reading references are provided in a printed index, for the following reasons:

(a) We can reasonably assume that a user who enters the index at a term such as 'Penguins' already knows that this concept belongs to a class called 'Birds', and hardly needs a reference to the broader term. In any case, that kind of information can be established easily by checking the narrower term in a dictionary.

(b) We cannot, however, expect a user who enters the index at 'Birds' to recall, on the instant, all the species that might have occurred as subjects of documents, nor can this information be obtained from a dictionary. A set of downward-reading references such as:

Birds
See also
Fulmars
Owls
Penguins
etc.

— therefore serves as an *aide memoire*, telling the reader which species of birds occurred as subjects in that particular issue of the index.

(c) Downward-reading references are economically more acceptable, since they are generated only when the narrower terms have actually occurred as subjects. Upward-reading references, if allowed, would undoubtedly overwhelm the index. A document on 'Birds', for example, would call for separate references from each of several species, such as:

Fulmars
  See also
    Birds

Owls
  See also
    Birds

Penguins
  See also
    Birds

etc.

— among many others.

A measure of choice is allowed when making references between terms linked by the *associative relationship*. A *See also* reference should be made in all cases *from the defining concept towards the term it helps to define*, e.g.

Birds
  See also
    Ornithology

Pain
  See also
    Analgesia

Aircraft
  See also
    Model aircraft

A need for references in this direction is based on the fact that a defining concept (such as 'Birds' and 'Pain' in the examples above) does not contain the defined concept as part of its meaning. Consequently, we cannot assume that a user who enters the index at a term such as 'Pain' will already have the concept 'Analgesia' in mind.

Supplementary references in the other direction, such as:

Ornithology
  See also
    Birds

Analgesia
  See also
    Pain

— are less essential, since we can reasonably assume that a user seeking documents on, say, 'Analgesia', will be aware that this concept is semantically related to 'Pain' before approaching the index. Nevertheless, extra references from defined concepts towards defining concepts are sometimes useful, especially when dealing with names of disciplines and their objects of study. These *two-way references* are least justified in the case of phrases containing syncategorematic nouns, since the defined concept (e.g. 'Model aircraft') contains the defining term (e.g. 'Aircraft') as part of its structure.

The construction of two-way references calls for the use of special codes and procedures introduced in Chapter 18 (p 258).

'Up-alphabet' and 'Down-alphabet' references

Even when a reference in a printed index is justified on relational grounds, it may be dropped if the source and target terms would occupy adjacent positions in the same column. The decision to drop or retain a reference depends on the direction in which it is read by the user. A distinction is made between:

(a) *Up-alphabet references*, e.g.

Welds
  See also
    Welding

— where the entry indicated by the target term ('welding') files earlier than the source term ('welds'). This kind of reference should be provided even when the reference and the entry to which it refers occupy adjacent positions in the index, e.g.

Welding
  Inert gas welding
Welds
  See also
    Welding

— on the grounds that a user searching for 'Welds', who happens to hit this term directly when approaching the index, will then read *away* from the related term since columns are read from top to bottom.

(b) *Down-alphabet references*, e.g.

Welding
  See also
    Welds

— where the entry indicated by the target term ('welds') files later than the source term ('welding'). These references can usually be dropped if the reference and the entry to which it refers occur consistently on successive lines in the index, e.g.

Welding
  See also
    Welds
Welds
  Testing. Use of ultrasonics

— on the grounds that users reading down a column, *towards* the target term, must 'overshoot' to ensure that they have examined *all* the potentially relevant entries. Although a printed reference may not be needed in these cases, a record of the relationship between the terms should still be added to the thesaurus, using special non-print codes described in Chapter 18.

Other products from the thesaurus file

A need to distinguish between features such as 'up-alphabet' and 'down-alphabet' references is clearly related to the use of the thesaurus file as the source of *See* and *See also* references in a printed index. The machine-held file has other potential uses, however:

(a) It constitutes a record of the preferred and non-preferred terms (excluding only some proper names) used in the indexes issued by a given agency. This could be of value not only to indexers but also users, such as those preparing search statements prior to on-line access. An alphabetical list of this kind, including definitions (where appropriate) and indications of some related terms, is issued bi-monthly by the British Library as the *PRECIS Vocabulary Fiche* †.

(b) The file could be organised and published as a fully-structured, stand-alone thesaurus supported by an alphabetical index, either on COM or as a printed page product. Some of the special codes and procedures described in Chapter 18 were developed with this form of output in mind.

(c) The information contained in the machine-held thesaurus could be displayed, as networks of related terms, to on-line users of the subject files. This kind of display is being developed by the National Film Board of Canada as part of their on-line information service (*FORMAT*), and it is also being investigated by other agencies using PRECIS.

---

† For details, contact:
The British Library, Bibliographic Services Division
Marketing and Support Group
2 Sheraton Street
London W1V 4BH, England

16. Thesaurus construction: components of input records

Introduction

This chapter deals mainly with the construction of a thesaurus intended as the source of *See* and *See also* references in a printed index. Establishing a file for this purpose involves a minimum set of codes and procedures that should be applied in any PRECIS thesaurus, regardless of output. Other kinds of output, reviewed at the end of the previous chapter, call for the occasional use of extra codes and procedures considered in later chapters.

The formats of typical *See* and *See also* references were explained earlier (p 18-19) and are summarised only briefly here. Each kind of reference consists of three parts:

— the *source term* (also known as the *referred-from term*);

— the *directive*, i.e. *See* or *See also*;

— the *target term* (or *referred-to term*).

These two kinds of reference differ, however, in layout and purpose:

(a) A *See* reference serves as an *instruction* to the user, directing attention away from a non-preferred term towards its preferred synonym: that is, towards the term that is used consistently in strings and entries. Concepts expressed by the terms on either side of a *See* directive are linked by the equivalence relationship (see p 200-203). A *See* reference is usually printed on a single line (with a necessary allowance for overruns), e.g.

Bufo *See* Toads

Other layouts are also possible and are shown in later examples.

(b) A *See also* reference links a pair of terms, each of which is capable of functioning in its own right as a lead in the index. This kind of reference is offered to the user an an *aide memoire* rather than a definite instruction. It directs attention to two classes of related concepts:

— subordinate concepts (kinds, parts or instances) belonging to the same hierarchy as the source term (see p 203-207);

— concepts linked to the source term by the associative relationship (see p 207-209).

A *See also* reference usually occupies three lines, e.g.

Broadcasting
  See also
    Television

Other (less common) formats are described later. If a given source term refers to more than one target term in the same issue of the index, the common components of the references (the source term and the directive) are suppressed automatically when the second or subsequent reference is generated. The target terms are then aligned as an alphabetical column, e.g.

Broadcasting
  See also
    Radio
    Television

Indexing strings and thesaurus records are held in separate files in the computer, and different programs are used to generate their outputs †. Consequently, some codes that were previously explained as instructions in strings will now be encountered again with different meanings (but no risk of confusion). For example, the code '$o' identifies a 'lead parenthetical difference' when it occurs as part of a string, but it indicates the hierarchical relationship within a thesaurus record. The meaning of a code can also vary *within* a record, depending upon its position. For example:

— *in a string*, the code $d indicates a place name when it occupies the final position in the primary manipulation code, but it indicates 'Date as a difference' when it is written, as a secondary code, after a term;

---

† Reasons for keeping these files separated are considered in the final chapter.

— *in a thesaurus record*, the code $d again identifies a place name when written as a prefix to a term, but it indicates a definition or scope note when it follows a term.

Components of input records

For the present we shall deal with the structure and contents of records as submitted to the computer. These differ in some respects from the records written by indexers and described in the next chapter. A computer input record can be visualised as a set of positions in a predetermined order, each holding a particular kind of code or data. The most commonly used components are introduced below in the order in which they are input. Some codes and data that are used only in special circumstances are deferred until later.

Position 1: Message code †

****
#RI# = Record input
#RA# = Record amend
#RD# = Record delete
#RP# = Report contents of record
****

At the time of its input to the computer, every record must begin with one of these codes to indicate the *kind* of message being submitted. We shall concentrate for the present on the contents of *standard input records* prefixed by the code #RI# — these account for the bulk of work in day-to-day practice. Every standard input record must contain codes or data in the first 4 positions:

---

† The symbol (#) in the 1st and 4th positions of each code is frequently used to mark the boundary between adjacent fields within a record, and/or the beginnings and ends of records.

Position 1: The message code (#RI#);

Position 2: A Reference Indicator Number *(RIN)*;

Position 3: A code indicating the type of term;

Position 4: The term itself, including typographic instruction codes if necessary.

Position 2: Reference Indicator Number (RIN)

A RIN consists of a 7-digit number, e.g. 0063614, the final character serving as a modulus-eleven check, similar to the check digit in an International Standard Book Number. As each new term is admitted to the thesaurus, the next available RIN is struck from a computer-generated list and written as part of the input record, where it indicates the address to which the term will be assigned in the random access file holding the thesaurus †.

The RIN functions as a surrogate for the term in some transactions. For example:

— If a term in a string calls for a reference, its RIN is written in a special field in the full indexing record described in a later chapter. The presence of a RIN in this field functions as an instruction, and directs the computer to the position in the machine-held thesaurus where the construction of references should begin;

— Relationships in the thesaurus are expressed as codes, but these are used to link the addresses (RINs) where terms are held, not the terms themselves. This allows shorter inputs (we shall see examples later), and also easier adjustments to terms and/or their relationships. For example, if a concept changes its name, the old term is overwritten by the new term at the same address, using an amendment procedure described later. The altered term is likely to be related to other terms in the file, but the relational data attached to these terms can be left intact, since they refer to the unchanged RIN, not to the altered term.

---

† This explains why the machine-held thesaurus is also known as the RIN-file. By a process of corruptive derivation, the construction of the thesaurus is sometimes called 'Rinning'; it is even said that 'Rinners' prepare 'Rinput'.

It should be remembered that RINs are simply addresses in a random-access file. They have no relational significance, and they cannot be compared with the notation of a library classification. A class number such as 621.381 (taken from DDC, 19th edition) performs two functions:

— it stands uniquely for the concept 'Electronic engineering' (to the extent that this number does not refer to any other concept);

— it also marks the concept as subordinate to 'Electronic and communication engineering', expressed by the shorter number 621.38.

These functions are separated in the PRECIS thesaurus. A RIN identifies a concept through its unique position in a machine-held file, but its relationships with other concepts are then conveyed by a separate system of codes considered later. Some writers have suggested that RINs should be more 'meaningful', and at least indicate levels of superordination and subordination. This, however, would seriously hinder the indexer's ability to add a new term to the system at any time, simply by assigning the next available RIN without concern for the hospitality problems usually associated with hierarchically-expressive notation.

Position 3: Term code

****

$a = Common noun
$b = Node label
$c = Proper name (other than place name)
$d = Place name
$k = 'Blanket' reference

****

Every term admitted to the thesaurus should be prefixed by one of these codes to indicate the class to which it belongs. Three of the codes ($a, $c and $d) were encountered earlier — they convey the same meanings in the final positions of primary manipulation codes (see p 192-193). The codes $b and $k occur only in the thesaurus, with special functions considered later. A thesaurus intended only as a source of *See* and *See also* references can be established without using the first 4 codes, but this is not recommended. The need to identify a class of terms is likely to arise at any time and cannot always be anticipated. This applies particularly to the proper names of persons, organisations, etc. — it may be necessary to isolate these terms, with minimum programming effort, for reasons such as the following:

— many of these names are subject to change when a new code of cataloguing practice is adopted;

— proper names account for a relatively high proportion of terms in most indexing vocabularies, and they tend to overload outputs such as alphabetical authority files, published thesauri, etc. They are therefore usually excluded from these products as a matter of policy †.

Position 4: Indexing term (including typographic codes)

Any term marked as a lead in a string is a potential candidate for the thesaurus, but different selection criteria, and different codes and procedures, are applied to: (i) proper names; (ii) common nouns and noun phrases. These are considered separately below.

Proper names of persons, organisations, etc. are not usually admitted to the thesaurus unless they are involved, as source or target terms, in references. It should be remembered that class-of-one terms are frequently context-established in strings by the names of their containing classes (see p 83-84). Any part of a proper name that calls for special typographic treatment is prefixed by one of the following instruction codes:

****

$e = Non-filing part in italic preceded by a comma
$f = Filing part in italic preceded by a comma
$g = Filing part in roman (i.e. bold), no preceding punctuation
$h = Filing part in italic preceded by a full point
$i = Filing part in italic, no preceding punctuation

****

† They might be issued as separate lists, or assigned to appendices in a published thesaurus.

These codes are also applied with the same meanings to proper names in strings.

Example: To generate the reference:

Guingand, *Sir* Francis de *See* De Guingand, *Sir* Francis

— the source and target terms should be input as follows:

Source term: #RI# 061744X $c Guingand $e Sir $g Francis de

Target term: #RI# 0617458 $c De Guingand $e Sir $g Francis

Note: The *See* directive would be generated by a relational code ($m) included among the data attached to the target term. This is considered later.

Common nouns and noun phrases marked as leads in strings should be admitted to the thesaurus as a matter of course, whether or not they are involved in references. A number of terms (called 'orphans') appear to lack relations when first admitted, but are later assigned to categories or recognised as members of equivalence sets, etc. Common nouns are input in slightly different forms in strings and thesaurus records. When these terms occur in strings they are written in lower case throughout, and the computer generates upper case initials where necessary; this can vary, depending upon which part of the term (focus or difference) appears in a filing position. Terms in references are not manipulated in this way, and should be input in the form required as output †.

There are no theoretical reasons why the typographic codes applied to proper names should not also be used in common noun phrases, but this rarely happens in practice — these two classes of terms are subject to different formal criteria ‡. Three special codes ($j, $p and $q) are

---

† Indexers in some agencies write their records in upper case throughout (as an aid to keyboarders), then underline the letters that should be input to the computer in upper case, e.g. BIRDS.

‡ They are also subject to different logical criteria. When an entity expressed by a proper name, such as 'Royal Sussex Regiment', is indexed (in accordance with cataloguing rules) as:

Great Britain. *Army. Royal Sussex Regiment*

— the term not only breaks the first (and otherwise mandatory) 'Rule of differencing' used in PRECIS, it also contravenes some of the recommendations on vocabulary control in national and international standards.

used to vary the layout and typography of references containing common nouns.

```
*******************************************
$j =  Simulate the appearance of a heading:
        1.  Print full point
        2.  Leave two spaces
        3.  Print the following word(s) in
              standard roman (not bold)
*******************************************
```

These instructions generate the appearance of a typical heading (lead + qualifier) in a PRECIS entry. A need for this layout in a reference can arise for reasons such as the following:

(a) *To refer from a non-preferred compound to its separate components printed as lead-plus-qualifier.* The 'Rules of differencing' (p 55 ff) call for a compound concept such as 'School libraries' to be factored into separate components, each expressed as a noun and assigned to its own position in a string, e.g.

String: (1) schools
(p) libraries

Entries: Schools
Libraries

Libraries. Schools

If the unfactored form of the concept is likely to be sought by users it should be admitted to the thesaurus as a non-preferred term and provided as a source term in a reference, e.g.

School libraries *See* Libraries. Schools

The correct typography and layout of the target term would be produced by the code $j included as part of its input record, e.g.

#RI# 0007676 $a Libraries $j Schools

(b) *To disambiguate homographs.* As noted earlier (p 82-83) the intended meaning of a homograph is usually indicated in an entry by the name of an appropriate broader concept printed in the qualifier, e.g.

(i) Seals. Engineering components

(ii) Seals. Mammals

These entries would be generated from the strings:

(i) (l) engineering components
(q) seals

(ii) (l) mammals
(q) seals

Broader terms are not marked as leads in these cases; the link between the name of the class (coded 'l') and its member (coded 'q') should still be handled by a reference extracted from the thesaurus, e.g.

(i) Engineering components
See also
Seals. Engineering components

(ii) Mammals
See also
Seals. Mammals

The correct forms of the target terms in these references are produced by the code $j in their input records:

(i) #RI# 0051977 $a Seals $j Engineering components

(ii) #RI# 0153060 $a Seals $j Mammals

Note that these input records do not yet contain the relational codes that would generate the *See also* references.

Compounds that include $j in their thesaurus records can also function as source terms in references, e.g.

Seals. Mammals
See also
Sea lions

****

$p = Simulate the appearance of a lead (bold) and a display (roman):
1. Assign the following word(s) to a second line in the target term
2. Indent 2 spaces
3. Print in standard roman

****

This code can be applied only to parts of target terms, not source terms. It produces a reference from a non-preferred compound to its separate (factored) components when these are printed on different lines corresponding to the lead and display positions in an entry. This kind of target term is needed in circumstances such as the following:

(a) A compound concept is factored into separate components assigned as a block to the string, but the second (or subsequent) term in the block has not been marked as a lead.

Example:

Compound concept to be factored but retained as a source term in a reference: Land law

String: (1) real property
(3) law

Entry: Real property
Law

Reference: Land law
See Real property
Law

Input for target term: #RI# 0370673 $a Real property $p Law

Notes: (i) In a legal context, 'Land' and 'Real property' are treated as equivalents.
(ii) It is assumed, as a matter of policy, that 'Law' is not selected as a lead when related to a specific legal problem.

Note that the *See* directive is printed on the second line in these cases. This is handled entirely by the computer; it avoids too many overruns when column width is restricted.

(b) When a compound concept is factored and re-expressed as a sequence of terms centred around an action, the terms in the string may be coded in such a way that —

— the entry under the first term in the sequence is generated in the standard format;

— the entry under the final term in the sequence is produced by the predicate transformation.

Each entry will then contain terms in the lead and display positions, but none in the qualifier.

Example:

Compound concept to be factored but retained as a source term in a reference: Computer aided design

String: (2) design
(s) applications $v of $w in
(3) computer systems

Entries: Design
Applications of computer systems

Computer systems
Applications in design

Reference: Computer aided design
  See Computer systems
    Applications in design

Input record for target term:

#RI# 0108375 $a Computer systems $p Applications in design

Note: In these situations the indexer is likely to face a choice of target terms, e.g.

(i) Computer systems $p Applications in design

(ii) Design $p Applications of computer systems

Other things being equal, the term that files nearer to the source term should usually be selected.

****

$q = Simulate the appearance of a lead (bold) and a display (italic):
1. Assign the following word(s) to a second line in the target term
2. Indent 2 spaces
3. Print in italic

****

This code, like $p, can be applied only to parts of target terms, not source terms. The instructions listed above parallel those attached to $p except for the choice of type face at Step 3. Italic is usually needed in the display position of a target term if a reference is made from a named historical period to a concept differenced by a date introduced by $d (see p 64).

Example:

Concept: Victorian England

String: (1) England $d 1837-1901

Entry: England
  1837-1901

Reference: Victorian England
  See England
    1837-1901

Input for target term: #RI# 0115800 $d England $q 1837-1901

Note that the *See* directive is printed on the second line when the target term contains the code $q.

Position 5: Definition or scope note

****
$d = Definition or scope note
****

A note which defines a term or restricts its use for indexing purposes should be added to a thesaurus record only when necessary. The majority of terms are unequivocal, and their intended meanings are generally conveyed by their contexts in index entries and/or their positions within hierarchies in the thesaurus. Two kinds of note (these occasionally overlap) can be attached to a term and identified by $d, as seen in the following examples.

1. *Definitions or restricted meanings*

Examples:

(a) #RI# 0507776 $a Indian languages $d Not a language group - use for comprehensive works on languages spoken in India, e.g. Indic plus Dravidian

(b) #RI# 0435635 $a Territorial minorities $d Groups forming minorities within states but majorities in smaller areas (e.g. Welsh in the UK)

(c) #RI# 0823988 $a Science parks $d Areas where manufacturing companies are located on campuses, allowing interchange of research etc. between the companies and the universities

(d) #RI# 0614750 $a Tachyons $d Theoretical particles moving faster than light

Note: The definition of a newly-emergent concept (as in *(c)* and *(d)* above) is usually taken from the first document on the topic if the term has not yet appeared in dictionaries, etc.

2. *Instructions to indexers (sometimes amounting to mini-policies)*

Examples:

(a) #RI# 0000507 $a Law $d Lead only when coded '1' (1st concept in string) or 'p' to a country. In other cases use a blanket reference

[Blanket references are explained later]

(b) #RI# 0078131 $a Acute abdomen $d A specific disease. Should be context-established by 'Abdomen (NU)' in the string

Unlike the 'qualifiers' introduced by $j (see p 221), a note prefixed by $d does not form part of the term to which it is attached. Consequently, it does not appear in printed indexes, but it should be included in other outputs, such as alphabetical authority files and systematic thesauri.

Position 6: Relational code + RIN for source term

The three basic relationships described in Chapter 15 are conveyed by the following codes in the machine-held thesaurus:

****

$m = Equivalence relationship

$n = Associative relationship

$o = Hierarchical relationship

****

The associative and hierarchical relationships can also be expressed by other codes with special meanings considered later.

Each of these codes must be followed immediately by the RIN of the term from which a reference should be made — indeed, the code plus its following RIN (e.g. $m 024757X) should be regarded as a unit. The relational code conveys the following instructions to the computer:

1. Proceed to the address (RIN) which follows the code;
2. Extract the term held at that address and print it as a source term in a reference;
3. Print the appropriate directive, determined by the relational code:
   $m = *See*
   $n & $o = *See also*
4. Complete the reference by printing, as a target, the term held in the 3rd position.

Example: If the following records have been input to the thesaurus:

(i) #RI # 024757X $a Aves #

(ii) #RI # 0241768 $a Birds $m 024757X#

— and if the RIN for 'Birds' (0241768) is quoted as part of the indexing data attached to a string on this concept, the computer will carry out the 4 instructions listed above and generate the reference:

Aves *See* Birds

A given concept can call for references from more than one term. An entry under 'Birds', for example, would be supported not only by the *See* reference shown above, but also *See also* references from:

— a broader term, e.g.
Vertebrates
See also
Birds

— an associated term, e.g.
Ornithology
See also
Birds

The record for 'Birds' will then contain three relational codes followed by their RINs, e.g.

#RI# 0241768 $a Birds $m 024757X $o 0245267 $n 0235194#

— where $o identifies the hierarchical relationship and $n the associative relationship. When a term is accompanied by more than one code-plus-RIN combination, these can be input in any order.

Variations in forms of references

As noted earlier, a *See* reference generated by $m is usually printed on a single line (with a necessary allowance for overruns) e.g.

Educational attainment *See* Academic achievement

Other formats are produced by the computer in the following circumstances:

(a) The input for the target term contains either $p or $q as a typographic code — see the examples on p 223-224.

(b) The source term refers to more than one target. This can occur if a compound concept which should be factored (see p 55 ff) represents a class with more than one species, and the index contains entries on two or more of the species. The directive will then be printed on a second line, with the target terms aligned as an alphabetical column, e.g.

School libraries
  See Libraries. Primary schools
      Libraries. Secondary schools

The *See also* references generated by codes such as $n and $o occur in only one form, e.g.

Vertebrates
  See also
    Birds

As noted earlier, if a source term refers to more than one target, the second and subsequent occurrence of the common parts of the reference (the source term itself, and the directive) are automatically cancelled, and the targets are aligned as an alphabetical column, e.g.

Mammals
  See also
    Horses
    Seals. Mammals
    Whales
    etc

See also references are printed before the entries that begin with the same term, e.g.

Birds
  See also
    Gulls
    Ornithology
Birds
  Anatomy
  Behaviour
Birds. Europe

When the source and target terms in a *See also* reference are linked by the hierarchical relationship, the computer can sometimes change its choice of a target term depending on factors considered in the next chapter.

Validation of records at input

Before a new term is accepted by the computer, its record is submitted to a series of validation checks of which the following are the most important:

(a) The RIN in *Position 1* (the address where the new term should be held) is tested for correctness on the basis of its modulus-eleven check digit. This is not entirely foolproof, but it detects simple copying errors in the great majority of cases.

(b) The computer ensures that the address indicated by the RIN is empty. It might already hold data if the indexer had failed to strike a RIN from the computer-generated list, and had then assigned the same number to a later term.

(c) If the record contains codes, such as $d and $o, these are tested for correctness. For example, a record containing a mistyped code-plus-RIN combination, such as '$z 0094676', will be detected and rejected, since '$z' does not appear among the codes allowed in the thesaurus.

(d) Every RIN that follows a relational code is subject to its own modulus-eleven check, and the indicated address is examined to ensure that it does, in fact, contain data. This elementary precaution guards against demands for *See* or *See also* references from nothing, but it also imposes a special constraint on the indexer, who must ensure that source terms are input *before* their target terms.

(e) If the source term represents a non-preferred synonym (indicated by the code $m among the data attached to the target term), its record must not contain any relational codes. This ensures that the user is never directed to a non-preferred term.

Any record which fails one or more of these validation checks is automatically rejected, and the indexer receives a warning message. If, for example, a record is submitted to an address that is already occupied (see check *(b)* above), the indexer receives a message stating:

- the reason for the rejection;
- the data comprising the rejected record;
- the data already held at that address.

Adding reciprocal relationships

Many of the input records used as examples above show that relational information recorded by an indexer points only in one direction: that is, from the target term to the source term. Reciprocal relationships are added by the computer during the validation routines described above — in particular, at Step *(d)*.

Example: Assuming that the following records have been input:

— #RI# 0008117 $a Photography#

— #RI# 0011762 $a Film making#

— #RI# 0112461 $a Motion picture films#

— #RI# 0011770 $a Cinematography $o 0008117 $m 0011762 $n 0112461#

— and assuming further (entirely for the sake of demonstration) that a reciprocal relationship can be represented by the symbol ℞ (replacing the $), the first 3 records shown above will be 'rounded-out' by the computer as follows:

— #0008117 $a Photography ℞o 0011770#

— #0011762 $a Film making ℞m 0011770#

— #0112461 $a Motion picture films ℞n 0011770#

These extra data allow the computer to scan up or down a hierarchy with equal facility, which speeds the production of references and also allows a faster response time if the thesaurus is searched on-line.

EXERCISES (For Answers, see Appendix 4, p 336)

Exercise 17

Using the terms and RINs in the left-hand column, prepare input records to generate the references shown in the right-hand column.

Example:

Terms & RINs	*References*
Flammability 0173193	Flammability *See* Inflammability
Fire 006775X	Fire *See also* Inflammability
Inflammability 0173207	

Input records (Answer):

#RI# 0173193 $a Flammability#

#RI# 006775X $a Fire#

#RI# 0173207 $a Inflammability $m 0173193 $n 006775X#

	Terms and RINs	*References*
(a)	Bears 0027790 Soft toys 0034584 Teddy bears 0549916	Bears *See also* Teddy bears Soft toys *See also* Teddy bears
(b)	Probabilistic models 0168491 Mathematical models 0009024 Stochastic models 0056421	Probabilistic models *See* Stochastic models Mathematical models *See also* Stochastic models
(c)	Office machinery 0067962 Sound recording equipment 0022829 Dictation machines 0067970	Office machinery *See also* Dictation machines Sound recording equipment *See also* Dictation machines

Exercise 18

If the records below have been input to the computer, what references would be produced if the indicated RIN is quoted as part of the data attached to a PRECIS string?

Example:

Input records: #RI# 0094676 $a Demand#

#RI# 0113565 $a Supply#

#RI# 0207764 $a Scarcity $n 0094676 $n 0113565#

Quoted RIN: 0207764

References (Answer):

Supply
See also
Scarcity

Demand
See also
Scarcity

(a) *Input records:* #RI# 0485063 $c Civil Service Commission $i (United States)#

#RI# 0485071 $c United States $h Civil Service Commission $m 0485063#

Quoted RIN: 0485071

(b) *Input records:* #RI# 008803X $a Propositions $j Logic#

#RI# 0378771 $a Hypotheses $o 008803X#

Quoted RIN: 0378771

(c) *Input records:* #RI# 0109843 $a Diurnal rhythms#

#RI# 0075337 $a Biological rhythms#

#RI# 0147753 $a Circadian rhythms $o 0075337 $m 0109843#

Quoted RIN: 0147753

17. Thesaurus construction: building the 'Penguin network'

This chapter deals with the construction of a network of terms linked by the basic thesaural relationships introduced in Chapter 15, using a selection of the components described in the previous chapter. These procedures will now be considered, however, more from the indexer's point of view than the computer's, which calls for the use of a different kind of record. The step-by-step account below is based upon two assumptions:

(a) Records containing new terms are written by indexers (for example, on cards), then forwarded in batches for input to the computer as a separate operation. This represents a 'most complex' case. On-line input would doubtless be faster and generally simpler. Each method has its advantages and disadvantages.

(b) The indexer responsible for the thesaurus is dealing with a PRECIS string containing the term 'Penguins', at a time when none of its broader or other related terms has yet been admitted into the system †.

Stage 1. Check term

The indexer in charge of the thesaurus is responsible not only for assigning terms to hierarchies, etc., but also for checking the acceptability of candidate terms, applying the various criteria for vocabulary

---

† It would have been a simple matter to choose a new example to demonstrate these procedures, abandoning the 'Penguin network' which has been used regularly as a teaching model on PRECIS courses. Nevertheless, and without apologies, 'Penguins' will again be used to demonstrate the building of a network, partly because it occurred as a genuine case (in the circumstances described in *(b)* above), partly because it illustrates all the salient points of thesaurus construction (changing the example would not change the principles or procedures), but chiefly because the 'Penguin', through repeated use, has almost acquired the status of an international PRECIS symbol.

control described in previous chapters, e.g.

— the choice of singulars or plurals (see p 104-106);

— the treatment of compound terms (see Chapter 4).

If string writing and thesaurus construction are handled by different people, the indexer responsible for the thesaurus should be able, when necessary, to take a string back to its indexer and ask for changes to one or more of its terms. As noted earlier, this editorial function is concerned not only with the consistency of the indexing vocabulary; it can also affect the hierarchies held in the thesaurus. For example, a term such as 'Lens polishing' should be factored, according to the *Second rule of differencing*, into two noun components, 'Lenses' and 'Polishing', the first of which would be assigned to a class of *things* called 'Optical equipment', and the second to a class of *actions* called 'Surface treatment'.

Stage 2. Record the term and assign its RIN

The records prepared at this stage serve as copy for the computer input messages considered in the previous chapter, but they differ from input messages in the following respects:

(a) The first component of the indexer's record consists of the term, not the RIN, e.g.

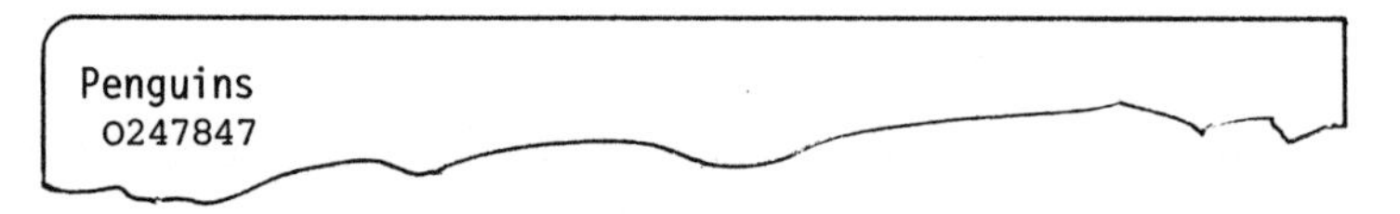

After this record has been keyboarded it is returned to the indexer and added to an authority file; the term then functions as the filing element.

(b) In a computer input message, a mandatory code in Position 3 indicates the class to which the term belongs ($a = common noun, $d = place name, etc.). In the records written by indexers, common nouns are not usually prefixed by the code $a. These represent the bulk of terms encountered in day-to-day practice, and insertion of this code is left to the keyboarder. Any other kind of term, such as a proper name or

place name, is distinguished by the appropriate code written as a prefix, e.g.

(c) Indexers' records for new terms do not contain #RI# message codes; these are added by the keyboarder at the time of input. Any other kind of input, such as an amendment, is identified by one of the special message codes considered later.

(d) In computer input messages, source terms are indicated only as code-plus-RIN combinations, e.g. $m 024757X. The source term itself is also written, as a reminder, on the indexer's record, but is ignored at the keyboarding stage (see later examples).

Stage 3. Establish related terms (if any)

The search for terms that should be provided as alternative access points can involve reference to standard works such as dictionaries, encyclopaedias, existing thesauri, classification schemes, etc. †. Specialists (preferably with a knowledge of indexing, such as librarians or information officers), can also be consulted, especially when dealing with newly-emerging concepts. At this stage the indexer is concerned with three classes of terms, corresponding to the three basic relations considered in Chapter 15:

- synonyms and quasi-synonyms *(equivalence relationship)*;
- broader terms *(hierarchical relationship)* ‡;
- other related terms *(associative relationship)*.

A dictionary check would reveal two terms directly related to 'Penguins':

---

† *Webster's Third New International Dictionary* is particularly useful as a first approach.

‡ When dealing with hierarchically-related concepts, the search is limited to broader, not narrower, terms (for reasons, see p 210-211).

— a synonym, 'Sphenisciformes';

— a broader term, 'Birds'.

Each of these terms should be recorded, and its RIN assigned:

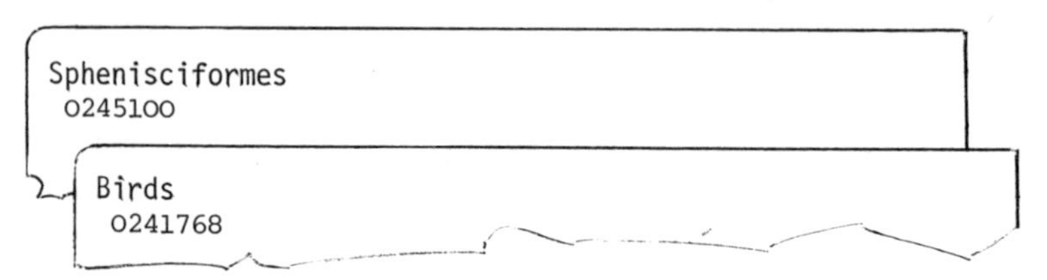

Assuming that preference is given to popular rather than scientific names, 'Sphenisciformes' now becomes a non-preferred term. This can be indicated on the indexer's record by an arrow pointing to its preferred equivalent, e.g.

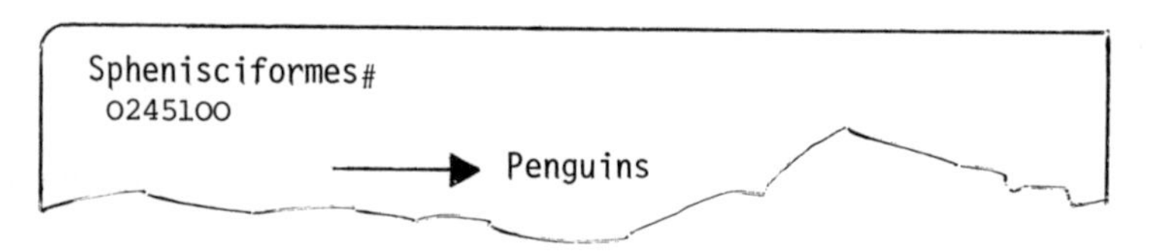

This addition is intended only as a warning to the indexer; it is not included among the data input at the keyboarding stage. Note that non-preferred terms should have data only in the first 4 (mandatory) positions in an input message. The record above would therefore be input as:

#RI# 0245100 $a Sphenisciformes#

These related concepts, together with their RINs preceded by appropriate relational codes, should then be added to the record for 'Penguins':

At this stage the RIN for 'Penguins' should also be added to a special field in the indexing record described in the final chapter.

Establishing further levels of concepts

Any contact with a broader or associated term, such as 'Birds' in the example above, introduces another 'level' of concepts, and calls for a repetition of the earlier stages. Each of these new terms should be considered as a potential target in its own right; it should be tested (or rather, re-tested) for acceptability, and a further level of new source terms should be established if necessary. A check of this kind applied to 'Birds' would reveal three further potential source terms:

- a synonym, 'Aves';
- a broader term, 'Vertebrates';
- an associated term, 'Ornithology'.

These new terms should be recorded, and their RINs assigned:

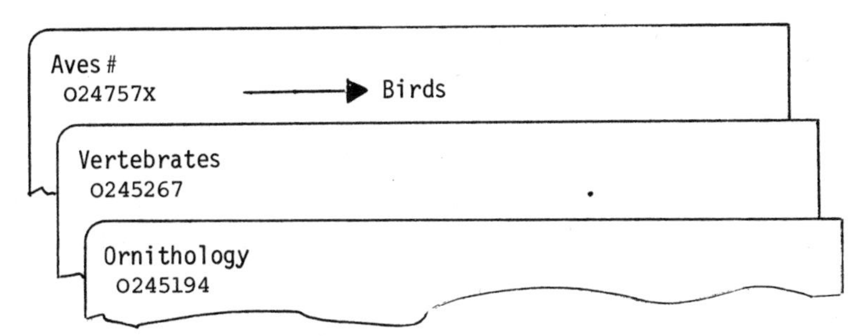

These terms, together with their RINs and the appropriate relational codes, should then be added to the record for 'Birds':

Birds	Aves	Vertebrates	Ornithology
0241768	$m 024757X	$o 0245267	$n 0245194

The same procedure would then be applied to the concepts 'Vertebrates' and 'Ornithology', and this would continue, level by level, to the point where the need for further terms appears to run out. Nearly all networks tend to be inadequate when first established, but we shall later consider simple procedures which allow new terms to be inserted into an existing hierarchy, or a hierarchy to be re-structured, whenever necessary. The need for extension or re-structuring usually becomes apparent when new documents throw further light on past decisions.

Ordering records prior to input

As noted in the previous chapter, terms must be input in an order which ensures that every source term has been assigned to its address before the record for its target term can be accepted (see Validation check *(d)* on p 229). This means that the records for 'Sphenisciformes' and 'Birds' must be in the system before the input record for 'Penguins' is submitted. A selection of records written in response to a lead on 'Penguins', and organised as an acceptable sequence, is illustrated on p 239 †. Note (again) that only essential data are selected from these records at the keyboarding stage. For example, the records for 'Birds' and 'Penguins' would be input in the form:

#RI# 0241768 $a Birds $m 024757X $o 0245267 $n 0245194#

#RI# 0247847 $a Penguins $m 0245100 $o 0241768#

After these records have been input, they are returned to the indexer for integration into a 'master' authority file. Most agencies using batch input procedures maintain a master file on cards, even when a fiche version is available and used as the principal working tool (see Note on p 213). A card file is invariably more up-to-date than its fiche equivalent.

Production and use of diagnostic printout

Provided that a record passes the various validation checks considered earlier, the computer will respond with a diagnostic printout showing the data it actually holds. This generally takes the form of a fully-formatted reference from each of the source terms in the input record, followed in each case by a copy of the input message itself. For example, the input for 'Penguins' would generate the diagnostic shown on p 240:

---

† Other orders that will satisfy this condition are also possible.

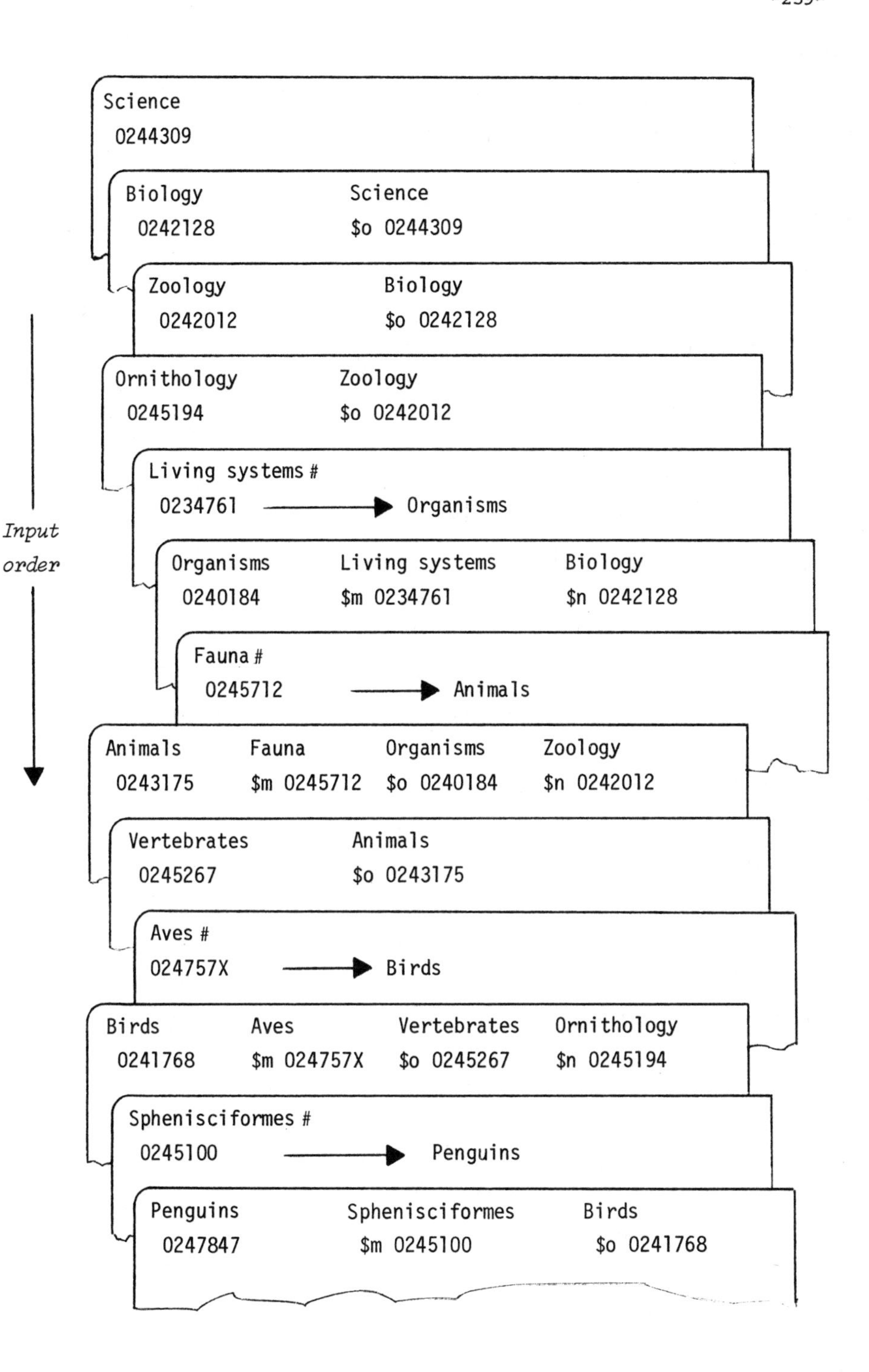
Science
0244309
Biology
0242128
Science
$o 0244309
Zoology
0242012
Biology
$o 0242128
Ornithology
0245194
Zoology
$o 0242012
Living systems #
0234761
Organisms
Organisms
0240184
Living systems
$m 0234761
Biology
$n 0242128
Fauna #
0245712
Animals
Animals
0243175
Fauna
$m 0245712
Organisms
$o 0240184
Zoology
$n 0242012
Vertebrates
0245267
Animals
$o 0243175
Aves #
024757X
Birds
Birds
0241768
Aves
$m 024757X
Vertebrates
$o 0245267
Ornithology
$n 0245194
Sphenisciformes #
0245100
Penguins
Penguins
0247847
Sphenisciformes
$m 0245100
Birds
$o 0241768
Input order

```
Sphenisciformes See ($m) Penguins
     0247847 $a Penguins $m 0245100 $o 0241768#

Birds
  See also ($o)
     Penguins
     0247847 $a Penguins $m 0245100 $o 0241768#
```

This is read for the kinds of error that cannot be stopped by validation routines, e.g. mis-spellings. The reference itself should also be read for commonsense. A nonsense reference would be produced from data which passed validation if the indexer failed to strike out a RIN as soon as it had been used, then assigned the same number to a later term. Let us assume, for example, that:

— an indexer had admitted the term 'Criminals' and assigned it to the address 0206970, but failed to strike out this RIN from the computer-generated list;

— the next document deals with 'Teachers' (a new term), which calls for a reference from the broader concept 'Professional personnel'. According to the list of RINs, the next available numbers are 0206970 and 0206989. These are assigned as follows:

```
#RI# 0206970 $a Professional personnel#
#RI# 0206989 $a Teachers $o 0206970#
```

Provided that the input record for 'Teachers' has been keyboarded correctly it will pass validation, since the RIN for its source term, 0206970, already holds data. The computer will then provide two clues to the fault in the system:

1. It will generate the diagnostic:

```
Criminals
  See also ($o)
     Teachers
     0206989 $a Teachers $o 0206970#
```

2. The input message for 'Professional personnel' will be rejected on the grounds that its address (the RIN 0206970) is already occupied (see bottom of p 229).

When errors are detected, the data on file should be corrected using the amendment procedures considered later.

Generating references from the 'Penguin network'

At first sight the records listed on p 239 do not appear to constitute the raw material for a systematic thesaurus. This may become more apparent, however, when the terms in these records have been reorganised, on the basis of their relational codes, into the 'Penguin network' shown on p 242. This network contains:

— two hierarchies indicated by $o, one consisting of discipline terms linked by the hierarchical whole-part relationship, the other containing names of organisms linked by the generic relationship;

— three associative relations indicated by $n;

— four non-preferred synonyms indicated by $m.

Constructing a network of this kind *ab initio* is a relatively time-consuming task, but it saves time in a number of ways once it has been established. In particular, it allows a full set of supporting references to be produced at any time simply by quoting a RIN in the appropriate field of a subject package †. The RIN for any preferred term in the network can be quoted in this way. If, for example, an indexer handles a document on 'Vertebrates' after the Penguin network has been established, quoting its RIN (0245267) will generate all the necessary references without the need for further decisions or input.

The production of *See* and *See also* references calls for a two-stage explanation:

— firstly, a description of the basic procedures involved in tracing a route step-by-step through a network, extracting data at each step and formatting the appropriate reference;

---

† RINs are also held in Field 692 of current MARC records.

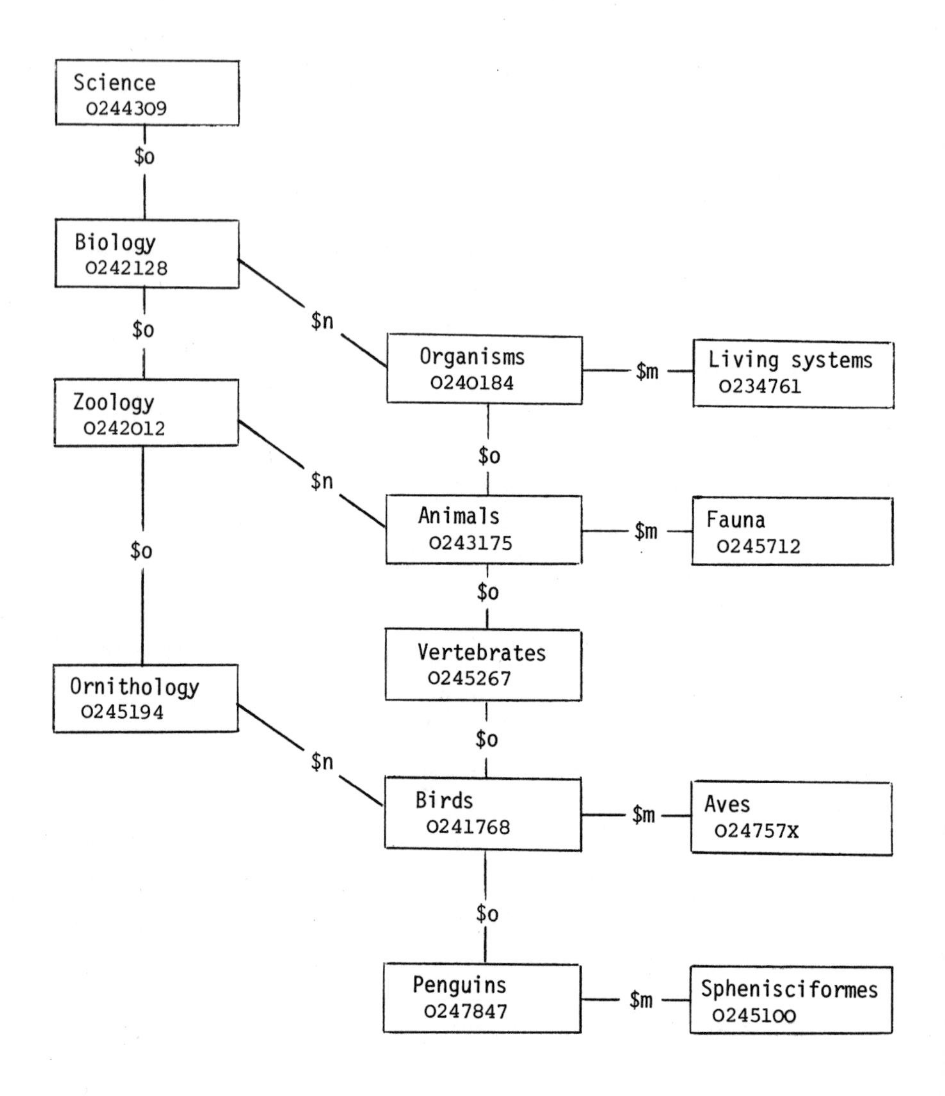

The Penguin network

— secondly, the introduction of a special routine which reduces, in some cases, the number of steps that a reader has to take when following a reference from a broader to a narrower term.

The explanations below are based upon two assumptions: (i) the network shown on p 242 is already held in the computer; (ii) the RIN 0247847 has been quoted in the appropriate field of a subject package attached to a PRECIS string containing a lead on 'Penguins'. The presence of a RIN in this field acts as an instruction, and triggers the following sequence of operations:

1. The computer is directed to the address 0247847 in the thesaurus, and checks it for the presence of relational codes. Two codes are present: $m and $o.

2. The machine is redirected, via $m, to the address 0245100. It extracts the term held at this address and formats the reference:

Sphenisciformes *See* Penguins

This path through the network is now effectively closed, since non-preferred terms must not be accompanied by further relational information.

3. The machine is also redirected, via $o, to the address 0241768. It extracts the term and formats the reference:

Birds
See also
Penguins

4. Tracing a route marked by a code such as $o takes the computer on to another (higher) level. The term 'Birds' is now treated as a potential target, and its address is checked for the presence of relational codes. The three codes present at this address generate the references:

$m = Aves *See* Birds

$n = Ornithology
See also
Birds

$o = Vertebrates
See also
Birds

5. The codes $n and $o again point the way to further levels. The addresses holding 'Vertebrates' and 'Ornithology' are therefore checked for the presence of relational codes:

— The address for 'Vertebrates' contains $o, which generates the reference:

Animals
See also
Vertebrates

— The address for 'Ornithology' also contains $o; this generates the reference:

Zoology
See also
Ornithology

6. This basic procedure is repeated level by level through the rest of the network, to the point where the computer encounters one or more *top terms* — these are recognised as preferred terms which lack any further relational information.

These various stages lead to the construction of the following references, organised into categories according to the relationships between their source and target terms:

'See' references produced by $m

Living systems *See* Organisms

Fauna *See* Animals

Aves *See* Birds

Sphenisciformes *See* Penguins

'See also' references produced by $n

Biology
See also
Organisms

Zoology
See also
Animals

Ornithology
See also
Birds

'See also' references produced by $o

Science
See also
Biology

Biology
See also
Zoology

Zoology
See also
Ornithology

Organisms
See also
Animals

Animals
See also
Vertebrates

Vertebrates
See also
Birds

Birds
See also
Penguins

The Bypass routine

The references shown above direct the reader one step at a time down a hierarchy, e.g. from 'Organisms' to 'Animals', 'Animals' to 'Vertebrates', and so on. This might be regarded as a reasonable route to 'Penguins' at the lowest point of the hierarchy provided that one or more index entries also occur at each (or most) of the intervening steps, but it should be rated as tedious, to say the least, if these step-by-step references appeared in an index which contains, in the subject fields covered by the 'Penguin network', *only* an entry for 'Penguins'. This potential source of irritation is relieved, at least in part, by a special procedure known as the *Bypass routine* and associated with the code $o.

This procedure can be explained, step by step, as a set of extra routines introduced into the output programs *before* any references based upon $o are formatted †:

1. *Compile List 'A'*. The computer reads the set of subject packages which comprise the source of the index. It extracts the RINs and organises these numbers as a list.

2. *Compile List 'B'*. The machine also checks through the relevant hierarchies in the thesaurus and extracts the RINs for all broader terms identified by $o. These, too, are organised as a list.

3. *Compare Lists 'A' and 'B'*:

— RINs common to both lists identify terms that should be printed as parts of *See also* references and *also* occur as leads in the index.

— RINs in List 'B' with no matches in List 'A' identify terms that should be printed as parts of *See also* references, but do *not* occur as leads in that particular issue of the index.

4. *Select targets*. Only terms that are common to both lists, and/or the lowest terms in hierarchies, are chosen as targets when references

---

† The step-by-step explanation above is offered as an aid to comprehension. It does not follow that the programs actually work in this way.

are constructed from broader to narrower terms linked by $o. The terms represented by unmatched RINs are *bypassed as targets* in these references, although they are still provided as source terms.

We can demonstrate this procedure by assuming that only 'Penguins' (of the terms in the network on p 242) has occurred as a lead in the index. Note that the bypass routine applies *only* to terms linked by $o; consequently, the one-step references produced by $m and $n, shown as two separate groups on p 244, will not be affected. The references from broader to narrower terms will, however, be modified as follows:

Science
See also
Ornithology

Biology
See also
Ornithology

Zoology
See also
Ornithology

Organisms
See also
Penguins

Animals
See also
Penguins

Vertebrates
See also
Penguins

Birds
See also
Penguins

These should be contrasted with the references produced if the index contains leads on, say, 'Penguins', 'Zoology' and 'Vertebrates'. Again, the one-step references produced by $m and $n will not be affected, but the references from broader to narrower terms will appear in the form:

Science
See also
Zoology

Biology
See also
Zoology

Zoology
See also
Ornithology

Organisms
See also
Vertebrates

Animals
See also
Vertebrates

Vertebrates
See also
Penguins

Birds
See also
Penguins

Note that none of the terms in the network has been lost as an access point — this procedure affects only the computer's choice of some target terms. It would have been a simple matter to reduce even further the number of steps taken by a user, and extend the bypass routine to terms linked by $n, but that would produce an occasional reference such as:

*Science
See also
Penguins

Extending a hierarchy

It is a simple matter to add a new term to an existing hierarchy at any time. An indexer might, for example, handle a document on 'Snakes' after the 'Penguin' network on p 242 has been established. The new concept can be accommodated by the addition of four extra terms:

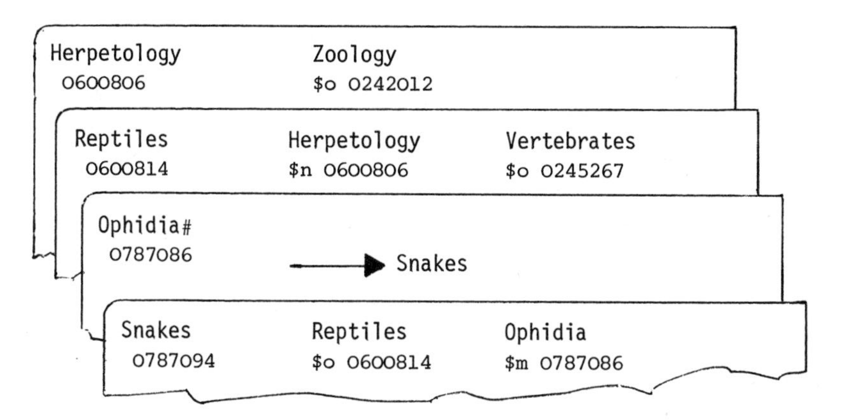

The terms 'Herpetology' and 'Reptiles' will then be grafted on to the appropriate hierarchies, since 'Zoology' and 'Vertebrates' are already in the system. The network would then be extended as follows:

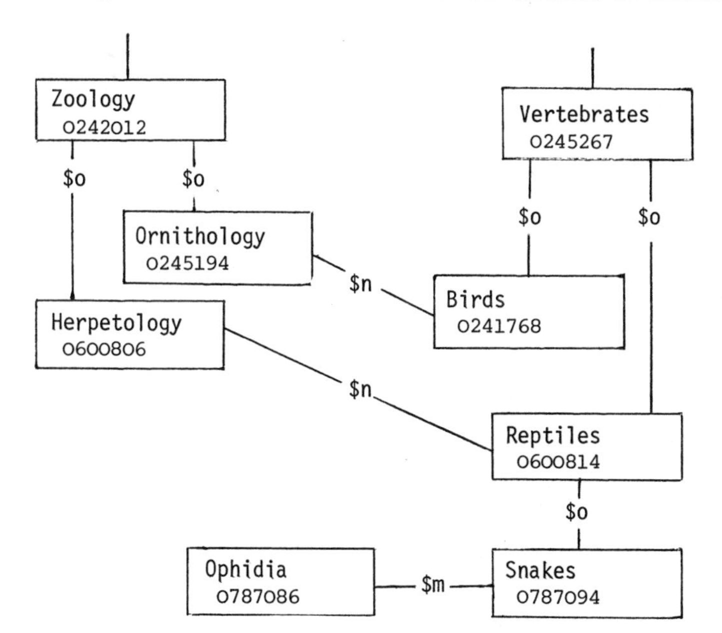

Experience shows that few entirely new hierarchies are likely to be established after the system has been applied to the first few hundred documents. The amount of input and effort decrease steadily as the thesaurus grows to the point where most references can be produced by quoting existing RINs, and new concepts can usually be attached to appropriate positions in previously established networks.

EXERCISES (For Answers, see Appendix 4, p 337)

Exercise 19

Using *only* the terms and RINs listed below:

(a) Organise the concepts into a network similar to the 'Penguin network' on p 242.

(b) Prepare and order the indexer's records that would assign these concepts to the thesaurus.

Books
0871001

Copyreading
087101X

Documents
0871028

Editing
0871036

Newspapers
0871044

Paperback books
0871052

Proofreading
0871060

Publications
0871079

Publishing
0871087

Serials
0871095

Exercise 20

Write the references that would be produced from the records above in an index containing leads on 'Newspapers' and 'Proofreading'.

18. Thesaurus construction: extra codes and procedures

This chapter deals with two different classes of codes and procedures:

— an extended range of 'standard' procedures used when building or amending a file intended as the source of *See* and *See also* references;

— extra codes and procedures, beginning on p 268, used only if the file is also (or mainly) intended as the source of a stand-alone thesaurus, e.g. on paper or COM.

As in the two previous chapters, this account deals with the preparation of 'messages' that are input to the computer as batches, on the understanding that batch input calls for the fullest explanations. On-line input would, without doubt, be simpler and faster, particularly where amendments to the file are concerned. However, on-line techniques are also more likely to vary from one agency to another, depending on local computer conventions.

Amendments to records on file

Amendment messages are identified by the prefix #RA#. Every amendment message must contain:

— the #RA# prefix;

— a RIN to indicate the record that needs correction;

— the code $v followed by data to be deleted;

— the code $w followed by data to be inserted.

An amendment message therefore takes the form:

#RA# [RIN] $v [data to be deleted] $w [data to be inserted] #.

The codes $v and $w must both be present in every amendment message, and they must be input in the order *$v before $w*. Either of the codes can, however, be 'empty' (that is, not followed by data), in which case —

— part of the record will be deleted if $v is followed by data, but nothing will be added if $w is empty;

— nothing will be deleted from the record if $v is empty, but characters will be added if $w is followed by data.

A straightforward amendment message would be used to correct a mis-spelt word noted during the reading of the diagnostic printout described on p 240. According to the procedures outlined in the previous chapter, the term 'Vertebrates' should be input in the form:

#RI# 0245267 $a Vertebrates $o 0243175

The diagnostic might show, however, that the following data are held in the computer:

Animals
See also ($o)
Vetebrates

0245267 $a Vetebrates $o 0243175

The spelling should then be corrected, using the message:

#RA# 0245267 $v e $w er #

This message conveys the following instructions to the computer:

— Proceed to the address 0245267;

— Trace and delete the *first occurrence* of the data prefixed by $v (i.e. the letter 'e');

— Replace the deleted character(s) by the data following $w (i.e. the letters 'er');

— Shift the rest of the record along to accommodate the extra character;

— Produce a new diagnostic printout.

Quoting a single letter was enough to locate the fault in the example above — the computer then traced and deleted the *first occurrence of the data following $v*. Any part of a term can be corrected in this 'minimal' way, provided that the indexer quotes a sufficient number of characters to pinpoint the error exactly. The nearest single letter cannot always be used as a position indicator. For example, the term 'Vertebrates' might have been miskeyed as 'Verterates' (where the error is adjacent to the second 'e', not the first). The message:

* #RA# 0245267 $v e $w eb #

— would then make matters worse, since the term will be changed into:

* Vebrterates

The correct result could be obtained by the message:

#RA# 0245267 $v te $w teb #

Other combinations of characters would achieve the same result, e.g.

$v ter $w tebr

If in doubt, the whole of the faulty word can be deleted and replaced by its correct version.

The ability to quote a fragment of a record, sufficient to pinpoint the position of an error, can be applied to any kind of verbal data, including indexing terms and scope notes. It cannot be used, however, to correct a fault in a relational code or its following RIN. If either of these contains an error, the code and the RIN must both be quoted as a unit. This is checked (as a safety measure) by a validation routine at the time of input. If, for example, the record for 'Vertebrates' had been keyed incorrectly as:

* #RI# 0245267 $a Vertebrates $n 0243175

— where $o (the link with 'Animals') had been miskeyed as $n, the code and RIN should appear in both parts of the amendment message:

#RA# 0245267 $v $n 0243175 $w $o 0243175 #

If necessary, an #RA# message can be used to correct more than one part of a record at the same time. If, for example, the record for 'Vertebrates' contained a mis-spelling, e.g. 'Vertabrates', and also the wrong relational code (as in the example above), these faults could be corrected simultaneously by the message:

#RA# 0245267 $v a $w e $v $n 0243175 $w $o 0243175 #

Corrections should then be written in the amendment message in the order in which they occur in the record being amended.

Either $v or $w can be input *without* following data, in which case material will be deleted from, or added to, the record depending on which of these codes is 'empty'. A straightforward 'empty' instruction would be used to delete one or more redundant characters from a term. For example, if 'Vertebrates' had been miskeyed as 'Verrtebrates', this could be corrected by the message:

#RA# 0245267 $v r $w #

The computer will then:

— delete the redundant 'r';

— close up the space left by the deletion;

— produce a new diagnostic showing the corrected version.

An #RA# message can be used to add one or more relationships to a term. For example, the record for 'Birds' (see p 239) might have been submitted in the form:

Birds	Aves	Vertebrates
0241768	$m 024757X	$o 0245267

This calls for a *See* reference from the non-preferred synonym 'Aves', and a *See also* reference from the superordinate concept 'Vertebrates', but the associative link with 'Ornithology' is missing. Provided that the term 'Ornithology' is already held in the system (at RIN 0245194), the missing link would be added by the amendment message:

#RA# 0241768 $v $w $n 0245194 #

— where $v is empty (so that nothing will be deleted), and $w is followed by the extra relational code and RIN.

The amendment procedures are sometimes used to replace the whole of a term. Let us assume that the file contained the following records:

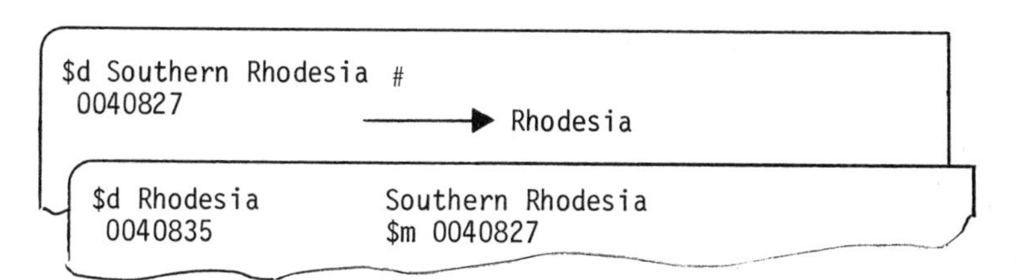

— at the time when 'Rhodesia' changed its name to 'Zimbabwe'. The old name can be kept as an access term, but it should be re-designated as a non-preferred synonym and assigned to a new address:

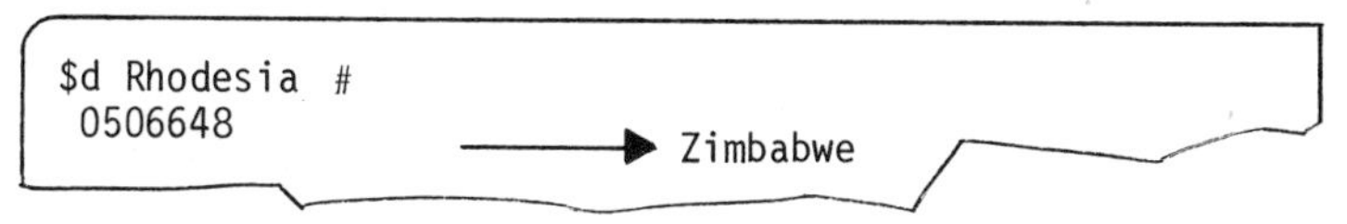

Two master records should then be changed to show the new preferred term:

(a)

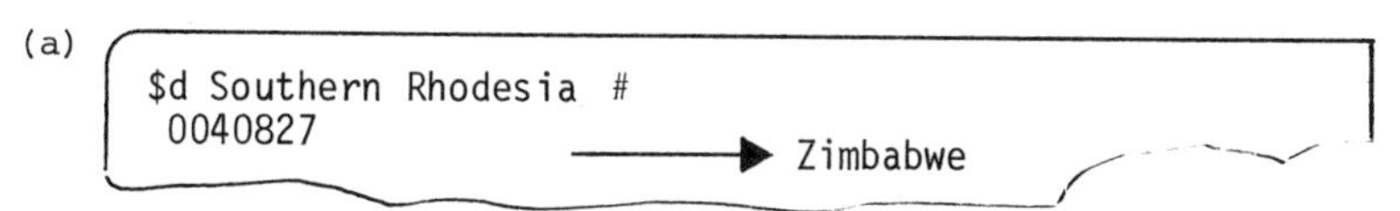

This change does not involve any correction to the machine-held data.

(b)

$d Zimbabwe — Rhodesia — Southern Rhodesia
0040835 — $m 0506648 — $m 0040827

This record should not be sent for keyboarding; instead, the original record should be corrected with the following message:

#RA# 0040835 $v $d Rhodesia $w $d Zimbabwe $v $w $m 0506648 #

This message contains two amendments:

— The first deletes 'Rhodesia' as the preferred term and replaces it by 'Zimbabwe';

— The second produces a new reference: Rhodesia *See* Zimbabwe

If this procedure is followed, the RIN for 'Rhodesia' can be left unchanged in any earlier subject packages that deal with this concept, although the term itself must be changed in all earlier strings.

Whenever the *whole* of a term is deleted or inserted in this way, the term code (e.g. $d in the example above) should be included as part of the amendment message.

Inserting terms into an existing hierarchy

The amendment procedures described above are also used when one or more extra terms are inserted into an existing hierarchy. The need for an insertion could arise if an indexer handles a document on 'Marine birds' after the 'Penguin network' on p 242 has been constructed, then realises, firstly, that 'Penguins' (together with other kinds of bird) belong to this newly-admitted class, and, secondly, that the class itself belongs to a wider category, 'Water birds', which is not yet present in the vocabulary. Before these new concepts can be admitted they should be recorded, their RINs should be assigned, and any appropriate related terms should be established:

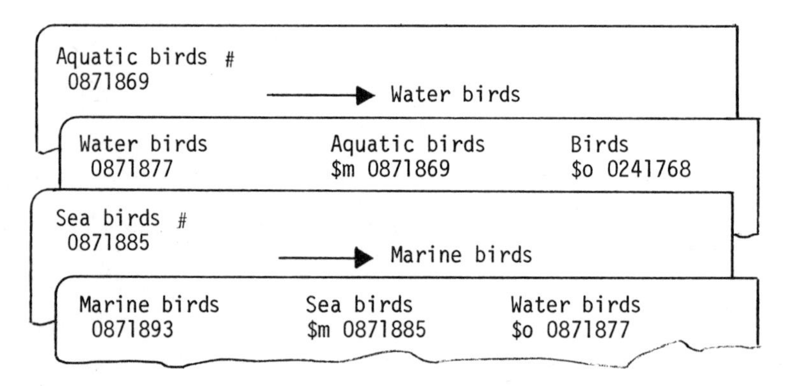

After these records have been input, the new set of terms will be attached to the previous network through the code-plus-RIN combination '$o 0241768'; this links 'Water birds' directly to 'Birds'. The lower part of the network will then have been restructured as follows:

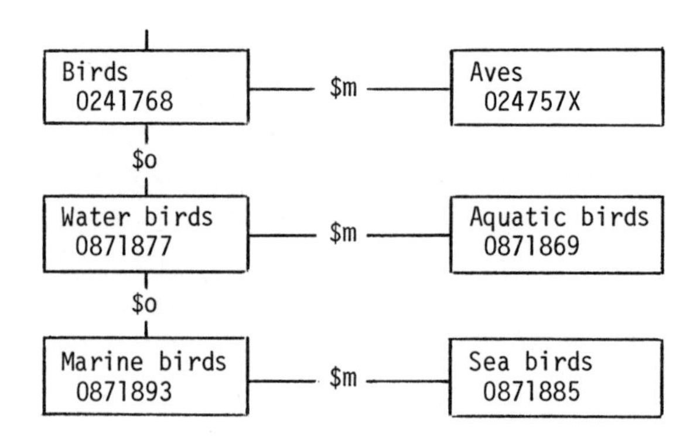

This still leaves the concept 'Penguins' directly subordinated to 'Birds'. Its record should therefore be rewritten:

Penguins 0247847	Sphenisciformes $m 024757X	Marine birds $o 0871893

— and returned to the master file; it should not be sent for keyboarding †. The new relationship should be established by an amendment message:

#RA# 0247847 $v $o 0241768 $w $o 0871893 #

This severs the previous connection between 'Penguins' and 'Birds', and replaces it by the new link to 'Marine birds'.

Deleting a record from the file: #RD#

A deletion message consists of the prefix #RD#, followed by: (i) the address of the record to be deleted; (ii) a final # to terminate the message, e.g.

#RD# [RIN] #

Two steps are involved in submitting a deletion message:

(a) The indexer should write a message in the form shown above;

(b) The RIN for the deleted record *must then be assigned immediately to the next term entering the system as an #RI# message*.

Deletion is a somewhat drastic step, and the second condition was introduced as a safeguard against the accidental removal of a record from the file if a different kind of message code, e.g. #RA#, is miskeyed as #RD#. Immediate re-use of the same RIN acts as a confirmation and declares the deletion to be intentional. Unless this condition is satisfied, the computer will not carry out the deletion instruction, but will print an error warning message instead.

---

† This record, if submitted as an #RI# input, would be rejected on the grounds that its address (RIN) is already occupied.

The use of an #RD# message will be illustrated by assuming (only for the sake of demonstration) that the indexer needs to remove the term 'Biology' from the network shown on p 242:

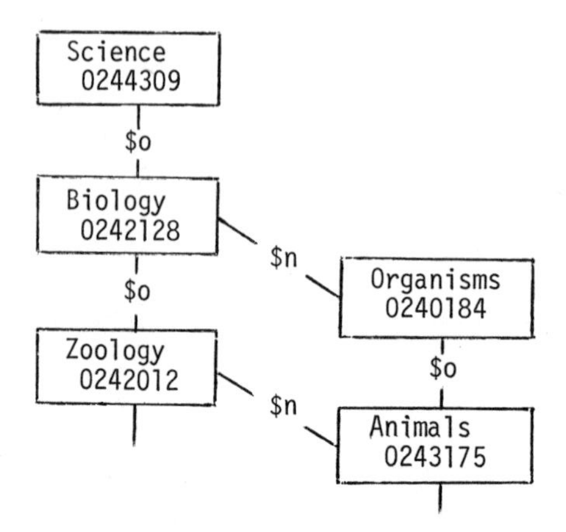

The procedure begins with the message:

#RD# 0242128 #

— followed immediately by an #RI# input to the same address, e.g.

#RI# 0242128 $a Buildings #

If the deletion instruction is accepted, the computer will respond with a confirmation, e.g.

THIS RECORD HAS BEEN DELETED 0242128
$a Biology $o 0244309

At the same time the computer will also proceed to any address which had formed part of the deleted record (e.g. the broader term 'Science', at RIN 0244309) and remove the reciprocal link. This is done automatically, just as reciprocals are assigned automatically in the first place.

Further decisions by the indexer are called for if the deleted term functioned as a source term in its own right — to the extent that 'Biology' served as the source term in references to 'Zoology' (a $o link) and 'Organisms' (a $n link). When links of this kind occur, the computer adds a further warning to the confirmation message shown above:

```
THE FOLLOWING RECORDS CONTAIN AN UPWARD LINK TO THE
DELETED TERM — PLEASE AMEND —
0240184 $a Organisms $n 0242128
0242012 $a Zoology $o 0242128
```

The computer does not attempt to change the data held at the addresses of these target terms, but it will not produce any references to or from these terms until the incorrect links have been removed by #RA# messages, e.g.

#RA# 0240184 $v $n 0242128 $w #

#RA# 0242012 $v $o 0242128 $w $o 0244309 #

These amendments effectively darn over the hole created by the deletion. The first message would break the connection between 'Biology' and 'Organisms' without offering a replacement. The second disconnects 'Zoology' from 'Biology' and replaces it by a direct connection to 'Science' at 0244309. As usual, the computer will then print out a new diagnostic showing the revised connections.

An #RD# message is rarely needed to change a network, as in the example above, but it can be useful if a record contains so much data that calls for correction (e.g. the whole of a complicated proper name, and/or a long scope note) that it is easier to delete the whole of the faulty record and immediately re-submit the corrected version as an #RI# message, rather than handle the corrections piecemeal using an #RA# amendment.

Report on the contents of a record: #RP#

It sometimes happens that the indexer no longer feels certain of the data held at a given address, especially if a record has been amended a number of times during the initial stages of setting up a network. This information can be ascertained at any time by submitting a *Record report message*. This consists of the message code #RP# followed by the RIN for the record and a terminal mark (#), e.g.

#RP# [RIN] #.

The computer responds with a report on the contents of the address, e.g.

REPORT ON RIN 0243175
$a Animals $m 0245711 $o 0240184 $n 0242012

None of the data held at that address will be changed, and references will be produced as normal from the network.

Production of two-way references: $x and $y

The Penguin network on p 242 contains three pairs of terms linked by the associative relationship ($n). This code generates a reference in only one direction, e.g. from 'Ornithology' to 'Birds' but not the other way round. In many cases, however, references between a pair of associated concepts should be provided in each direction. Establishing these *two-way references* calls for the use of an #RA# amendment message and also introduces two new relational codes.

****

$x = Two-way associative relationship between sibling terms belonging to the same hierarchy

$y = Two-way associative relationship between terms belonging to different hierarchies

****

The reason why extra codes, with special instructions, are needed to generate two-way references can be explained most simply by assuming that an indexer tried to use one of the codes considered earlier (e.g. $n) to generate references in each direction between a pair of sibling concepts such as 'Carpets' and 'Rugs'. These might form part of a network such as the following:

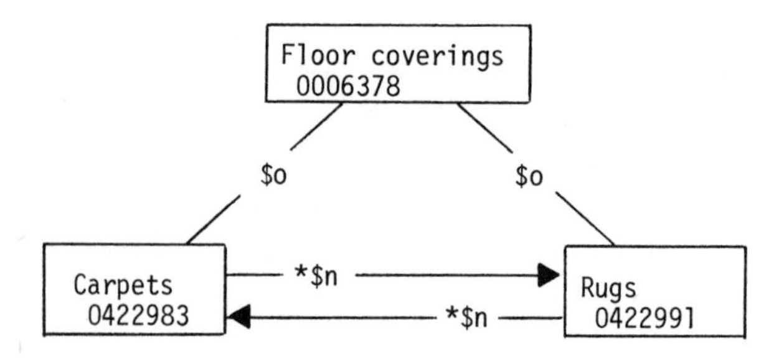

Quoting the RIN for 'Carpets' (0422983) would start the sequence of operations described on p 243-244:

Step 1. The computer would proceed to the address 0422983 and check it for the presence of relational codes. The two codes present would generate the references:

$o = Floor coverings
See also
Carpets

$n = Rugs
See also
Carpets

So far, so good.

Step 2. The address for 'Floor coverings' contains no relational codes, which means that the route through that part of the network is closed. The address for 'Rugs', however, contains two further codes which generate the references:

$o = *Floor coverings
See also
Rugs

$n = *Carpets
See also
Rugs

These references are likely to be misleading — there is no guarantee that the index contains an entry at 'Rugs'. Worse is to come, however —

Step 3. — the computer is directed, via the code+RIN combination $n 0422983, back to the address for 'Carpets'. This leads inevitably to the production of the references already generated at Step 1, and it also restarts the whole cycle. In effect, a loop has been introduced into the operation, and Steps 1, 2 and 3 will be repeated continuously unless it can be broken in some way.

The loop can be broken quite simply by changing the code $n into $x whenever the indexer wishes to generate two-way references between sibling concepts. The network would then take the form:

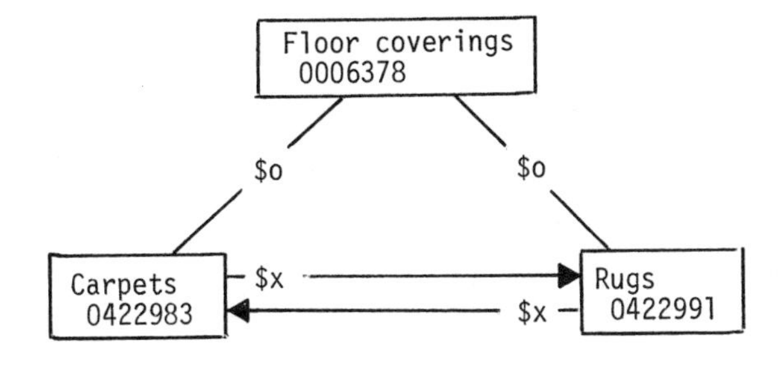

The loop is broken by a special instruction embodied in the code $x:

$x = Print a *See also* reference from the term at the following address. Ignore all relational codes at that address with the exception of $m.

The final part of this instruction would have generated a *See* reference to 'Rugs' if it happened to possess a non-preferred synonym. All other references would be blocked. Quoting the RIN for 'Carpets' would then produce only two references:

Floor coverings *See also* Carpets	Rugs *See also* Carpets

The code $y carries exactly the same instruction, and is used when the indexer needs to generate two-way references between terms belonging to different hierarchies (e.g. 'Birds' and 'Ornithology'). The two codes identify, as sources of two-way references, the two kinds of associative relationship described on p 208. This distinction is necessary if the file will be used as the source of a systematic thesaurus — otherwise, two-way references can be handled consistently by one of these codes, e.g. $x.

The records for the terms in the revised network would appear as follows in the master file:

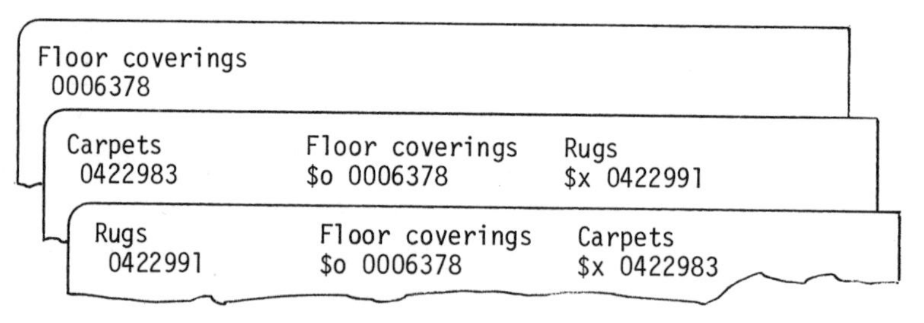

They cannot, however, be submitted in exactly this form, since one of the inputs would fail validation. The input for the first sibling term to enter the system (e.g. 'Carpets') would be rejected on the grounds that the record contains a RIN (0422991) which has not yet been occupied. This RIN must therefore be dropped from the record when 'Carpets' is first submitted, and added later using an #RA# amendment:

#RA# 0422983 $v $w $x 0422991 #

Redirect references: $r and $s

Given the following network:

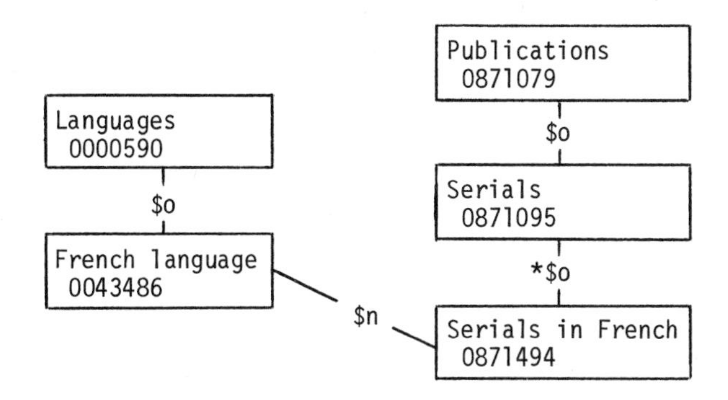

— and assuming that the index contains entries at 'Serials' and also 'Serials in French' (so that the bypass routine is effectively blocked; see p 245), the index would contain the following references:

Languages
See also
French language

French language
See also
Serials in French

Publications
See also
Serials

*Serials
See also
Serials in French

The final reference, from 'Serials' to 'Serials in French', can hardly be justified, since —

— the source and target terms begin with the same word;

— these terms are likely to file on adjacent lines in the index;

— the target term is also down-alphabet from the source term (see p 212).

The unnecessary final reference can be suppressed without affecting the output from the rest of the network if the hierarchical link between 'Serials' and 'Serials in French' is expressed by $r instead of $o. This change can be seen in the final record of the following set:

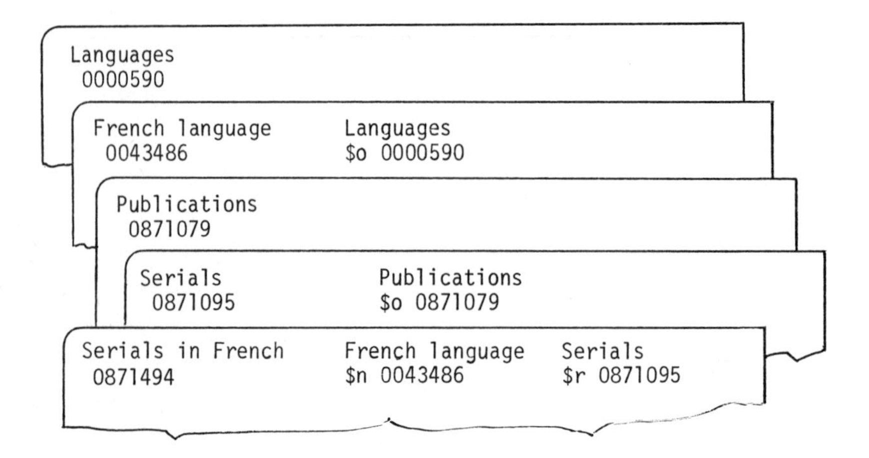

The *redirect codes* $r and $s differ from any of the relational codes considered earlier insofar as they do *not* generate references from the terms held at their following addresses. Instead, they convey the following instructions to the computer:

— Proceed to the address that follows the code (e.g. 0871095);

— Do not make a reference *from* the term at that address (e.g. 'Serials'), but begin the production of references *to* that term.

The same procedure could be used to suppress an unwanted reference from 'Betting' to 'Betting at racecourses' while still providing a reference from, say, 'Gambling' to 'Betting'. These terms would be recorded as follows:

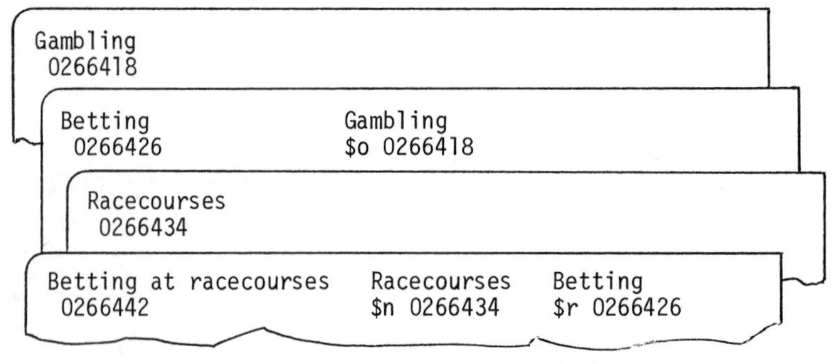

Quoting the RIN for 'Betting at racecourses' (0266442) would generate the following references:

— *a reference between a pair of associated terms, produced by $n:*

Racecourses
See also
Betting at racecourses

— *a reference from a broader to a narrower concept produced by $o:*

Gambling
See also
Betting

— but *not* the unnecessary down-hierarchy reference:

*Betting
See also
Betting at racecourses

In the examples above the code $r was used to suppress unwanted references between concepts linked by the hierarchical relationship (usually expressed by $o) †. The code $s conveys the same redirect instructions, but is used to suppress unwanted references between pairs of terms linked by the associative relationship (usually expressed by $n, $x or $y). A redirect instruction coded $s occurs in the final record of the following set:

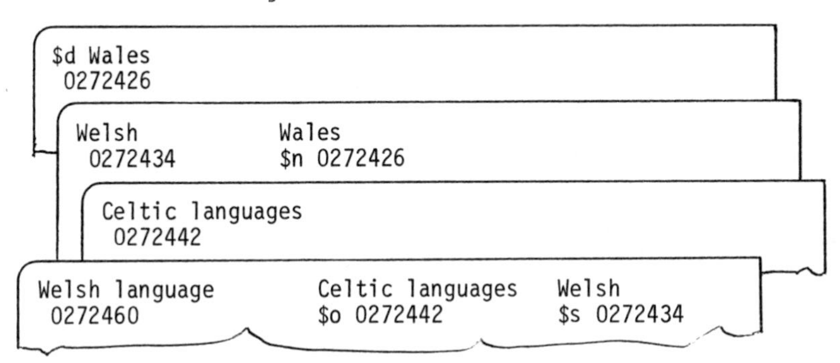

Quoting the RIN 0272460 would then generate the references:

Celtic languages
See also
Welsh language

Wales
See also
Welsh

The same RIN would also be quoted in an appropriate field in subject

† This is the normal relationship between a concept expressed by a prepositional phrase (e.g. 'Betting at racecourses') and its focal noun (e.g. 'Betting').

packages dealing with a range of related concepts such as 'Welsh music', 'Welsh literature', 'Welsh folklore', etc.

Blanket references: term code $k

We have so far encountered two circumstances in which the user is offered a less-than-direct approach to a concept:

(a) A reference generated by a redirect code involves a measure of indirectness. The example on p 263 shows how a user who enters the index at a term such as 'Wales' would be directed, through a *See also* reference, not to the term which actually occurred as a lead, but to the less specific concept 'Welsh' †.

(b) In the chapter on differencing we saw how the link between the focus of a compound term and the term as a whole can be made explicit in the entry, e.g.

Industries
  Aircraft industries

— but is sometimes provided less directly by a once-for-all reference such as:

Industries
  See also
    Aircraft industries

The second option should be chosen if the number of display lines in the merged entries under a common lead are likely to exceed a common-sense limit, such as 25 to 30.

A *blanket reference*, such as:

Industries
  See also
    Names of specific industries

— represents the final step in what might be called a controlled retreat from direct access — it leaves the reader to think of the terms

---

† The adjective 'Welsh' cannot be accepted as a preferred term in its own right. This is the only circumstance in PRECIS where an adjective minus its noun is allowed as part of a reference.

that might have occurred as leads. The blanket instruction is identified by the term code $k written as a prefix on its input record (see example below).

This kind of reference should be provided only when a source term would be followed by so many target terms that the user would be hindered (or at least irritated) by a total listing. Experience suggests (again) an upper limit of some 25-30 target terms under a common source †. Blankets should then be used to handle references to concepts that are linked hierarchically, as subordinate terms, to the source concept. This hierarchical relationship is expressed by the code $o on the record containing the blanket:

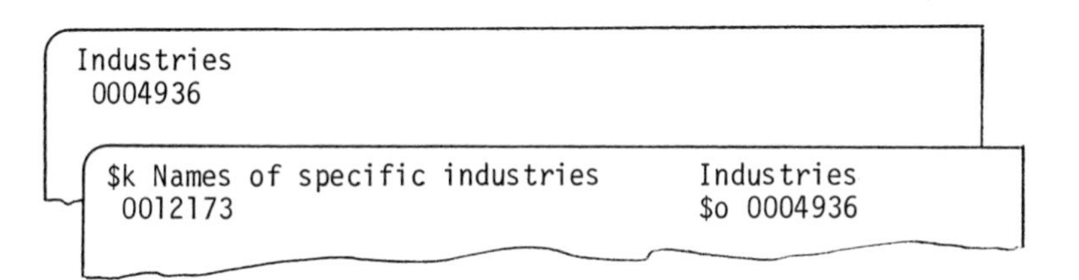

Industries
0004936
$k Names of specific industries
0012173
Industries
$o 0004936

Blankets should not be used to handle the other kinds of basic relationship. For example, an associated concept (identified by $n, $x or $y) should still be printed in the usual way:

Industries
See also
Names of specific industries
Industrialization

Two features of this example should be noted:

(a) Since a blanket cannot function as an entry term it should be printed in a different and less distinctive typeface, e.g. standard roman rather than the bold face generally used for leads and targets (such as Industrialization in the example above). This change of typeface is controlled by the term code $k;

---

† In the index to a cumulating bibliography, such as *BNB*, this would be related to the number of references expected in an annual volume containing some 40 000+ citations.

(b) The blanket is also printed before the other, more usual, target terms, even when this appears to run contrary to alphabetical order. This, too, is controlled by the term code $k †.

A blanket reference is sometimes generated through the redirect code $r. In an English language index, the link between 'United States' and each of the individual states would usually be handled by a blanket, e.g.

United Sates
  See also
    Names of individual states

Unless this procedure is adopted, most (if not all) of the states would be listed in an alphabetical column under the common source term, and the index would begin to resemble a geography lesson rather than a retrieval tool. The blanket reference can be generated through a redirect instruction included in the records for the individual states, e.g.

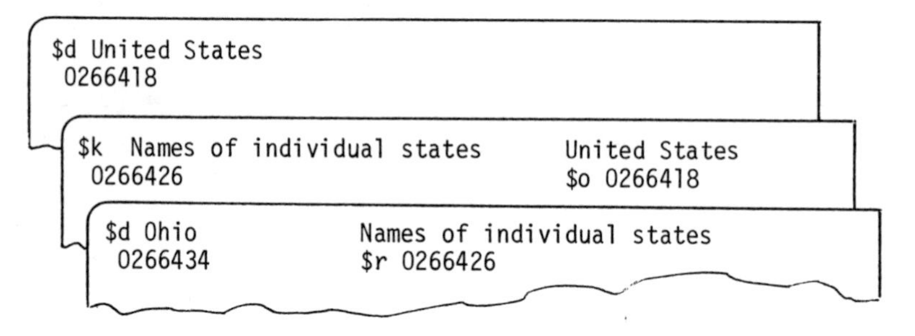

This allows 'Ohio' to be registered in the thesaurus as subordinate to 'United States' ($r and $o both indicate the hierarchical relationship) without producing any unnecessary references.

---

† This does not call for special filing concessions associated with $k terms. The width of a printed character is measured in *units*; more units are allocated to 'm' (the widest letter) than 'i' (the narrowest). Given the size of the typeface typically used in an index, a unit is approximately a hairsbreadth wide. The code $k conveys a special instruction: Align the blanket with other target terms, then *indent by an extra space one unit wide*. The standard filing principle, 'Nothing before something', then ensures that blankets, preceded by the extra space (with a value of nothing) file before other target terms. The extra indention is barely detectable on the printed page.

A blanket reference can be used to direct the reader towards the entries containing a term that has *not* been marked as a lead, usually for economic reasons. In most general indexes a term such as 'Design' would be so heavily used that it should be marked as a lead only when it occurs as the first core concept in a string, e.g.

String: (2) désign *Entry:* Design

It should not be marked as a lead when related to a specific object:

String: (1) digital computers
(p) keyboards
(2) design

Entries: Digital computers
Keyboards. Design

Keyboards. Digital computers
Design

This and similar entries could be supported, at least to a limited extent, by a blanket reference such as:

Design
See also
Design *under the names of specific objects*

This would be generated from the following records:

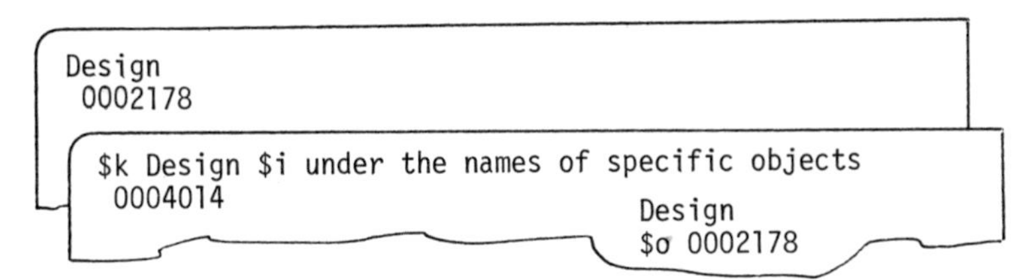

The two codes in the record for the blanket carry typographic instructions:

— $k causes the term 'Design' to be printed in standard roman — its appearance in the reference then matches its appearance in the display part of an entry.

— the rest of the blanket is printed in italic in response to $i (note that italic is used, again, as a de-emphasising device).

The RIN for the blanket should then be quoted as part of any subject packages containing 'Design' as a non-lead term.

Extra codes used in the production of a structured thesaurus

Some of the procedures described above can be initiated by more than one code. For example:

— two-way references can be generated by $x or $y. These two codes allow the indexer to distinguish between the two varieties of the associative relationship (see p 208);

— $r and $s convey the same redirect instructions. The former identifies the link between hierarchically related concepts; the latter identifies the associative relationship.

In both these cases, either code could be used to generate the *See also* references needed in a printed index. The 'extra' code was introduced to make a relational distinction that has practical significance only if the file is used as the source of a structured thesaurus. These extra codes are supplemented by the three (final) codes considered below. These play no part in generating references, and were established entirely for thesaural purposes.

Non-print hierarchical relationship: $t

Chapter 4 covered two different but equally logical approaches to the treatment of a compound term such as 'Primary schools':

(a) The parts of the term could be coded as a focus and its difference:

(1) ✓schools $21 primary

Each word would then be printed as a direct access point in the index:

Schools
  Primary schools
Primary schools

(b) The compound term could be written in natural language order in the string, e.g.

(1) ✓primary schools

— and access through the noun would be provided by a reference:

Schools
  See also
    Primary schools

The first of these approaches offers a more direct route to the user, but it could also involve a kind of relational 'loss' from the viewpoint of the thesaurus if the hierarchical link between 'Schools' and 'Primary schools' is left unrecorded on the grounds that a printed reference is not required.

This link can be registered without generating a reference by submitting the following records:

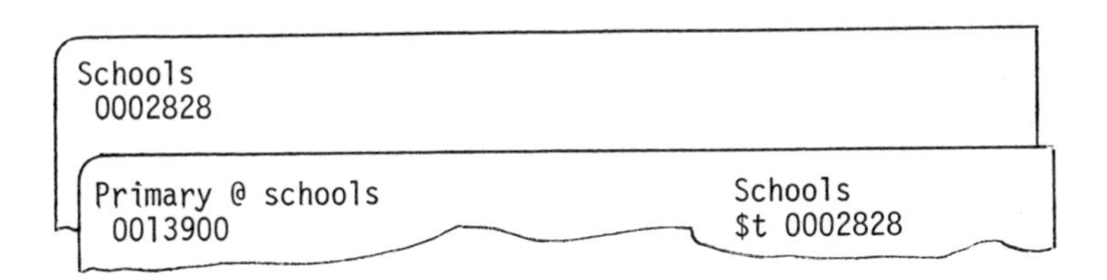

Two features of the record for 'Primary schools' should be noted:

(a) An arbitrary symbol, '@', follows the part of the term that would be coded as a lead difference in the string. This symbol is added only as a reminder to the indexer; it should not be keyboarded.

(b) The link between the narrower term 'Primary schools' and the broader term 'Schools' is indicated by the code $t. This records a hierarchical relationship only for the sake of the thesaurus; the code does not generate a printed reference in the index.

The same technique would be applied to a term containing differences on more than one level. A separate record should then be prepared for each of the embedded noun phrases marked as a lead. For example, if the term 'Silk-screen printed fabrics' is indexed as follows:

String: (1) fabrics $21 printed $22 silk-screen

Entries: Fabrics
  Silk-screen printed fabrics

Printed fabrics
  Silk-screen printed fabrics

Silk-screen printed fabrics

— the following records should be written for the thesaurus:

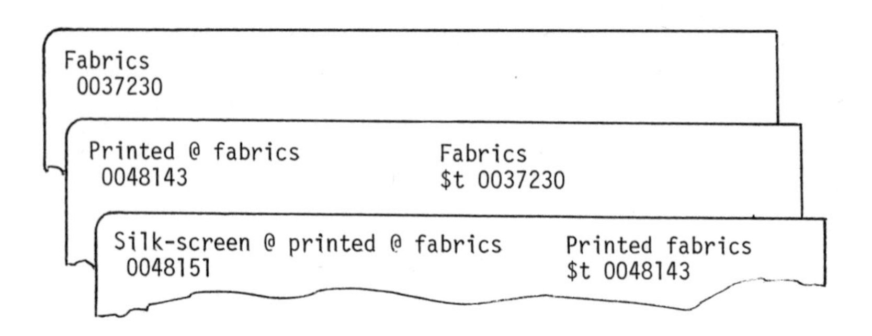

Non-print associative relationship: $u

A similar procedure would be applied, less frequently, when concepts are linked by an associative relationship that should be recorded in the thesaurus, yet their terms share so many common filing characters (usually a common stem) that a *See also* reference would not be justified. It might be decided, for example, that a reference from 'Evaporation' (the action) to 'Evaporated milk' (the product) should not be provided, even though it would be up-alphabet, if these are the only terms in the system beginning with this stem. The relationship between these concepts could still be registered in the thesaurus by submitting the following records:

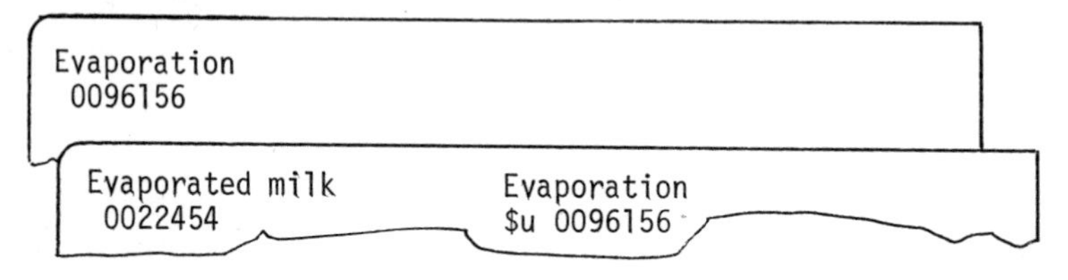

The non-print codes $t and $u are also used in records for node labels (described below).

Node labels: term code $b

The Draft International Standard on thesaurus construction defines a *node label* as ...

> "... a dummy term not assigned to documents when indexing, but inserted into the systematic section of some types of thesauri

to indicate the logical basis on which a category has been divided".

Node labels are needed only in a structured thesaurus where terms are organised systematically into hierarchies supported by an alphabetical index. Two classes of node label are recognised, each with its own function:

(a) *Hierarchical node labels* usually begin with the preposition 'By'. They are inserted into a hierarchy to show the logical basis on which it has been divided. The terms on either side of the node label refer to *concepts of the same basic type.*

Example: Aircraft
By payload
Freight aircraft
Passenger aircraft
By user
Civil aircraft
Military aircraft

In this example, *By payload* and *By user* function as node labels and explain how species of 'Aircraft' were collocated as subgroups.

(b) *Associative node labels* are used to insert *concepts of a different type* into a hierarchy to ensure that they are collocated close to the concepts with which they are usually associated.

Example: Textiles
Operations
Felting
Knitting
Weaving

– where *Operations* functions as a node label. In these cases, the node label collocates associated, not narrower, concepts.

If node labels are needed in a systematic thesaurus constructed from the RIN-file, they should be identified by the term code $b written as a prefix, e.g.

$b By payload
0779938

There is no need for separate term codes to distinguish between the two kinds of node label considered above; the difference can be indicated clearly by the relational code that links the label to the earlier term in the schedule:

(a) *Hierarchical node labels* are identified by —

— the term code $b;

— the code $t written as a prefix to the RIN for the earlier term, e.g.

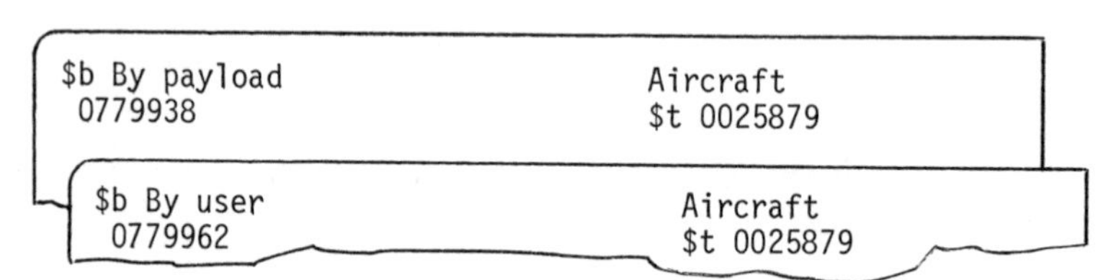

$b By payload
0779938
Aircraft
$t 0025879
$b By user
0779962
Aircraft
$t 0025879

The code $t identifies a non-print hierarchical relationship (see p 268).

(b) *Associative node labels* are identified by —

— the term code $b;

— the code $u written as a prefix to the RIN for the earlier term in the schedules, e.g.

$b Operations 0053104 — Textiles $u 0006378

The code $u identifies a non-print associative relationship (see p 270).

These are the only data allowed in the record for a node label.

The link between a node label and the terms it collocates is indicated by the code $t, followed by the RIN for the node label, among the data on their records, e.g.

Freight aircraft 0040355	Aircraft $o 0025879	$b By payload $t 0779938
Military aircraft 0064300	Aircraft $o 0025879	$b By user $t 0779962
Weaving 0013854	Textiles $n 0006378	$b Operations $t 0053104

Note that these records also contain the 'standard' relational codes ($n and $o) used in the production of *See also* references. This means that each of the target terms (e.g. 'Freight aircraft' and 'Weaving') is linked to its source term in two different ways:

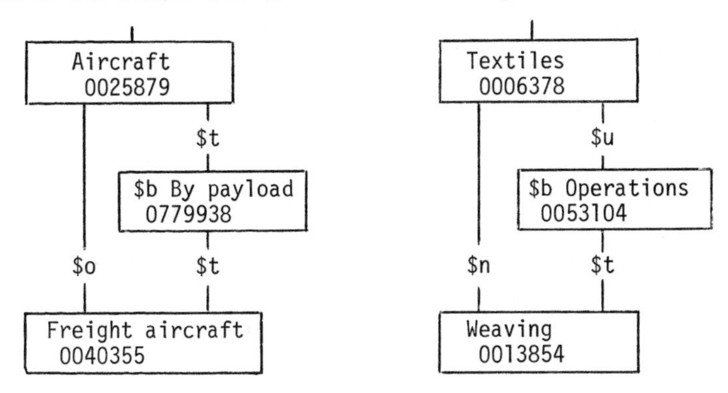

The standard codes in these networks, $n and $o, mark the routes that should be followed when the computer generates references for a printed index. When the machine is switched to the production of a systematic thesaurus, it follows the alternative route marked by the codes $t and $u; this is confirmed as a node label route by the term code $b. This would generate the hierarchies shown on p 271.

It is most unlikely that indexers could anticipate the node labels needed in a given thesaurus — this depends entirely on the numbers and kinds of concepts admitted into the system †. Networks should therefore be constructed in the first place without regard for node labels, and the labels should be added later as additions and amendments. If, for example, the file contains the term 'Freight aircraft' linked by $o to the broader term 'Aircraft' (as in the diagram above), the extra route could be added in two stages:

— the node label itself should be admitted into the system:

$b By payload	Aircraft
0779938	$t 0025879

— the alternative route via the node label should then be added as an amendment to the record for 'Freight aircraft':

#RA# 0040355 $v $w $t 0779938 #

---

† The presence of several 'orphan' terms within the same subject area would usually point to a need for node labels.

Forms of output

The principal standards on thesaurus construction (see footnote on p 200) refer to three basic forms of output:

- *alphabetical display;*
- *systematic display;*
- *graphic display.*

The standards note that many published thesauri contain features of more than one of these general types.

It is doubtful whether terms could be organised by the computer into an entirely satisfactory graphic display, such as an arrowgraph or tree structure. The other two forms are amenable to computer production based on the codes described in this and the previous two chapters. For example, the addresses that hold the terms in the Penguin network on p 242 contain enough relational information (including the reciprocal relationships described on p 230) to generate the following outputs:

Organisation as an alphabetical thesaurus

Animals
  UF Fauna
  BT Organisms
  NT Vertebrates
  RT Zoology
Aves *USE* Birds
Biology
  BT Science
  NT Zoology
  RT Organisms
Birds
  UF Aves
  BT Vertebrates
  NT Penguins
  RT Ornithology
Fauna *USE* Animals
Living systems
  USE Organisms
Organisms
  UF Living systems
  NT Animals
  RT Biology
Ornithology
  BT Zoology
  RT Birds
Penguins
  UF Sphenisciformes
  BT Birds
Science
  NT Biology
Sphenisciformes *USE*
  Penguins
Vertebrates
  BT Animals
  NT Birds
Zoology
  BT Biology
  NT Ornithology
  RT Animals

Note: The layout above is modelled on examples in BS 5723 and ISO/DIS 2788. Relationships, expressed in the RIN-file by machine-readable codes such as $o and $n, have been translated into the conventions usually seen in English-language thesauri:

- Equivalence relationship = *USE/UF* (Use/Use for)
- Hierarchical relationship = *BT/NT* (Broader term/Narrower term)
- Associative relationship = *RT* (Related term).

Organisation as a systematic thesaurus

Hierarchy 1:

345 Science
346 Biology
RT Organisms
347 Zoology
RT Animals
348 Ornithology
RT Birds

Hierarchy 2:

7789 Organisms
UF Living systems
RT Biology
7790 Animals
UF Fauna
RT Zoology
7791 Vertebrates
7792 Birds
UF Aves
RT Ornithology
7793 Penguins
UF Sphenisciformes

Note: For obvious reasons, a systematic thesaurus must be supported by an alphabetical index. In the example above, it is assumed that the computer assigned the running numbers shown in the left-hand column. These would then be transferred, as addresses, into the index, e.g.

Animals 7790
UF Fauna
RT Zoology (347)
Aves *USE* Birds (7792)
etc.

Published systematic thesauri vary considerably in the amount of relational information offered in their indexes. The example above excludes references to broader and narrower terms, since these are clearly displayed in the systematic schedules.

A thesaurus generated as a stand-alone product from the RIN-file would have various uses. In particular, it would serve as —

— a working tool for indexers (in which case terms should be accompanied by their RINs);

— an aid to users, especially if PRECIS data can be searched on-line. This is considered further in the next (final) chapter;

— a source of terms and relationships offered for use by other agencies, avoiding a good deal of duplicated effort. With this end in mind, it is important to ensure that the vocabulary is controlled in accordance with a set of neutral principles, such as those described in the standards taken as models throughout this *Manual*.

19. Management aspects of PRECIS

This final chapter deals only occasionally with the techniques of indexing and thesaurus construction, and covers instead a range of topics falling within a loose definition of management, with particular reference to —

— the organisation of indexing and related tasks;

— forms of output, including the role of PRECIS in on-line searching;

— further developments of the system, mainly in the field of new languages.

Organisation of an indexing workflow

This account is based upon the flow of work through the Bibliographic Services Division (BSD) of the British Library, although this hardly rates as a typical indexing agency, for reasons such as the following:

(a) The Division does not select the kinds or amounts of materials it processes; these are determined by the deposit of newly published items for copyright purposes;

(b) Documents are routed through a sequence of offices, each responsible for a particular set of library techniques. For example, one office deals only with descriptive cataloguing; another (the Subject Systems Office) handles all classification and indexing. This should be seen in contrast to the majority of libraries and documentation centres, where the same person(s) may be responsible for all kinds of bibliographic processes;

(c) The Subject Systems Office is itself divided into sections, again on the basis of particular techniques. Together, these produce a range of subject data, only a selection of which is used in British Library products, such as the *British National Bibliography*.

For these and other reasons, the organisation of work in BSD is generally more complicated than in most other agencies, but this has advantages from the present point of view:

— a more complex situation calls (again) for the fullest explanations;

— it is easier to extract relevant simple parts from an overfull description than to infer the correct approach to a complex procedure (if needed) from an oversimplified account.

When a document is handled by the Descriptive Cataloguing Office, its details are recorded on a standard worksheet, organised by MARC fields, such as that reproduced on p 278-279. A glance at this worksheet will show that none of its fields are allocated to subject data — the link between the description of the item as a physical entity and a record of its subject is provided through a single field (Field 691, at the bottom of side 2) with a special function considered later. This worksheet accompanies the item during its progress through the various sections of the Subject Systems Office. These are identified down the right-hand side of the flow diagram on p 280 — it can be seen that the indexers in one section write PRECIS strings and assign the appropriate DDC numbers; a different section constructs and maintains the thesaurus; a third assigns Library of Congress subject data.

A document is handled first by the indexers in the PRECIS/DDC Section; they are responsible for the subject analysis which serves as the basis for all later decisions taken in the Office. Their examination of a document follows the procedures described in Chapter 2, and generally conforms to the approach recommended in the International Standard on techniques for subject analysis (1). At this stage, the indexer has two main objects in mind:

— to establish the subject of the document;

— to determine whether or not that subject has occurred in the past and

---

(1) International Organization for Standardization. Methods for examining documents, determining their subjects, and selecting indexing terms: ISO/DIS 5963. Geneva, I.S.O., 1982

BL CATALOGUING INPUT — MONOGRAPHS		Item number	
ISBN 001	#R1 # 0 00 685445 1	BNB issue no. 039	$p $a
Uniform title 240 243			
Title 245 (245.14) 245.3	The bird table $b attracting birds to garden or balcony. how to recognize and feed them $e [painted by Terence Lambert ; ... written by Hermann Heinzel] #		
Part title 248			
Edition 250			
Imprint (260) 260.1	[London] $b Fontana $c 1979		
Physical description 300	$f 1 $n folded sheet $a [12]p (\$b) col. ill $i chart coat of arms facsim form geneal.table map music plan port sample (\$c) 25 cm # $e pbk cased spiral unbound		
Linking ISBN 021		BNB serial no. 015	
Language 041		LC card no. 010	
Price 350	£0.35 #	Receipt date (957)	821210c#
Notes 5XX			
Information codes 008	$a s1979 (\$b) en $c $d (\$e) 0 (\$f) 0 (\$g) 0 (\$h) 0 (\$i) 1 $j $k (\$l) eng $m (\$o) a (\$p) W #		

BSD PC4/2

MARC cataloguing input record (Side 1)

Amendment message 018	
Access points 1XX/7XX 100 1	Lambert $h Terence #
Series 4XX/8XX 440	Domino $v 5 #
References & analytical added entries	
Supplementary tracing 790	
Correction message 017	
SIN 691	2407698 #

Subject Indicator Number (SIN) in Field 691

MARC cataloguing input record (Side 2)

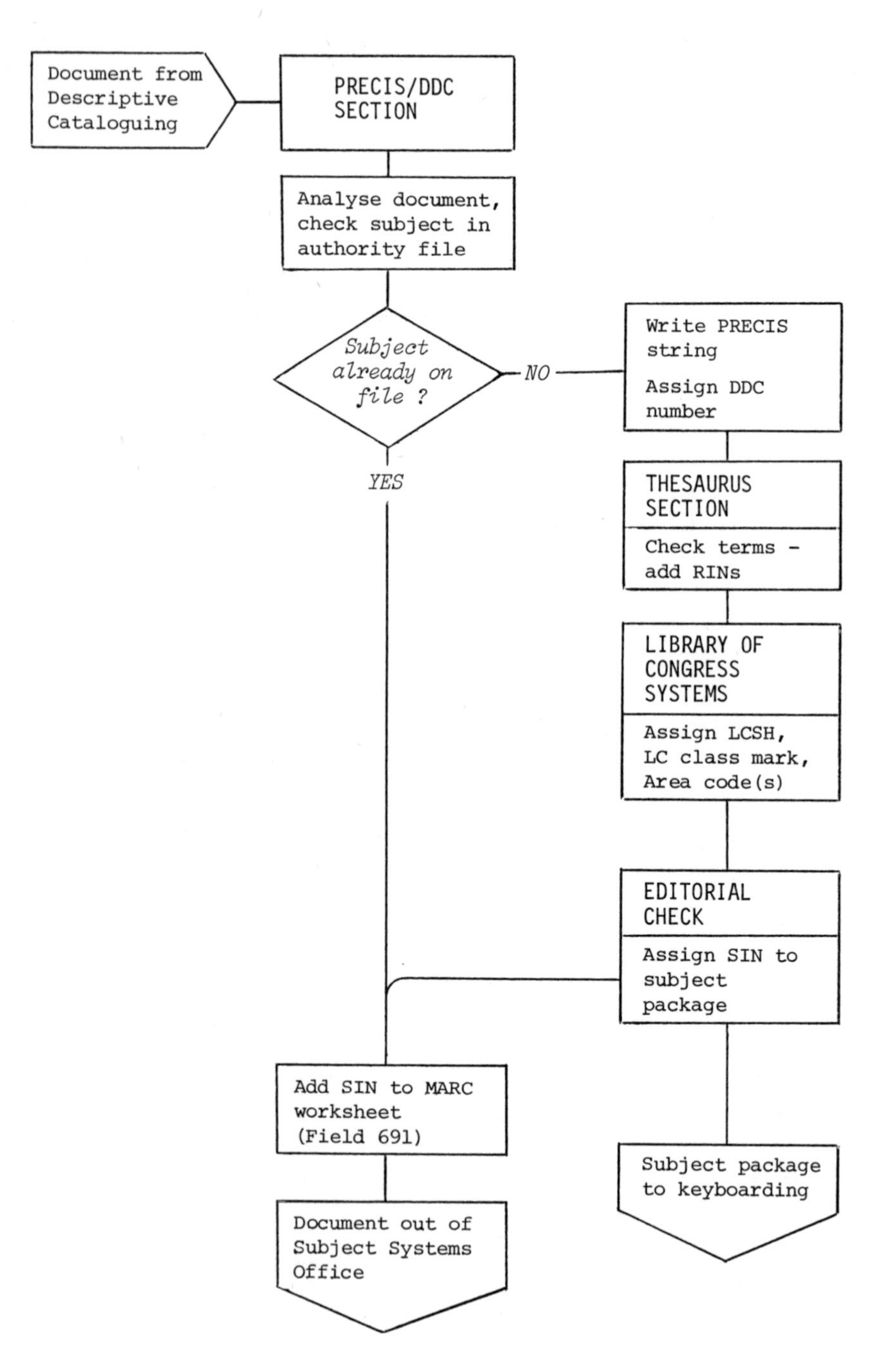

Workflow through the Subject Systems Office (The British Library)

appears in one of the authority files provided by the computer (we shall see examples of these authorities later).

This brings us to the question, "Is the subject already on file?", near the top of the flow diagram on p 280. For the sake of easier explanations, we need to make two assumptions at this point: firstly, the indexer is dealing with the document described on the MARC worksheet on p 278-279; secondly, the answer to the question is 'No', which means that the indexer faces a new topic.

This answer takes us across to the right-hand side of the flow diagram, to the point where the indexer expresses the subject in the form of a PRECIS string. This is written in Field 690 on the input form shown on p 282. Expressing the subject first as a PRECIS string has important implications from a management point of view. Studies have shown that the most time consuming, and therefore most expensive, part of any subject approach based upon a controlled vocabulary (this includes selecting class marks as well as assigning indexing terms) consists in studying the document and establishing its subject. This is regarded as more demanding than translating the subject, once it has been established, into the terms or symbols of an indexing language or classification scheme †. The initial stage of subject analysis is done only once in the Subject Systems Office, where the PRECIS string is taken as the basis for all later decisions. None of the other systems applied in BSD is capable of assuming this role. The PRECIS string —

— is usually the fullest statement of the subject;

— consists of terms appropriate to the topic in hand (the system is based on an open-ended vocabulary);

— is organised in a form sufficiently close to natural language to allow any of the indexers or classifiers in later sections to understand the subject at a glance.

---

† The following comment is typical of several quoted by Bakewell (see footnote on p 8): "... The problem is knowing what the book is about; having established that, PRECIS is easy to apply. The role operators are easy to use and also act as a check on correct indexing".

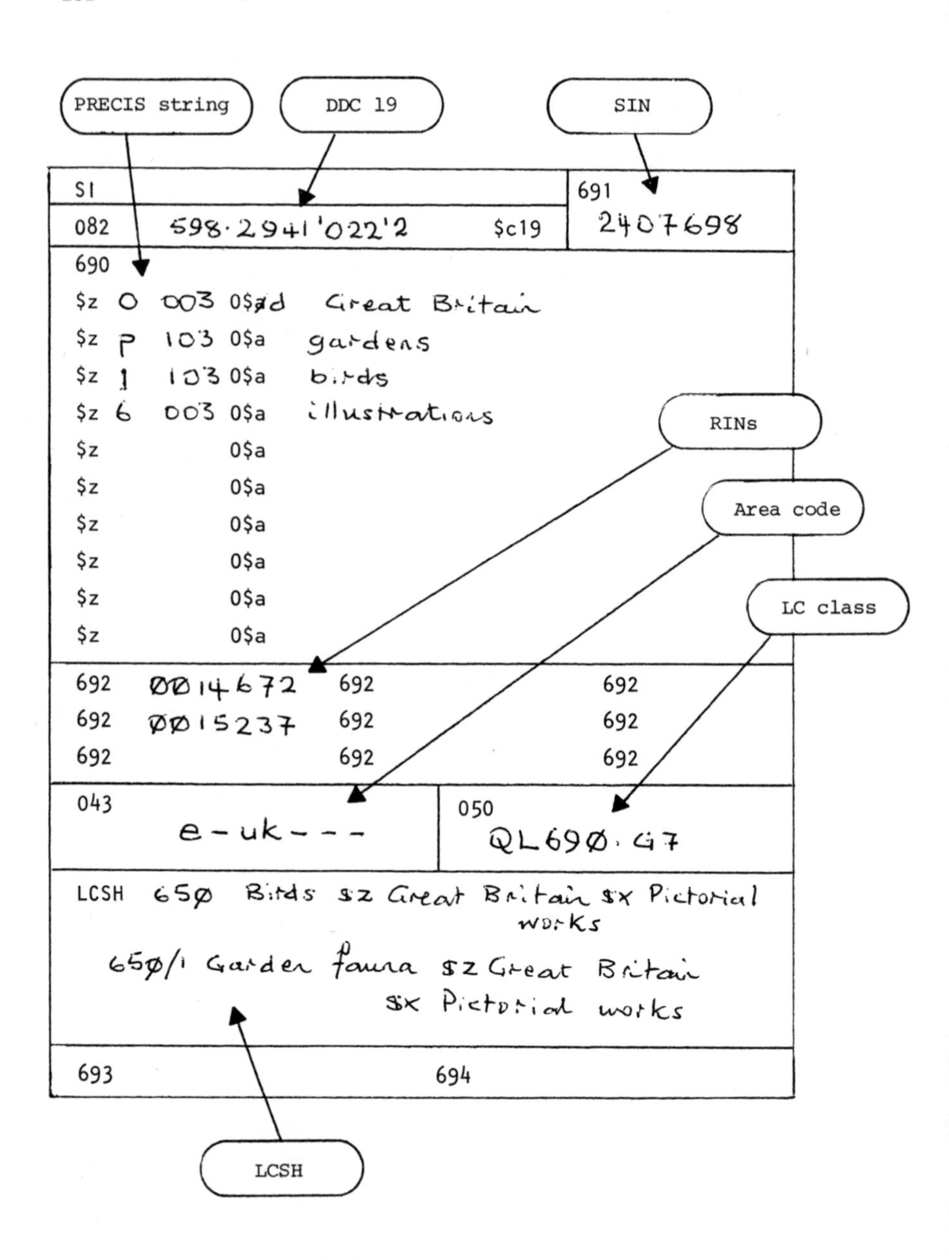

Indexing form containing 'subject package' based on PRECIS string

The indexer who writes the PRECIS string also assigns the appropriate DDC number (one class mark per string); this is added to Field 082 in a box near the top of the indexing record on p 282. Indexers do not expect their class marks to match the specificity and/or exhaustivity of their PRECIS strings. Less than 10% of strings in the BSD files can be matched, concept for concept, by their DDC numbers, even when synthesis is used to its fullest extent. The example on p 282 is fairly typical; the number 598·29410222 represents 'Illustrations of British birds', but does not contain the concept 'garden birds'. This apparent 'loss' is not regarded as important. The subject is sufficiently expressed by the entries generated from the string; the class mark then has a different and complementary function — it adds, as a piece of ancillary information, "... and this is where we decided to shelve it" †. These numbers serve two purposes in the printed issues of *BNB*:

(a) They organise catalogue entries in the classified sequence, where the grouping of citations by subject field offers a basis for stock selection. The extract at the top of p 284 shows part of a classified listing which includes the entry for the book described on the MARC worksheet on p 278-279. This extract also shows that the 'meaning' of each class mark is explained by a string of words, known as the *verbal feature*, immediately following the symbol. The feature is constructed by the computer from the terms in the PRECIS string selected in input order. If a string contains coordinate themes (identified by the theme codes 'x' and 'y' — see p 41-44), the feature consists of terms selected only from the first theme in the string.

(b) The DDC class mark also functions as an address in the subject index. Extracts from an index containing the entries that would be generated from the string on p 282 are reproduced on the next page. This is known as a *two-stage index*, since the user is directed, via the class number, to a position in a second file containing the relevant catalogue entry or entries. Alternative forms of output are considered later.

In a limited number of cases the DDC schedules contain instructions

---

† This view is also held by a number of DDC users, who see the scheme essentially as a mark-and-park system.

ʾirds. Observation.

ʻs guide / John
ı, 1980. —
ʼm

: £6.95
3.50 B81-13594

ʼkling. Birds.
dence, diaries,

ʼon of birds : a
ʻ and Lodge. —
ʼolson, c1980. —
ʼrts ; 19x21cm
ʼudes index
B81-03047

ʼirds. Observation

s diary : the
Millington. —
. — 192p : ill

598.294 — Europe. Birds — *Illustrations*

Burton, Philip, *1936-*. Small birds : a colour guide to common small birds of Britain and Northern Europe / [painted by Philip Burton]. — [London] : Fontana, 1979. — 1folded sheet ([12]p) : col.ill ; 25cm. — (Domino ; 1)
ISBN 0-00-685441-9 : £0.85 B81-20748

598.294 — Western Europe. Birds — *Field guides*

Hayman, Peter. The Mitchell Beazley birdwatcher's pocket guide / Peter Hayman. — London : Mitchell Beazley in association with the Royal Society for the Protection of Birds, c1979. — 192p : col.ill ; 20cm
ISBN 0-85533-148-8 : £3.95 B81-01574

598.2941 — Great Britain. Birds

A **Notebook** of birds 1907-1980 / with a commentary by Jim Flegg ; and illustrations by Norman Arlott, Robert Gillmor and Laurel Tucker. — London : Macmillan, 1981. — vii,184p : ill ; 23cm
Selections from British birds. — Includes index
ISBN 0-333-30880-8 : £6.95 : CIP rev.
B81-13809

598.2941 — Great Britain. Gardens. Birds — *For children*

Gill, Peter, *1924-*. Birds in the garden / by Peter Gill ; illustrated by the author. — Cambridge : Dinosaur, c1981. — 24p : col.ill ; 16x19cm. — (Althea's nature series)
ISBN 0-85122-274-9 (cased) : £1.85 : CIP rev.
ISBN 0-85122-258-7 (pbk) : £0.70 B81-02671

598.2941'022'2 — Great Britain. Gardens. Birds — *Illustrations*

Lambert, Terence. The bird table : attracting birds to garden or balcony, how to recognize and feed them / [painted by Terence Lambert ; ... written by Hermann Heinzel]. — [London] : Fontana, 1979. — 1folded sheet([12]p) : col.ill ; 25cm. — (Domino ; 5)
ISBN 0-00-685445-1 : £0.85 B81-20740

598.29411'35 — Scotland. Shetland. Birds

Tulloch, Bobby. A guide to Shetland birds / by Bobby Tulloch and Fred Hunter. — Rev. ed., Repr. with minor amendments. — Lerwick ([Prince Alfred St.], Lerwick, Shetland [ZE1 0EP]) : Shetland Times, 1981, c1979. — 45,[16]p of plates : ill ; 22cm

Extract from classified listing in *BNB* △

Extracts from PRECIS index to *BNB* ▽

that can affect the content or coding of the PRECIS string. This has been noted where appropriate at various points throughout the *Manual*. For example:

— coordinate concepts are sometimes linked by the operator 'f' rather then 'g' if the DDC number acts as a 'binding concept' (see p 99-100);

— a subject containing a two-way interaction, such as 'foreign relations', is sometimes expressed by two strings, rather than a single string centred on the operator 'u', if the interrelated concepts belong to different places in the schedules (see the example on p 145-146).

This occurs far less frequently than some teachers of indexing have suggested, and in no case does it lead to a 'distortion' of PRECIS logic.

Adding the DDC number to the indexing record (see p 282) means that two fields have been contributed to what might be called a *package* of subject information based on the PRECIS string. A check against the flow diagram on p 280 will show that the document, accompanied by its MARC worksheet and the indexing record, is handled next by the Section responsible for the thesaurus. Any term marked as a lead in a string is checked in the authority file, and a new record is created if necessary, using the procedures described in Chapters 15 to 18. RINs are added to Field 692 on the indexing record — the two RINs in the example on p 282 would generate references such as:

	Ornithology	Plants	
Aves *See* Birds	*See also*	*See also*	*etc.*
	Birds	Gardens	

Indexers in this Section are responsible for more than the production of satisfactory *See* and *See also* references. They also have an editorial function, and check all terms marked as leads (these qualify automatically as candidates for the thesaurus) to ensure that they comply with the recommendations on vocabulary control described at various points throughout the *Manual* and laid down in both national and international standards (see footnote on p 200). They will, if necessary, take a string back to its indexer and ask for changes to one or more terms. Reference to recognised standards is particularly important in an agency such as the British Library where the RIN-file is used as the source of a controlled vocabulary by a number of different organisations, including outside agencies as well as other Divisions of the Library.

Further fields are completed on the indexing record when the document is handled next by the Section responsible for Library of Congress subject data †. This team completes three new fields:

— Library of Congress Subject Headings (LCSH) assigned to fields in the 6XX range;

— Library of Congress class marks, held in Field 050;

— Area codes, in Field 043.

These can be seen in the indexing record shown on p 282. Adding these data does not involve a further stage of subject analysis; the LC data are based again on the original analysis represented by the PRECIS string.

A glance down the right-hand side of the diagram on p 280 will show that the workflow is nearly complete. The subject package is checked to ensure that all the necessary fields contain appropriate data, and the whole of the package is then assigned to its own address in another random-access file. This address is indicated by a *Subject Indicator Number* (inevitably shortened to *SIN*) which functions exactly like a RIN. It consists of a seven-digit number (including a modulus eleven check digit) struck from a computer-generated list and written in Field 691 in the top right-hand corner of the record shown on p 282. It is also added immediately to Field 691 in the descriptive catalogue record (see p 279). Adding the SIN to the MARC worksheet effectively ties together the descriptive cataloguing data held in one file and the subject data held in a separate file. Whenever the cataloguing data are processed — for example, when producing MARC exchange tapes or the issues of *BNB* — the machine is directed by the SIN to the exact position in a random-access file where all the necessary subject data can be located and extracted.

---

† Library of Congress subject data are used largely by some academic libraries in Britain. They are virtually unknown in continental Europe.

The SIN-repeat procedure

To understand why these different kinds of data are assigned to separate files we should return to the diagram on p 280 and visualise a different situation, assuming that the question near the top of the work flow led to 'Yes' as an answer. This means that the indexer, after examining a document, found a match for its subject in the authority file. Various kinds of authority are available, including on-line access to any word or term in the PRECIS strings attached to UK-MARC records. For the sake of demonstration we should again assume that the indexer handled a work consisting of illustrations of British garden birds, and checked its subject in the PRECIS authority file on fiche. Parts of two frames from this fiche are reproduced on p 288, with arrows pointing to entries at 'Birds' and 'Gardens'. A check of the entry at 'Birds' will show that the whole of the subject package is reproduced at each point, including not only the PRECIS string, the DDC number, LCSH, etc., but also the SIN — this is the number 2407698 printed on the third line of each entry. The indexer would then write the SIN directly into Field 691 on the MARC worksheet, and the document would be routed down the left-hand side of the flow diagram, by-passing all the decision-making stages listed down the right-hand side. There is hardly need to stress the management implications of a procedure that allows an indexer to extract a relatively complex package of subject information from a computer simply by copying a number from an authority file †.

When a new subject package is written, it rarely involves entirely original indexing. Given a reasonably well-established file, it will be found that a high proportion of new subject packages are based on models already in the system — we refer to this as *indexing by analogy*. For

---

† The effectiveness of the SIN-repeat procedure is carefully monitored in the British Library. At the time of writing (1983) over 60% of documents passing through BSD are routed down the left-hand side of the flow diagram on p 280. This mechanism, plus the fact that the initial subject analysis is carried out only once, accounts for an apparently disproportionate allocation of staff in the Subject Systems Office. Three indexers in the Thesaurus Section, plus three in the Library of Congress Section, handle the output of 12 indexers in the PRECIS/DDC Section.

F10

```
9866'5ƒc18     Birds.  Gardens. Great Britain
                 - For children
                1087061                                 082000      598.2941ƒc19
               083000ƒaGreat Britain. Gardens. Birdsƒb- For children
0ƒaBirdsƒzG    690000ƒz00030ƒdGreat Britainƒzp1030ƒagardensƒz11030ƒabirdsƒz6003
               0ƒafor children
               692000ƒa0014672 692000ƒa0015237 043000ƒae-uk--- 050000ƒaQL690.G7
               650000ƒaBirdsƒzGreat BritainƒxJuvenile literature
2'94174ƒc18
               Birds.  Gardens. Great Britain
                 - Illustrations
                2407698                           082000      598.2941'022'2ƒc19
               083000ƒaGreat Britain. Gardens. Birdsƒb- Illustrations
               690000ƒz00030ƒdGreat Britainƒzp1030ƒagardensƒz11030ƒabirdsƒz6003
               0ƒaillustrations
               692000ƒa0014672 692000ƒa0015237 043000ƒae-uk--- 050000ƒaQL690.G7
.966'51ƒc19    650000ƒaBirdsƒzGreat BritainƒxPictorial works 650000ƒaGarden fau
               naƒzGreat BritainƒxPictorial works

00ƒaBirdsƒ     Birds.  Gardens. Great Britain
                 Care
                0564109                              082000      639.9'782941ƒc19
               083000ƒaGreat Britain. Gardens. Birds. Care
               690000ƒz00030ƒdGreat Britainƒzp1030ƒagardensƒz11030ƒabirdsƒz2003
66'51ƒc19      0ƒacare
               692000ƒa0014672 692000ƒa0015237 043000ƒae-uk--- 050000ƒaQL690.G7
               650000ƒaBirdsƒzGreat Britain 650000ƒaGarden faunaƒzGreat Britain
00ƒaBirdsƒ
               Birds.  Gardens. Great Britain
                 Observation - Manuals
                0354627                            082000      598'.07'23441ƒc19
.2941ƒc19      083000ƒaGreat Britain. Gardens. Birds. Observationƒb- Manuals
               690000ƒz00030ƒdGreat Britainƒzp1030ƒagardensƒz11030ƒabirdsƒz2103
rds            0ƒaobservationƒz60030ƒamanuals
ƒaQL690.G7     692000ƒa0014672 692000ƒa0015237 692000ƒa0049786 043000ƒae-uk---
t Britain      050000ƒaQL677.5 650000ƒaBird watchingƒzGreat Britain

               Birds.  Gardens. United States
                 Care
.2941ƒc19       0115703                              082000      639.9'782973ƒc19
               083000ƒaUnited States. Gardens. Birds. Care
rdsƒz6003      690000ƒz00030ƒdUnited Statesƒzp1030ƒagardensƒz11030ƒabirdsƒz2003
               0ƒacare
aBirdsƒzG      692000ƒa0014672 692000ƒa0015237 043000ƒan-us--- 050000ƒaQL676.5
               650000ƒaBirdsƒzUnited States

               Birds.  Gardens. Western Europe
                 - For children
                2810816                                 082000      598.294ƒc19
  (B)          083000ƒaWestern Europe. Gardens. Birdsƒb- For children
               690000ƒz01030ƒdWestern Europeƒzp1030ƒagardensƒz11030ƒabirdsƒz600
               30ƒafor children
               692000ƒa0014672 692000ƒa0015237 043000ƒaew----- 050000ƒaQL690.A1
               650000ƒaBirdsƒzEuropeƒxJuvenile literature 650000ƒaGarden faunaƒ
               zEuropeƒxJuvenile literature
```

```
      ...20 0ƒa001..237 692000ƒa00..672 69..00..a00..85 ... 30..ƒa. uk ...
      050000ƒaQL690.G7 650000ƒaBirdsƒzGreat Britain 650000ƒaForest bir
      ds 693000ƒa00 219025 7 (1)

      Gardens.  Great Britain
        Birds
       0787213                                  082000      598.2941ƒc19
      083000ƒaGreat Britain. Gardens. Birds
      690000ƒz00030ƒdGreat Britainƒzp1030ƒagardensƒz11030ƒabirds
      692000ƒa0014672 692000ƒa0015237 043000ƒae-uk--- 050000ƒaQL690.G7
      650000ƒaBirdsƒzGreat Britain 650000ƒaGarden faunaƒzGreat Britain

      Gardens.  Great Britain
 (A)    Birds - Field guides
       2283271                                  082000      598.2941ƒc19
      083000ƒaGreat Britain. Gardens. Birdsƒb- Field guides
      690000ƒz00030ƒdGreat Britainƒzp1030ƒagardensƒz11030ƒabirdsƒz6003
      0ƒafield guides
      692000ƒa0014672 692000ƒa0015237 043000ƒae-uk--- 650000ƒaBirdsƒzG
      reat BritainƒxIdentification

      Gardens.  Great Britain
        Birds - For children
       2503204                                  082000      598.2941ƒc19
      083000ƒaGreat Britain. Gardens. Birdsƒb- For children
      690000ƒz00030ƒdGreat Britainƒzp1030ƒagardensƒz11030ƒabirdsƒz6003
      0ƒafor children
      692000ƒa0014672 692000ƒa0015237 043000ƒae-uk--- 050000ƒaQL690.G7
      650000ƒaBirdsƒzGreat BritainƒxJuvenile literature 650000ƒaGarde
       faunaƒzGreat BritainƒxJuvenile literature 693000ƒaDO NOT USE: U
      SE 1087001

      Gardens.  Great Britain
        Birds - For children
       1087061                                  082000      598.2941ƒc19
      083000ƒaGreat Britain. Gardens. Birdsƒb- For children
      690000ƒz00030ƒdGreat Britainƒzp1030ƒagardensƒz11030ƒabirdsƒz6003
      0ƒafor children
      692000ƒa0014672 692000ƒa0015237 043000ƒae-uk--- 050000ƒaQL690.G7
      650000ƒaBirdsƒzGreat BritainƒxJuvenile literature

      Gardens.  Great Britain
        Birds - Illustrations
       2407698                            082000      598.2941'022'2ƒc19
      083000ƒaGreat Britain. Gardens. Birdsƒb- Illustrations
      690000ƒz00030ƒdGreat Britainƒzp1030ƒagardensƒz11030ƒabirdsƒz6003
      0ƒaillustrations
      692000ƒa0014672 692000ƒa0015237 043000ƒae-uk--- 050000ƒaQL690.G7
      650000ƒaBirdsƒzGreat BritainƒxPictorial works 650000ƒaGarden fau
      naƒzGreat BritainƒxPictorial works
```

Print from subject authority file on fiche

example, an indexer may be dealing with a 'Field guide to garden birds in Western Europe', and cannot find an exact match on the authority fiche reproduced on p 288, which means that a new string has to be written. But this can be based with confidence on some of the models already in the system. The fiche contains:

— a *field guide to garden birds* in Britain (marked 'A');

— a children's book of *garden birds in Western Europe* (marked 'B').

These existing packages serve as models not only for the PRECIS string but also the other systems later in the workflow, e.g. DDC, LCSH, etc..

The diagram on p 290 shows how different kinds of data are assigned to separate files in the computer. Catalogue records are held in one file, subject packages in another, and the thesaurus in a third. This deliberate use of separate files relates not only to the special characteristics of each of these different kinds of data but also to the chance that data taken from one file might be used or re-used in another. It is reasonable to assume that every document record exists as a unique entity, to the extent that if we detect an exact match between two catalogue records we can infer that one of the records should not have been written. We do not expect this kind of uniqueness when we create a subject package — in fact, these packages are assigned to a separate file in the expectation that they will be re-used (by quoting a SIN) as soon as another document on the same topic occurs. There is an even greater chance that the terms comprising a new string have all occurred in other subjects in the past and are already present in the thesaurus. The data base is constructed so that any of these data can be extracted and re-used whenever necessary, simply by quoting their addresses (i.e. their SINs or RINs).

Forms of output

A two-stage index, such as that shown in the extract on p 284, is typically used to support a classified file of citations. Examples can be seen in publications such as the *British National Bibliography*, the

Files

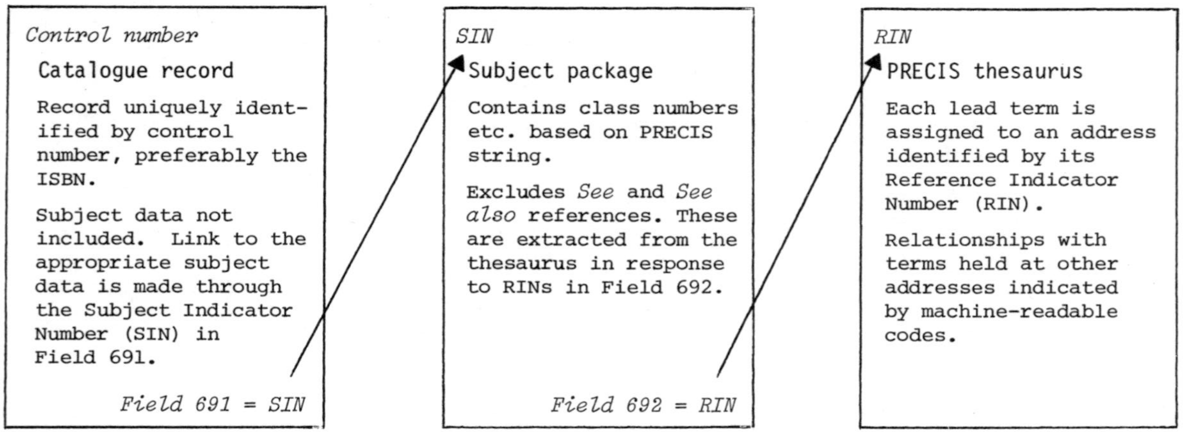

Control number

Catalogue record

Record uniquely identified by control number, preferably the ISBN.

Subject data not included. Link to the appropriate subject data is made through the Subject Indicator Number (SIN) in Field 691.

Field 691 = SIN

SIN

Subject package

Contains class numbers etc. based on PRECIS string.

Excludes *See* and *See also* references. These are extracted from the thesaurus in response to RINs in Field 692.

Field 692 = RIN

RIN

PRECIS thesaurus

Each lead term is assigned to an address identified by its Reference Indicator Number (RIN).

Relationships with terms held at other addresses indicated by machine-readable codes.

Outputs

1. MARC tapes
   Each MARC record consists of the catalogue record plus its appropriate subject package(s). It does not (at present) contain references extracted from the thesaurus. The fields on these tapes are assigned to an inverted file for on-line searching.
2. Printed products (including COM)
   (a) Authority files, e.g. PRECIS authority fiche, RIN fiche, DC fiche, name authority list.
   (b) Catalogues & bibliographies, e.g. *British National Bibliography*, *British Education Index*, *Audio-visual Materials for Higher Education*, etc.

Machine-held files of bibliographic data (British Library used as example)

Australian National Bibliography, *Audio-visual Materials for Higher Education*, and others. Other agencies prefer a more user-friendly, one-stage approach, where at least a brief citation is offered immediately after each entry in the subject index (similar to a traditional subject heading system). The first one-stage PRECIS index, produced for a network of school libraries in York County, Ontario, proved that this form of output is less demanding, in terms of space, than had been expected. The method is now used regularly in products such as:

— the *British Education Index*, covering current journals in the field of education (see extract on p 292);

— separate indexes in English and French to the films and videotapes produced by the National Film Board of Canada, with each entry followed by one or more titles (see extract from a French sequence on p 292);

— an index to recently-acquired printed books held in the Reference Division of the British Library (the first issue, on COM, covers over 300 000 items).

The production of a one-stage PRECIS index in German is also being investigated by the Deutsche Bibliothek in Frankfurt.

All these outputs consist of printed, pre-coordinated indexes of one kind or another, either on paper or COM. Pre-coordination also has a role to play in on-line systems. An on-line search is usually based on keywords linked by the standard Boolean operators (AND, OR, NOT). These operators allow the user to identify records where a given set of terms co-occurred in designated fields, but they cannot show *how* the concepts were interrelated. Consequently, some of the citations are likely to be irrelevant. This can be largely avoided if the user can call for the display of a pre-coordinated subject statement, as a kind of filter, during the search procedure. An example of a search containing this filter stage is reproduced on p 293. This shows part of a printout from an on-line search of the UK-MARC files for documents on 'Women's attitudes', starting from the statement 'WOMEN AND ATTITUDES' constructed from two PRECIS words (PW) linked by a Boolean AND. The fifth line of the printout reports a total of 23 hits containing both terms, but the user cannot yet distinguish between the documents that

TEACHING AIDS. General studies. Secondary schools
Simulation games
Who's afraid of simulations? / Ken Jones. — *Gen. Educ.*, No.35 : Autumn 81. — p1-8
Bibliography: p8

TEACHING AIDS. Home economics. Polytechnics
Microcomputer systems
To the rescue of quality control / by Barbara Fisk. — *Educ. Comput. (London)*, Vol.2, no.9 : Oct 81. — p21-22
'Home economics'

TEACHING AIDS. Home economics. Secondary schools
Microcomputer systems
Drawing the strings together / by Jacky Watson. — *Educ. Comput. (London)*, Vol.2, no.9 : Oct 81. — p20-21
'Home economics'

An **ideal** medium for teaching microelectronics / by Lynda Golightly. — *Educ. Comput. (London)*, Vol.2, no.9 : Oct 81. — p19-20
'Home economics'

TEACHING AIDS. Home economics. Universities
Microcomputer systems
Home economics at the touch of a button / Bonnie D. Brandi. — *Home Econ.*, Vol.27, no.1 : Jan 81. — p4-5

TEACHING AIDS. Industrial studies. Schools
— Case studies
Aids to learning about industry / Roy Palin, Chris Hackworth. — *Ind./Educ. View*, No.11 : Spring 82. — p8-10

TEACHING AIDS. Language skills. Multiply handicapped pupils. Special schools
Paget-Gorman Sign System
The **Paget-Gorman** Sign System / Jacqueline Rowe. — *Spec. Educ.*, Vol.8, no.4 : Dec 81. — p25-27

TEACHING AIDS. Language skills. Pupils
Computer games
Creator of contexts for language work / Tony Gray and Derek Blease. — *Educ. Comput. (London)*, Vol.2, no.11 : Dec 81. — p31-32
'CAL tutorial'

TEACHING AIDS. Modern languages. Secondary schools
Microcomputer systems
The **use** of microcomputers for the teaching of modern languages / Gareth W. Roberts. — *Br. J. Lang. Teach.*, Vol.19, no.3 : Winter 81. — p125-129

TEACHING AIDS. Nuclear power. Secondary schools
Simulation games — Case studies
The **nuclear** debate : a new educational package for teachers / Henry Ellington and Eric Addinall. — *Simul./Games Learn.*, Vol.11, no.3 : Autumn 81. — p120-125

TEACHING AIDS. Open University
Cassette sound tape recordings
Audio-tapes for teaching science / Robert Haines, Sheila Wright. — *Teach. Distance*, No.20 : Winter 81. — p78-81

TEACHING AIDS. Open University
Telephones
Telephone tutoring in the Open University : a review / Bernadette Robinson. — *Teach. Distance*, No.20 : Winter 81. — p57-65

TEACHING AIDS. Primary schools
Microcomputer systems. Attitudes of pupils
Reactions to the Commodore Pet / Bob Campbell and Margaret Wellard. — *Educ. Comput. (London)*, Vol.3, no.3 : Apr 82. — p17

TEACHING AIDS. Primary schools
Microcomputer systems. Organisations: Micros and Primary Education *(Group)*
Going MAPE? / by Ron Jones. — *Educ. Comput. (London)*, Vol.2, no.8 : Sep 81. — p58-59

TEACHING AIDS. Professional education. Physiotherapists
Closed circuit television
Closed circuit television (CCTV) : is it really worth the effort? / B. Brockie. — *J. Furth. High. Educ. Scotl.*, Vol.6, no.2 : May 82. — p41-46

TEACHING AIDS. Professional education. Teachers
Simulation games
Simulations, games and the professional education of teachers / Jacquetta Megarry. — *JET. J. Educ. Teach.*, Vol.7, no.1 : Jan 81. — p25-39

Extract from *British Education Index* (The British Library)

CONDITION FÉMININE. Canada
Ce que femme veut.

CONDITION FÉMININE. Québec
– Perspectives historiques
Les Filles du Roy.
– Témoignages de femmes
J'me marie, j'me marie pas.
Souris, tu m'inquiètes.

CONDITION FÉMININE. Régions rurales. Inde
Shakti.

CONDITION HUMAINE
Eli, Eli, lamma sabachtani?
L'Homme nouveau.
– Films d'animation
Au bout du fil.
Déclin.
Jeu de coudes.
Ô ou l'Invisible Enfant.
L'Œil.
Rencontre.
Rien qu'une petite chanson d'amour.
– Films expérimentaux
Dans le labyrinthe.
Exprimée par le mime – *Traitement humoristique – Films d'animation*
Baxter gagne son ciel.

CONDITION PHYSIQUE
– Traitement humoristique – Films d'animation
Sports divers.

CONDITION PHYSIQUE. Canadiens
Joie de vivre.

CONDITIONNEMENT PHYSIQUE
Voir aussi
EXERCISES PHYSIQUES
SPORTS

CONDITIONNEMENT PHYSIQUE
En pleine forme.
Parcours de conditionnement physique. Construction et planification
Parcours de conditionnement.

Amélioration par des programmes spéciaux – *Exemples étudiés: Tembec, Steinberg et Hunter Douglas*
Ça prend du vouloir.

CONDITIONS DE TRAVAIL. Travailleurs. Industrie forestière. Québec
Manifestations, *1971*
La Revanche.

CONDUITE *Voir* **COMPORTEMENT**

CONDUITE AUTOMOBILE. Hiver
Mesures de sécurité
La Conduite en hiver: gardez votre sang-froid.

CONFÉDÉRATION. Canada
Voir aussi
CENTENAIRE DE LA CONFÉDÉRATION

CONFÉDÉRATION. .Canada
Entrée de la Nouvelle-Écosse
Charles Tupper (Le Magnanime).
Rôle de Cartier, Georges-Étienne
Georges-Étienne Cartier (Le Lion du Québec).
Rôle de Galt, Alexander
Alexander Galt (L'Idéaliste impénitent).
Rôle de Lafontaine, Louis-Hippolyte
Louis-Hippolyte Lafontaine.
Rôle de Macdonald, John A.
John A. Macdonald (L'Intuition fantastique).
Rôle de Tupper, Charles
Charles Tupper (Le Magnanime).

CONFESSION. Église catholique. Acadie
Effets sur les jeunes acadiens – *Films de fiction*
La Confession.

CONFLIT DE GÉNÉRATIONS
– Films de fiction
Mon amie Pierrette.

CONFLIT DE GÉNÉRATIONS. Familles
– Films de fiction
La Déchirure.
Eddie.
Un fait accompli.

CONSERVATION. Eau
Élément 3.

CONSERVATION. Eaux douces. Canada
Recherche scientifique. Rôle du Centre canadien des eaux intérieures
Notre deuxième territoire.
Technologie des eaux usées.

CONSERVATION. Énergie
Projets – *Régions étudiées: Québec et Danemark*
Économies ou Échecs.

CONSERVATION. Faune. Canada
Compte à rebours.
Gardiens de la faune.

CONSERVATION. Forêts. Canada
L'Autre Visage de la forêt.
Un œil sur nos forêts.

CONSERVATION. Grues blanches d'Amérique
Ce grand oiseau blanc.

CONSERVATION. Oiseaux aquatiques. Provinces des Prairies
Les oiseaux aquatiques sont menacés.

CONSERVATION. Poissons. Gaspésie. Québec
Techniques de fumage
Boucanerie.

CONSERVATION. Ressources énergétiques. Canada
Mesures
L'Administration de l'énergie pour l'avenir.

CONSERVATION. Ressources marines. Canada
Maintenant ou Jamais.
Rôle du ministère des Pêches et des Océans
Les Sciences de la mer.

CONSERVATION. Ressources marines. Saint-Laurent *(golfe)*
Mesures. Points de vue de Cousteau, Jacques-Yves
Les Pièges de la mer.

CONSERVATION. Saumon
Du saumon pour l'avenir.
Effets de la pêche commerciale
Richesse à sauver.

Extract from *Catalogue 1983* (Office national du film du Canada)

PROG:

SS 1 / C ? *[Computer requests 'Search statement 1' or 'Command']*

USER: (PW) WOMEN AND ATTITUDES *[Find set of documents indexed by PRECIS words 'Women' AND 'Attitudes']*

PROG:

SS 1 PSTG (23) *[Search statement 1 = 23 postings (i.e. hits)]*

SS 2 / C ?

USER: PRT VF *[Print verbal features]*

PROG:

1 VF - SOCIETY. ROLE OF WOMEN. ATTITUDES OF CHRISTIAN CHURCH - FEMINIST VIEWPOINTS

2 VF - GREAT BRITAIN. FAMILY LIFE. ATTITUDES OF WOMEN

3 VF - GREAT BRITAIN. WOMEN. PORTRAYAL BY ADVERTISING MEDIA. ATTITUDES OF WOMEN CONSUMERS

4 VF - FRANCE. MOTHERHOOD. ATTITUDES OF WOMEN, 1680-1980

5 VF - WOMEN. ATTITUDES OF SOCIETY - FEMINIST VIEWPOINTS

6 VF - WOMEN. HEALTH. ATTITUDES OF SOCIETY, 1860-1973 - FEMINIST VIEWPOINTS

7 VF - SOCIETY. ROLE OF WOMEN. ATTITUDES OF MARXISTS RELATED TO THEORIES OF FREUD, SIGMUND ON WOMEN'S SEXUAL BEHAVIOUR

8 VF - FICTION IN ENGLISH, TO 1968. SPECIAL THEMES: ATTITUDES OF SOCIETY TO WOMEN

9 VF - YEMEN (ARAB REPUBLIC). SAN'Ā'. SOCIAL CHANGE. ATTITUDES OF WOMEN

PROG:

CONT. Y OR N ? *[Computer pauses, requests instruction to continue]*

Printout of features from an on-line search for 'Women' AND 'Attitudes'

deal with 'Attitudes *of* women' (the subject of the enquiry) and 'Attitudes *to* women'. This distinction can be made quite simply by asking the computer to display, for each hit, a pre-coordinated subject statement generated from the PRECIS string that contains both terms. This statement consists, in fact, of the *verbal feature* used to explain a class number in the classified section of *BNB* and similar bibliographies (see p 283). It is displayed in response to the instruction 'PRINT VF'. The rest of the printout on p 293 consists of a numbered sequence of features for the first nine responses to the enquiry. These show that five of the responses (for example, 1 and 5) can be rejected as irrelevant without paying the costs of retrieving their catalogue entries — they deal with 'Attitudes *to* women'. Probable hits have occurred, however, with citations such as 2 and 3. These deal with 'Attitudes *of* women' in one way or another, and although some of them may be too specific, this, too, can be judged from the features †.

Applications of PRECIS in new languages

Readers familiar with the first edition of the *Manual* will have noted some new codes and procedures in the present account; in particular:

— number differences (see note on p 72);

— two new operators: 'u' (two-way interactions) and 'f' (bound coordinate concepts;

— downward-reading substitutes.

Tests confirm that these extensions to the system allow both faster and easier indexing (by removing the need to devise a complex stratagem when the indexer faces a situation that should be handled by one of the new codes), and they also lead to shorter input strings. Nevertheless, they must be rated as relatively minor additions to a basically unchanged

---

† This procedure does not depend on 'features' constructed as explanations of class numbers. The same facility is offered by the National Film Board of Canada as part of their FORMAT system, but the equivalent of a feature is devised entirely for on-line use.

system. It is doubtful whether further developments of equal significance will be needed for indexing in English. This can be stated with reasonable confidence against a background of extensive tests of PRECIS in new languages.

Extending or adapting an indexing language, such as PRECIS, for use as a multilingual system calls for equally satisfactory advances on each of two fronts, corresponding to its two main components:

— the thesaurus, with particular reference to the general applicability of the rules for vocabulary control and the handling of inter-concept relationships;

— the syntactical side of the system, and a need for codes and procedures leading to input strings that are capable of generating entries in new languages that would be judged as acceptable by native speakers.

These two aspects are considered separately and briefly below.

Experience suggests that the thesaural procedures used in PRECIS can be applied, without modification, in other languages. There are two main reasons for advancing this view:

(a) The PRECIS thesaurus is based upon rules and relationships that are recognised in international standards as both culture- and language-independent. The Draft International Standard on multilingual thesauri contains no rules for vocabulary control, nor does it deal with inter-concept relationships (1). These are regarded as sufficiently covered in the standard on monolingual thesauri, which is taken as the basic text. This leaves the multilingual standard free to concentrate on problems (encountered some 10% of the time in practice) related to the translation of indexing terms encountered in one language into acceptable equivalents in another. In some cases the proposed solution calls for reference to the rules for vocabulary control contained in the monolingual standard — in particular, the rules for factoring compound terms (these correspond to the Rules of differencing in PRECIS). It is

---

(1) International Organization for Standardization. Documentation: Guidelines for the establishment and development of multilingual thesauri: ISO/DIS 5964. Geneva, I.S.O., 1983

generally easier to translate a complex expression in one language into acceptable equivalents in other languages if the original term is first factored according to these rules. For example, an attempt at direct translation of the German term 'Lehrerbildungsgesetz' into English and French would call for complicated paraphrases, e.g. 'Law of professional education of teachers' and 'Loi sur la formation des enseignants'. Neither of these would be regarded as a satisfactory indexing term. A shorter expression, closer to the original German, can be achieved in English ('Teacher education law'), but not in French. According to the Rules of differencing, the German term should have been factored in the first place into three separate noun components; these can be translated far more readily into the new languages:

German	*English*	*French*
Lehrer	Teachers	Enseignants
Ausbildung	Professional education	Formation
Gesetz	Law	Loi

(b) The relational codes used in the PRECIS thesaurus are, by their nature, language independent. In all the examples used so far the code $m generated a *See* reference, and $n and $o generated *See also* references, but these directives are no more than local expressions of the basic relationships that underlie the codes. The same relationships could be conveyed by any appropriate phrase, as seen in the following examples of references based on the associative and hierarchical relationships taken from demonstration indexes:

French: Primates
Voir aussi
Lémuriens

Polish: Prasa
Zob. też
Czasopisma

Spanish: Edificios
Ver también
Casas
Palacios

Portuguese: Política
Ver também
Movimentos políticos

German: Botanik
Siehe auch
Vegetation

Danish: Fysisk geografi
Se også
Landskabsformer

Swedish: Naturresurser
Se även
Energiresurser

Experiments in the generation of entries from PRECIS strings in non-English languages began in the early 1970's (some were reported in the first edition of the *Manual*), but although the results were encouraging, these early investigations could hardly be rated as serious. This situation changed with increasing contacts with indexers in non-English-speaking countries, leading to the production of test indexes, prepared by native speakers, in a range of European and non-European languages. The results were often aesthetically pleasing, as seen in the following Farsi example †:

String:

✓ (0) ایران
✓ (1) صنعت نفت
✓ (p) کارگران ماهر
✓ (2) آموزش حین خدمت
(5) مورد مطالعه
✓ (q) پالایشگاه تهران

Entries:

ایران
صنعت نفت ، کارگران ماهر ، آموزش حین خدمت **ـ موردمطالعه ؛ پالایشگاه‌تهران**

صنعت نفت ، ایران
کارگران ماهر ، آموزش حین خدمت **ـ موردمطالعه ؛ پالایشگاه تهران**

کارگران ماهر . صنعت نفت ، ایران
آموزش حین خدمت **ـ موردمطالعه : پالایشگاه تهران**

آموزش حین خدمت . کارگران ماهر . صنعت نفت ، ایران
ـ موردمطالعه : پالایشگاه تهران

پالایشگاه تهران . موردمطالعه
ایران . صنعت نفت . **کارگران ماهر** . آموزش حین خدمت

These experiments showed that acceptable results could

---

† This deals with the topic 'In-service training of skilled workers in the Iranian oil industries, based on studies in the Tehran Refinery'. The string and entries are read from right to left. The example is taken from :
Moradi, Nurolla. [PRECIS]. *Iranian Library Association Bulletin*, X(3) Autumn 1977 *and* X(4) Winter 1978 *(in Farsi)*

usually be achieved using procedures developed originally for English (these were the only procedures available at the time). In some cases, however, the production of grammatically acceptable entries called for the writing of long and complicated strings and an unorthodox use of the operators and codes. It became clear that extra codes and procedures would be needed to generate 'natural' entries from strings that appear (from the indexer's point of view) as straightforward as their English-language counterparts. This led to the writing of specifications for a range of new codes and procedures, many of which have been programmed and tested †, but these will probably remain unknown (as quite irrelevant) to the majority of English-language indexers. These studies showed a need to draw a sharp distinction between two facets of the syntactical side of PRECIS:

— fundamental relationships between concepts, conceived in terms of their roles and represented by the primary and secondary operators in the right-hand panel of Appendix 1 (p 307);

— secondary adjuncts, not strictly concerned with the roles of terms but used to explicate these roles in selected outputs. These are represented (in English) by some of the secondary codes in the central box of the left-hand panel — in particular, the number differences and the connective codes.

The fundamental relationships represented by the role operators appear to be language-independent, and the order of concepts imposed by these operators (for example, object before action before performer) has provided a basis for meaningful entries in all the languages tested. Some changes have been made to this part of the schema since the first edition of the *Manual* (such as the introduction of operators 'f' and 'u', and a broadening of the scope of operator 'r'), but these were introduced for practical reasons that apply in any language, and they do not affect the logic on which the system is based. Contacts with new languages have not revealed a need for further extensions to this side of the system, and none of these operators has remained unused in the

---

† Particularly in the programs developed by Mr Fred Smith of the Department of Library and Information Studies, Loughborough University, England.

various languages studied. The special routines attached to some of the operators, such as the predicate transformation, are also needed, and operate successfully, in all the languages tested.

This view of the operators as expressions of language-independent relations is supported by researches which indicate parallels between the roles used in PRECIS and certain *deep cases* proposed by linguists and regarded as linguistic universals, meaning that they occur in all human languages. A distinction is drawn in modern linguistics between:

— a finite set of basic inter-concept relationships (whether explained as roles or deep cases). These are said to exist at the *deep structure* level of all languages;

— adjuncts and conventions used to convey these basic relationships in *surface outputs* (speech or writing).

Surface adjuncts and conventions (but not deep structure relations) vary from language to language, which explains why different languages need their own prescriptive grammars and their own rules for recognising well-formed sentences. Some languages convey relationships through prepositions, whereas others use postpositions; some require their nouns to be inflected; others, such as Chinese (and to some extent English) rely largely on word order. Many languages employ combinations of these different devices — German, for example, possesses a rich repertory of prepositions and also inflects its nouns †. Faced by the variety of these surface conventions, we can hardly expect a set of codes and procedures developed to handle adjuncts in English to be adequate, or even appropriate, in all other languages. For example, the connective codes $v and $w are generally used to introduce prepositions written as separate words and inserted into outputs so that they precede the terms to which they are directly related. These codes cannot be used as they stand in languages characterized by different conventions, such as:

— adjuncts that function like prepositions, but are conjoined to their following terms, becoming *prefixes* (as in Hebrew);

---

† Inflections on nouns indicate *surface cases*, such as accusative, dative, etc. These are not the same as the deep cases proposed by linguists, such as patient, agent, instrument, location, etc.

— adjuncts that *follow* the terms to which they relate. These can be printed either as separate *postpositions* (as in Finnish), or conjoined as *postfixes* (as in Hungarian).

Encounters with these various situations led to a specification for *generalized connective codes*, based upon $v and $w but extended by an extra number taken from the following grid †:

	Space-generating	Close-up
Prepositional	0	1
Postpositional	2	3

This does not affect the workings of the present connectives in English, but the codes in English strings should be converted, by the computer, into '$v0' and '$w0' in the unlikely event that they occur in the same data base as strings in a language using a different convention.

This account of the generalized connectives is offered only as an example of the kinds of codes that have been specified to cope with the surface features of certain languages but have no relevance at all for English-language indexers. Other codes and procedures have been devised to deal with surface features and adjuncts such as:

— inflections on nouns (e.g. in German and the Slavonic languages);

— infixes inserted into some compound terms to show how their parts are related (e.g. in Danish);

— special function words (called 'explicatives' in the specification) that are sometimes needed to resolve a potential ambiguity in a language, such as Danish, which possesses a very limited range of prepositions (compared with, say, English or German), and does not use inflections on nouns to indicate roles;

— a set of new term codes to identify special kinds of action terms that should be printed in entries *after* the names of their objects

---

† This generalized coding system was proposed by Jutta Sørensen (now Jutta Austin), who was also involved in the development of the generalized differences described on p 48. The two systems show obvious parallels.

and/or performers. A need for this has been detected in Finnish, Hindi, Tamil and Sinhala.

Whenever one of these situations was encountered and the necessary codes had been specified, the routines attached to the codes were tested not only in the new language but also, by simulation, in English. This has benefitted the 'English' side of the system; the number differences were, in fact, first formulated to handle Komposita (single-word compounds) in German.

Indexing in a non-English language does not necessarily incur the need for extra codes to handle its surface features. Indexers in a language such as French (and, by analogy, closely related Romance languages such as Italian, Portuguese and Spanish) use the same codes and procedures as indexers in English, but different parts of the system carry different loads. This applies particularly to the treatment of adjectival compounds. Access to parts of these terms is usually provided by differencing in English, but calls for a greater use of the thesaurus in French and similar languages. The need for this less direct approach can be attributed to two factors:

(a) Normal left-to-right reading conventions mean that when an adjectival phrase, such as 'Pasteurised milk', is truncated right-to-left, each part, as it is isolated, consists of a noun or noun phrase, i.e.

Milk Pasteurised milk

These are, of course, the leads that would be generated from a string containing a differencing code, e.g.

(1) ✓milk $21 pasteurised

The equivalent phrase in French, 'lait pasteurisé', cannot be handled in this way. Since the adjective follows its noun, application of right-to-left truncation would immediately isolate an adjective minus its noun:

*Pasteurisé Lait pasteurisé

This would contravene a recommendation in the International Standard on thesaurus construction, which stipulates that indexing terms should consist, as far as possible, of nouns or noun phrases.

(b) Adjectives in French, as in a number of other languages, must agree with their nouns in number and gender. This means that an adjective, if accepted as a lead, could vary depending upon its noun and file at different positions, e.g.

Pasteurisé *(masc. singular)*
Pasteurisée *(fem. singular)*
Pasteurisés *(masc. plural)*
Pasteurisées *(fem. plural)*

Both problems are usually resolved in French indexes by converting the adjective, where possible, into the noun form of the concept from which it was derived (e.g. 'pasteurisation'), then using the thesaurus to extract a reference from this noun to the full form of the term, e.g.

Pasteurisation
Voir aussi
Crème pasteurisée
Lait pasteurisé
Produits pasteurisés

A similar reference, taken from an index in Portuguese, can be seen at the bottom of p 296. The source and target terms are invariably linked by the associative relationship in these cases.

A program for indexing in French needs a minor routine added to those employed in English. Connectives in French are conventionally accompanied by articles, e.g. 'de la' and 'par les'; these are sometimes combined as a single word, such as 'des' or 'du'. Cases like these do not call for extra procedures; the appropriate article is simply written as part of the connective, e.g.

String: (1) énfants
(2) développement $w des
(s) rôle $v des $w dans le
(3) párents

Entries: Enfants
Developpement. Rôle des parents

Developpement. Enfants
Rôle des parents

Parents
Rôle dans le developpement des enfants

When an article ends in a vowel, however, this vowel is suppressed and replaced by an apostrophe if the following word begins with a vowel; the following word is then printed immediately after the apostrophe (i.e. without an intervening space), e.g.

String: (1) enfants
(2) education $w des
(s) rôle $v des $w dans l'
(3) parents

Entries: Enfants
Education. Rôle des parents

Education. Parents
Rôle des parents

Parents
Rôle dans l'education des enfants

The article-noun combination 'l'education' in the display line of the final entry is produced by an extra routine which suppresses the space that would otherwise be inserted between the connective and the following term *whenever the connective ends in an apostrophe*. This extra instruction is usually incorporated into the standard routines used to generate outputs in English, where it remains virtually hidden except when needed.

One final point concerning syntax calls for emphasis. The so-called 'problems' encountered in new languages are all related to the *surface features* of their outputs, which explains why the codes developed to handle these problems belong to the class of secondary codes in the left-hand panel of Appendix 1. The core of the system, represented by the operators in the right-hand panel, has not been affected, and the soundness of the premises on which the system is based, explained in terms of context-dependency related to roles, has been tested and confirmed by these contacts with new languages. The consequence of these developments could not have been anticipated when the first edition of the *Manual* was published in 1974. The *Manual* then described the whole of the system. This has changed, and the present edition deals with what Sørensen called "... an English *sub-grammar* extracted from a *macro-grammar*". It is almost inconceivable that indexers in a given language community would need access to the full range of options that has been specified.

A note on PRECIS software

When PRECIS was first developed, access to a mainframe computer was regarded as a necessary prerequisite for its successful application. This position has changed, for reasons such as the following:

— Hardware has developed to the point where minicomputers can handle workloads that once demanded mainframe machines. The efficiency of microcomputers is also rising, although they suffer (at present) from two disadvantages: lack of space for storing files of entries and references prior to merging and printing, and slow operating times.

— Programs are more efficient and/or programmers are cleverer. The first PRECIS software, in a low level (assembly) language, was written in piecemeal fashion, and consisted of sets of routines, each associated with one of the algorithms which determine the choice of leads and the formats of entries. Analysts and programmers now take a different, more economical approach — they study the system as a gestalt and search for general procedures within particular cases. For example, the following input and outputs:

String: (1) Canada
(u) foreign relations $v with $w with
(1) China

Entries: Canada
Foreign relations with China

Foreign relations. Canada
With China

Foreign relations. China
With Canada

China
Foreign relations with Canada

— are based on routines that can be generalized and applied at various points in the system:

(a) *Entries 1 and 2* are in the *standard format*;

(b) the routines that generate *Entry 3* would also produce a lead on a *directional property* coded 's' (see the example of an entry under 'Attitudes' on p 155);

— *Entry 4* invokes the *predicate transformation*.

There is little point in reporting on software in use at present, except as examples of types:

(a) Programs for *mainframe machines* are held in the British Library, the National Library of Australia, and the University of Toronto Library Automation Systems, but these are not available to other agencies;

(b) A complete suite of programs for a *minicomputer* has been written, in Basic, at the Department of Library and Information Studies, Loughborough University. This covers all the syntactical procedures described in this *Manual*, plus a number of extra routines for dealing with new languages;

(c) Some PRECIS (or 'PRECIS-like') programs have been written for *microcomputers*, but their facilities are limited in one way or another; they may, for example, handle only a selection of operators, or only one level of differencing. A program has been written in Pascal by students at the Statens bibliotekskole (State Library School) at Oslo, and generates indexes in Norwegian. Other programs for micros have been reported, but their outputs have not been evaluated.

These various programs have been based upon the algorithms printed as an Appendix in the first edition of the *Manual*. These have been re-thought and updated, and a new version is offered here as *Appendix 5* (p 340). Algorithms for the PRECIS thesaurus have not been developed; these would be relatively straightforward.

Further readings

The sections on workflow are based on a paper presented by Derek Austin at the 1983 General Assembly of LIBER (Ligue des Bibliothèques Européennes de Recherche). This has been reprinted in the *LIBER Bulletin*, and a version in German appeared in *Bibliothek: Forschung und Praxis*.

The application of PRECIS as a multilingual system was introduced in a series of four papers, under the covering title 'PRECIS in a multilingual context', published in consecutive issues of *Libri:*

Part 1. Austin, Derek. PRECIS, an overview. *Libri*, 26(1), 1976, p 1-33

Part 2. Sørensen, Jutta & Austin, Derek. A linguistic and logical explanation of the syntax. *Libri*, 26(2), 1976, p 108-139

Note: This part referred to a system of deep cases proposed by Johansen. This proved to be inadequate in the light of further researches, and the system was later abandoned by its author. The paper also introduced a theory proposed by Sørensen, called 'Time of conceptualisation', to explain the order of concepts in PRECIS strings. This remains sound, but has not been covered in this *Manual*.

Part 3. Sørensen, Jutta & Austin, Derek. Multilingual experiments — proposed codes and procedures for the Germanic languages. *Libri*, 26(3), 1976, p 181-215.

Part 4. Lambert, Germaine. The application of PRECIS in French. *Libri*, 26(4), 1976, p 302-324

A selection of the codes developed to handle surface features in non-English languages was described in:

Sørensen, Jutta. Multilingual aspects of PRECIS. *In* The PRECIS index system: principles, applications and prospects. Proceedings of the International PRECIS Workshop held in the University of Maryland, October 1976, *edited by* Hans H Wellisch. New York, H. W. Wilson, 1977

Parallels between the roles used in PRECIS and systems of deep cases proposed by linguists have been studied in:

Austin, Derek. PRECIS as a multilingual system: a search for language-independent explanations. Thesis submitted to the Department of Information Studies, University of Sheffield, 1982. [Available in the Library Association Library, London]

This also contains the fullest account to date of the various codes and procedures developed for new languages.

APPENDIX 1. PRECIS OPERATORS AND CODES

CODES IN PRECIS STRINGS

Primary codes

Theme interlinks	$x	1st concept in coordinate theme
	$y	2nd/subsequent concept in theme
	$z	Common concept
Term codes †	$a	Common noun
	$c	Proper name (class-of-one)
	$d	Place name

Secondary codes

Differences

Preceding differences *(3 characters)*

1st and 2nd characters :

$0	Non-lead, space generating
$1	Non-lead, close-up
$2	Lead, space generating
$3	Lead, close-up

3rd character = number in the range 1 *to* 9 *indicating level of difference*

Date as a difference	$d	
Parenthetical differences	$n	Non-lead parenthetical difference
	$o	Lead parenthetical difference
Connectives	$v	Downward-reading connective
	$w	Upward-reading connective

Typographic codes †

$e	Non-filing part in italic preceded by comma
$f	Filing part in italic preceded by comma
$g	Filing part in roman, no preceding punctuation
$h	Filing part in italic preceded by full point
$i	Filing part in italic, no preceding punctuation

† These codes are also used in the thesaurus

SCHEMA OF OPERATORS

Primary operators

Environment of core concepts	0	Location
Core concepts	1	Key system *Thing when action not present. Thing towards which an action is directed, e.g. object of transitive action, performer of intransitive action.*
	2	Action; Effect of action
	3	Performer of transitive action *(agent, instrument);* Intake; Factor
Extra-core concepts	4	Viewpoint-as-form; Aspect
	5	Selected instance, *e.g. study region, sample population*
	6	Form of document; Target user

Secondary operators

Coordinate concepts	f	'Bound' coordinate concept
	g	Standard coordinate concept
Dependent elements	p	Part; Property
	q	Member of quasi-generic group
	r	Assembly
Special classes of action	s	Role definer; Directional property
	t	Author-attributed association
	u	Two-way interaction

Note on prefixes to Codes. The codes in the left-hand panel are marked as instructions, as opposed to data, by their preceding symbols. These are shown as dollar signs ($) to reflect current practice in many PRECIS files, but any non-alpha-numeric character will serve the same purpose. The draft version of the *UNIMARC Manual* (referring to PRECIS data in Field 670) states that "signs used as subfield codes (in UNIMARC, the $) *should be avoided*".

APPENDIX 2. WORD ORDER IN ENGLISH ADJECTIVAL COMPOUNDS

A footnote to Chapter 4

Word order in English adjectival phrases is never in doubt when the noun is modified by preceding adjectives which can be specified only as first and second level differences. The natural left-to-right order is then:

2nd level difference — 1st level difference — focus

— that is, each word modifies the next component of the phrase. Changing the order of adjectives either invokes a different concept, to the extent that the term *Concrete reinforced structures* differs semantically from *Reinforced concrete structures*, or the expression tends to baffle immediate comprehension, as in **Shaped heart flowers* rather than *Heart shaped flowers*.

Problems arise only rarely when a noun is qualified by two or more differences on the same level; for example, when each of two adjectives is related directly to the focus, neither adjective modifying the other. In these cases adjectives tend to be ordered according to generally recognised criteria which are not, perhaps, stated explicitly in standard grammars, but are apparently understood and applied intuitively by both speakers and listeners. An adjectival phrase such as *English folk songs* appears to be natural, whereas **Folk English songs* does not, yet both adjectives function as first level differences; that is, each serves independently to specify a class of songs:

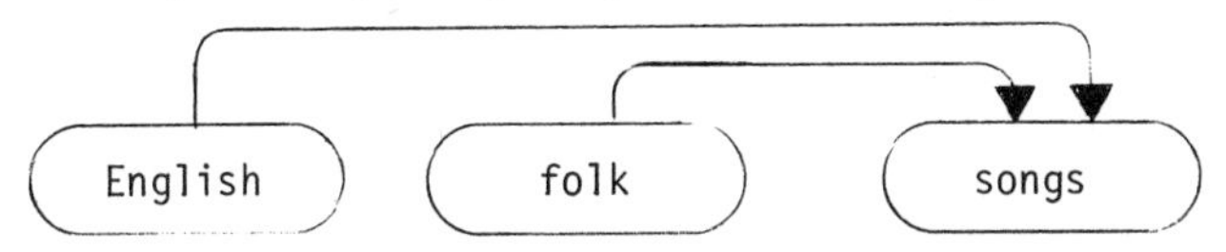

Occasionally, however, the order of words in an adjectival construction is less obvious, especially when dealing with the names of unfamiliar or newly-emerging concepts. Largely as a theoretical exercise, but also as a possible step towards teachably consistent practice in these cases, a sample of adjectival constructions was collected during the research which led to PRECIS, then examined for any evidence of underlying principles which might govern the order of adjectives. The selected sample was not limited to phrases that indexers would regard as significant candidates for a controlled vocabulary, but covered compound terms of any kind, gathered from sources as diverse as newspaper headlines and modern poetry. Analysis of these terms, based on introspective (but shared) judgements, strongly suggested that the order of words in adjectival compounds is more than a matter of chance, and cannot be explained only in terms of speech conventions. Instead, this order appears to be subject to rules which can themselves be related to an internal categorial system, where differences are organised into classes based upon factors such as parts of speech (e.g. adverbs *versus*

adjectives), words that express the viewpoint of the speaker rather than refer to an intrinsic attribute of the noun, and certain logical relationships between the difference(s) and the focal concept. When a compound term is constructed *ab initio*, its elements seem to be selected from among these categories in a preferred order. To illustrate this point, a system of categories was established empirically, the classes being set down in the order in which it appears that their members are normally cited when more than one occurs within a term. These categories are listed below as a Table.

Ordered categories of adverbs and adjectival differences

Categories of differences		*Examples*		
		1	*2*	*3*
11	Adverbs			very
10	Evaluatives			useful
9	Relatives			small
8	Properties		flexible	
7	Place of origin	Russian		
6	Agents of past actions			hand-
	Past actions (focus as object)		extruded	made
4	Materials		aluminium	brass
3	Parts	swing-wing	channelled	
2	Actions by or within focus	vertical take-off		
1	Function or purpose (inc. user)	military		travelling
0	FOCUS	aircraft	sections	clocks

Note: Categories are numbered in PRECIS input order reading up the columns. Natural language order (output) is read down the columns.

Once the table had been established, it was found that the order of words in adjectival phrases conformed with a high level of consistency to that predicted by the sequence of categories. Rare exceptions could usually be explained in one of the following ways:

(a) even in written English, an order of words that would lead to an awkward combination of speech sounds was sometimes avoided;

(b) consecutive adjectives, each representing a first level difference, were sometimes transposed if the 'logical' order could be misinterpreted as a second level difference qualifying a first level difference. Even in these situations, however, the predicted order was liable to occur, the writer/speaker depending upon the context to resolve the latent ambiguity. For example, *large garden sheds*, which is potentially ambiguous, is not generally misinterpreted as *sheds for large gardens*.

Supporting evidence which suggests that the order of words in adjectival phrases is governed by an internal categorial system has also been traced in accounts of research by linguists †.

Two points of practical significance emerged from this largely theoretical exercise:

1) It was suggested (p 52) that the parts of multi-word terms should be input in the order that produces the most 'natural' phrasing at output. In the light of these researches, this suggestion appears less likely to lead to subjective variations than might have been expected. On the whole, natural language seems more 'logical' than many classificationists have allowed.

2) The Table identifies and isolates three classes of words (categories 9, 10 and 11, at the head of the column) that call for special care when indexing. Words in these classes should usually be avoided as components of indexing terms, even when they are freely used by authors.

(a) Adverbs (Category 11) cannot refer to nouns, and can therefore function only as second or higher level differences. They are defined in Chambers' as words "... added to a verb, adjective or other adverb to express some modification of its meaning". They are frequently used in adjectival phrases to introduce a note of emphasis rather than a higher level of specificity; consequently, they have little value as indexing terms except when they have acquired specific meanings within a jargon, as in '*very* high frequency'.

(b) Evaluatives (Category 10) are grammatically related to nouns, but they do not, in fact, speciate the focal concept in terms of its intrinsic attributes, but rather express an observer's opinion of the focus, e.g. as *unethical* or *beautiful*. Since views of this kind are variable and context-dependent upon the observer, these words should also be avoided in indexing.

(c) Relatives (Category 9) serve to identify a point on a continuum. These words also tend to express variable, and to some extent observer-oriented, concepts: a 'large' river in England would not be regarded as such in the United States. These words should also, therefore, be avoided in indexing except when they have acquired specific meanings within a jargon, as in '*new* products', '*small* firms', and '*low* tar cigarettes'.

---

† See, for example:
Crystal, David. Linguistics. London, Penguin, 1971

The table has been used occasionally as a basis for decisions in cases of doubtful order, although it is realised that the categories are too broad to deal with the most difficult situations. In particular, they cannot predict an order when a given noun is qualified by two or more differences on the same level and drawn from the same category; for example, two or more past actions, as in '*powdered skimmed* milk'. Further refinement of the categories might form an interesting line of future enquiry, aimed at classes that are so mutually exclusive that it should not be possible to modify a given focus by differences drawn from the same category. To do so would introduce the kind of logical contradiction contained in the first three words of Chomsky's often-quoted sentence, *Colorless green ideas sleep furiously*. Apart from the fact that an abstract concept, 'ideas', cannot be modified (giving a subclass) by a physical property such as 'green', a further semantic restriction prohibits the simultaneous possession by an entity of properties, such as 'green and 'colourless', drawn from the same category (assuming that 'colourless' would logically be assigned, as an antonym, to a class called 'colours').

APPENDIX 3. FUNDAMENTAL RELATIONSHIPS

A footnote to Chapter 7, including references to examples in later chapters

As noted in Chapter 7, the various roles indicated by the PRECIS operators can be explained in terms of a limited set of fundamental or 'primitive' relations. Two main classes of relations between concepts have been established empirically and appear to be common to many kinds of subject statements, including indicative sentences in natural language, terms organised as networks in thesauri and classification schedules, sequences of terms in pre-coordinated indexes, etc. †:

Grammatical relations

- Predicative *(to be)*
- Possessive *(to have)*
- Active *(to do)*
- Locative *(to occur at/in)*

Logical relations

- Coordination *(and)*
- Disjunction *(or)*
- Negation *(not)*

Relations comprising the class labelled as 'logical' are probably familiar as the Boolean functions commonly used to link indexing terms in on-line searches. Only one of these is represented explicitly by codes or operators in PRECIS: the *and* relationship links not only coordinate concepts (operators 'f' and 'g'), but also coordinate themes (indicated by the theme codes 'x' and 'y'). The grammatical relations occur at various points in the system, and have already been encountered among examples in Chapters 2 to 7, not only in index strings and entries, but also in references extracted from the thesaurus:

— the *to be* relationship links a genus to its species. This applies equally to the true generic relationship usually handled by the thesaurus (e.g. All rats *are* rodents), and also to concepts linked by the quasi-generic relationship expressed by the operator 'q'. For example,

---

† Since at least the time of the Ancient Greeks, classificationists and philosophers have proposed various schemata of basic concept types and fundamental relationships. Some of the relationships found in these systems do not occur in indexing. Others can be reduced, for practical purposes, to the more primitive relations considered above.

the following string:

(1) pets
(q) snakes

- expresses the author's view that at least some snakes *are* pets.

— a *to be* relationship also links a compound term to its focus. For example, 'skimmed milk' *is* a kind of 'milk', just as 'steel containers' *are* 'containers'.

— the *to have* relationship links wholes to their parts or properties. As noted earlier, this relationship is sometimes handled by a reference extracted from the thesaurus, e.g.

Vascular system
See also
Arteries

More often, however, it is handled within a string and indicated by the operator 'p', e.g.

(1) teachers
(p) career prospects

Some examples of strings have contained actions *(to do)* and locations *(to locate)*; these are covered more fully in later chapters.

The fact that the number of roles expressed by the operators exceeds the number of underlying relationships can be attributed mainly to the reciprocal nature of all relationships. A relationship must, by definition, link at least two concepts, each of which generally assumes a different role. Most of the basic relations are capable of linking only *pairs* of concepts, one on each side of the relation:

— *To be* can link: (i) a broader and narrower concept; (ii) the terms comprising a synonym pair (known as the *preferred term* and *non-preferred term*).

— *To have* links a possessed concept (part or property) with its possessor.

— *To locate* links a located concept with its environment.

— the logical *and* relationship links concepts as coordinated pairs. This remains logically true even if a coordinate block contains more than two terms.

The *to do* relationship (involving an action) is different, insofar as it can interrelate varying numbers of concepts depending upon the class to which the action itself belongs. For example, an intransitive action, such as 'hibernation' or 'sleep', can be linked only to its performer; it cannot involve an object or instrument in the usual sense. This should be contrasted to an action such as 'repair', which can involve two or more other concepts, each possessing a different role. We can see this in a sentence such as 'John used a wrench to repair the refrigerator for Mary', which contains concepts with roles as follows:

'repair' = *action*

'refrigerator' = *patient (direct object)*

'Mary' = *beneficiary (indirect object)*

'John' = *agent*

'wrench' = *instrument*

Despite the apparent diversity of these roles, they can all be seen as surface manifestations of a single underlying *to do* relationship. They would be handled in PRECIS by selecting appropriate operators and arranging the terms as a sequence, or *operator pattern*, typical of the actions belonging to this class. Other classes of action call for different operator patterns. Some are indicated by their own operators ('s', 't' and 'u') and generate special formats described in later chapters.

These basic relations begin to acquire more than a purely theoretical interest when we note that three of the common grammatical relations (*be*, *have*, *do*) seem to vary in what might be called their *relational strengths*. This can be represented by the diagram:

Be > Have > Do

- which indicates that *be* is stronger than *have*, and *have* is stronger than *do*. 'Strength', in this context, refers to a system of implied priorities among these relations: one that is capable of throwing light on certain aspects of index use, and also helps to explain some indexing procedures.

It was suggested (p 14) that the order of terms in a PRECIS entry, and their assignment to three basic positions (the lead, qualifier and display) allows a user to approach a sequence of entries in a step-by-step fashion, testing each entry in turn for relevance/non-relevance. This explanation can now be reinforced by referring to the part played by relational priorities in conveying a subject to the user. An explanation along these lines seems particularly necessary when an entry consists of adjacent nouns or noun phrases separated by punctuation marks but lacking any of the adjuncts, such as prepositions, which function as relational clues in natural language. This would apply to an entry such as the following:

Women. Teachers

It is suggested that a reader encountering this entry is more likely to perceive its meaning as 'Teachers who *are* women' (*to be*) rather than 'Teachers who *teach* women' (*to do*). Similarly, the entry:

Costs. Teaching

— is likely, at a first reading, to be interpreted as 'Costs *of* teaching' (*to have*) rather than 'Teaching the subject of costs' (*to do*). It is realised that a user who approaches an index with a subject such as 'Teaching the subject of costs' already in mind would probably register a hit when encountering the entry shown above. This kind of relational confusion associated with users' expectations accounts for many of the false drops (and also the frustration) reported by subscribers to on-line systems where terms used as retrieval keys are linked only by the logical relations (*and, or, not*), without reference, whether stated or implied, to their grammatical relations.

A recognition of these implied priorities is, in fact, built into the programs used to generate PRECIS entries, to the extent that some of the sub-routines are executed in a pre-determined order based on these priorities to ensure that terms are organised into entries which match, as closely as possible, the user's expectations. We can illustrate this by looking ahead to an example used in Chapter 11, where all three grammatical relations intersect within a single string. The following subject occurs as Example 8 on p 150-151:

Subject: Software packages for microcomputer systems applied to school administration

String: (1) schools
(2) administration $w of
(s) applications $v of $w in
(3) computer systems $31 micro
(p) software packages

What might be called a clash of relational priorities occurs when the focal component of the performer term, i.e. 'computer systems' (coded '3'), is considered as a lead †. The computer then faces a 'choice' among three different procedures for deciding which term or phrase should be selected as the first component of the display. Each of these sub-routines deals with a single relational situation; two have already been described; the third is covered in a later chapter, but is summarised below:

1. A familiar routine associated with the standard format calls for the display to start with the name of a dependent element (coded 'p', 'q' or 'r') when its context-establishing term appears in the lead. This procedure, described on p 75, would favour the choice of 'software packages'.

2. Another routine is associated with the differencing codes (see Chapter 4). This favours the choice of the full form of a compound term (e.g. 'microcomputer systems') as the first component of the display when only part of the term (e.g. 'computer systems') appears in the lead.

3. A third basis for choice is associated with a special formatting procedure known as the *predicate transformation* (described in Chapter 10). This is applied whenever the name of a performer (e.g. 'computer systems', coded '3') appears in the lead. The computer then checks the operator assigned to the next preceding term in the string; if this indicates an action (coded '2', 's', 't' or 'u') the action term is printed

---

† For the sake of demonstration, only this element has been marked as a lead in the string above. The full set of entries that would be generated from this string is shown on p 151.

at the start of the display — it is not shunted into the qualifier, as with the standard format. This would favour the choice of 'applications' (operator 's'), followed by any components linked to this term by upward-reading connectives, giving the phrase 'Applications in administration of schools'.

Each of these procedures can be seen as the computer's response to a specific relational situation identified by a characteristic pattern of operators. These different situations can themselves now be explained in terms of the primitive relations considered above. These relations are marked as insertions in the string below:

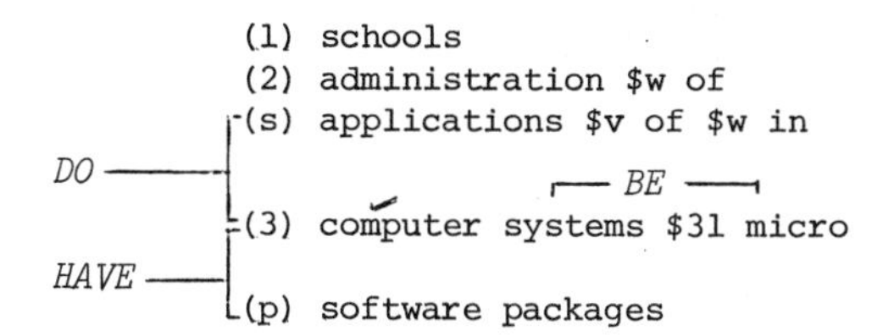

Following the system of inbuilt priorities considered earlier, the subroutines in the program are applied in the order:

1. Complete the differenced term *(to be)*
2. Select the dependent element *(to have)*
3. Apply the predicate transformation *(to do)*.

This generates the entry:

Computer systems
 Microcomputer systems. Software packages. Applications in administration of schools

Experiments have been conducted using different priority values, but these generate outputs that seem to be less idiomatic, if not less comprehensible, than the entry seen above, e.g.

*Computer systems
 Software packages. Microcomputer systems. Applications in administration of schools

— where the order is *Have-Be-Do*, or:

*Computer systems
 Applications in administration of schools. Microcomputer systems. Software packages

— where the order is *Do-Be-Have*.

Most languages allow some flexibility at the output stage, to the extent that a given idea can frequently be expressed by more than one surface form. On a purely structural level, these different forms can often be seen as apparent shifts in the basic grammatical relations considered above. For example, the notion conveyed by the active sentence 'The boy *admires* the teacher' (*to do*), can also be expressed by sentences such as:

— The teacher *has* the boy's admiration *(to have)*

— The boy *is* the teacher's admirer *(to be)*.

These outputs emphasise different concepts, but they would generally be regarded as referring to a single phenomenon. The same applies to entries in pre-coordinated indexes: a given subject can sometimes be expressed by more than one sequence of terms. For example, the topic 'Employment of unskilled personnel in the steel industries' can be represented in PRECIS by the strings:

(a) (1) steel industries ⎤ — *Have*
(p) unskilled personnel ⎦⎤ — *Do*
(2) employment ⎦

(b) (1) unskilled personnel ⎤
(2) employment $v by $w of ⎥ — *Do*
(3) steel industries ⎦

Like the sentences above, these strings also convey different emphases; the second tends to stress the action 'employment' *(to do)* without explicating the possessive relationship that links 'steel industries' to their 'unskilled personnel'. It might be possible to detect such a bias in some of the documents we index; nevertheless, we can regard the meanings of the two strings seen above as sufficiently close to justify choosing one *or* the other as a standard approach when indexing documents on this topic. Where a choice of this kind exists, it will usually be found that a string based more obviously upon a relatively strong *have* or *be* relationship, such as (a) above, leads to entries that are clearer and less prone to misinterpretation.

Earlier examples have shown that potential ambiguities can sometimes be avoided by choosing appropriate terms and arranging them in such a way that a latent *be* and/or *have* relationship is made more explicit. When the topic 'Soaps in supermarkets' *(have)* was considered on p 85, it was anticipated that the entry:

*Soaps. Supermarkets

— might be misinterpreted as 'Soaps *for use in* supermarkets' *(do)*. The correct relationship was then made explicit by inserting the name of a quasi-generic group *(be)* which explained, in effect, the *have* relationship between 'supermarkets' and 'soaps':

(1) supermarkets ⎤ — *Have*
(p) merchandise ⎦⎤ — *Be*
(q) soaps ⎦

A similar procedure was applied to an example on p 97, where it was anticipated that the heading:

*Serials. National libraries

— might be misinterpreted as 'Serials *describing* national libraries' *(do)*, rather than the intended subject 'Serials *in* national libraries' *(have)*. Again, the intended topic was brought out by inserting the name of a quasi-generic group which explicated the *have* relationship between 'national libraries' and 'serials':

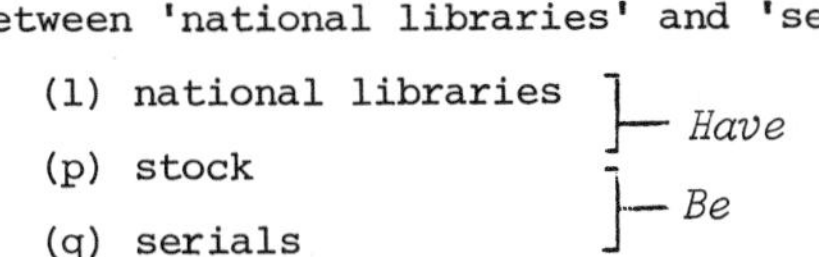

The examples above show strings adapted to produce an apparent shift in a basic relationship at the output stage. Variations in output can also occur when working within a single basic relationship. For example, the subject 'Women teachers', based on a clear *to be* relationship between the term as a whole and its focal noun, can be indexed in three different ways, each of which is equally valid in terms of PRECIS logic.

(a) The subject can be factored into two separate terms:

String: (1) teachers] — *Be*
(q) women]

Entries: Teachers
Women

Women. Teachers

(b) It can be handled as a compound term, with the focus and difference coded separately:

Be

String: (1) teachers $21 women

Entries: Teachers
Women teachers

Women teachers

(c) The compound term can be written 'straight through' (i.e. without factoring or differencing):

Be

String: (1) women teachers

Entry: Women teachers

This entry could then be supported by a reference extracted from the thesaurus:

Teachers
See also
Women teachers

None of these can be rated as the more correct, nor even the preferred, technique. The choice of one procedure rather than another is largely determined by the needs of the community of users served by the index; it is not prescribed by the indexing system *per se*:

— The strings at (a) and (b) both offer 'teachers' and 'women' as direct access points, but the former would generally be rated as the 'safer' approach. It allows an indexer room to manoeuvre if either concept is encountered at a higher level of specificity in other documents, e.g.

String: (1) teachers $01 part-time
(q) women $21 married

Entries: Teachers
Part-time teachers: Married women

Women. Part-time teachers
Married women

Married women. Part-time teachers

This approach might therefore be adopted in an index covering all disciplines, where terms in the field of education are encountered, but not to the extent that they become overused.

— The string shown at (b) would be more appropriate when indexing in a limited subject field *outside* the area of education, where educational terms are encountered only occasionally, so they are not likely to be overused, and higher levels of complexity would not be expected.

— The approach shown at (c) is probably more appropriate for a special index in the field of education, where 'teachers' would probably be rated as a heavily-used term. The *See also* reference would then act as an off-loading device.

These different approaches are equally valid from a logical point of view: they all express the same *to be* relationship.

As shown by some of the examples above, a reference to these basic relations can occasionally be useful when testing an indexing decision after it has been taken. It is not suggested, however, that subjects should be checked for their underlying relations (as opposed to the roles of their concepts) during the stage of document analysis. This excursion into theory is offered as an aside for indexers who are interested not only in 'How?' but also 'Why?'. It should be stressed that a knowledge of these underlying relations is not in any sense necessary for the successful application of PRECIS.

Further reading

The concept types discussed in Chapter 7, and the primitive relations considered above, are examined further in:

Austin, Derek. Basic concept classes and primitive relations. *In* Universal classification, subject analysis and ordering systems: Proceedings of the 4th International Study Conference on Classification Research ... Augsburg, 1982, *ed* I Dahlberg. 2 vols. Frankfurt, Indeks Verlag (for FID/CR), 1982. (Vol. 1, p 86-94)

APPENDIX 4. ANSWERS TO EXERCISES

NOTE: After Exercise 2, different choices of leads do not count as 'wrong' answers

---

Exercise 1 (p 44)

(a) (1) children
(2) mental development
(2) assessment

(b) (0) France (NU)
(p) Paris
(1) art galleries

(c) (0) Cornwall
(1) castles (LO)
(q) Pendennis Castle
(6) visitors' guides

Exercise 2 (p 45)

Strings	*Entries*
(a) (1) coal (2) mining (sub 2↑) (2) coal mining (2) operations research	Coal Mining. Operations research Mining. Coal Operations research Operations research. Coal mining
(b) (1) films (2) indexing $w of (2) automation	Films Indexing. Automation Indexing. Films Automation Automation. Indexing of films
(c) (z) (1) offices (x) (p) electronic equipment (y) (2) maintenance (x) (p) stationery (y) (2) purchasing	Offices Electronic equipment. Maintenance Electronic equipment. Offices Maintenance Offices Stationery. Purchasing Stationery. Offices Purchasing Purchasing. Stationery. Offices
Entries produced when common headings cancelled	Offices Electronic equipment. Maintenance Stationery. Purchasing

Answers to exercises (cont)

Exercise 3 (p 73)

	Strings	*Entries*
(a)	(1) coins $21 gold	Coins Gold coins Gold coins

(b)	(1) songs $21 folk $21 English	Songs
		  English folk songs
		Folk songs
		  English folk songs
		English songs
		  English folk songs

(c)	(1) plays $21 one-act	Plays One-act plays One-act plays
(d)	(2) genetics $31 pharmaco	Genetics Pharmacogenetics Pharmacogenetics

(e)	(1) panels $21 reinforced
	$22 fibre $33 glass-
		Panels
		  Glass-fibre reinforced panels
		Reinforced panels
		  Glass-fibre reinforced panels
		Fibre reinforced panels
		  Glass-fibre reinforced panels
		Glass-fibre reinforced panels

(f)	(1) houses $21 manor
	$d 1600-1700
		Houses
		  Manor houses, *1600-1700*
		Manor houses
		  1600-1700

Exercise 4 (p 73)

(i) Differencing can be applied to the following terms:

(a) Decorated porcelain

String: (1) porcelain $21 decorated

Entries: Porcelain
  Decorated porcelain
Decorated porcelain

Answers to exercises (cont)

Exercise 4 (cont)

(c) Public libraries

String: (1) libraries $21 public

Entries: Libraries
  Public libraries

Public libraries

(ii) According to the *Rules of differencing*, the following terms should be factored:

(b) Frog migration

String: (1) frogs
(2) migration

Entries: Frogs
  Migration

Migration. Frogs

(e) Library buildings

String: (1) libraries
(p) buildings

Entries: Libraries
  Buildings

Buildings. Libraries

(iii) The term 'Toy soldiers' contains a syncategorematic adjective, and should not be differenced.

String: (1) toy soldiers

Entry: Toy soldiers

A (weak) case might be made for a supporting reference:

Soldiers
  See also
    Toy soldiers

Exercise 5 (p 90)

	Category 1 (handle by references)	*Category 2 (handle by 'q' in string)*
(a)	Granite/Rocks	Granite/Building materials
(b)	Molasses/Syrups	Molasses/Health foods
(c)	Jewellery/Ornaments	Jewellery/Gifts
(d)	Paintings/Graphic arts	Paintings/Investments
(e)	Maps/Documents	Maps/Teaching aids

Answers to exercises (cont)

Exercise 6 (p 91)

	Strings	*Entries*
(a)	(1) hippies (r) communes (sub 2↑) (1) hippy communes (p) leadership	Hippies Communes. Leadership Communes. Hippies Leadership Leadership. Hippy communes
(b)	(2) management (p) decision making	Management Decision making Decision making. Management
(c)	(0) developing countries (1) milk $21 skimmed (p) prices	Developing countries Skimmed milk. Prices Milk. Developing countries Skimmed milk. Prices Skimmed milk. Developing countries Prices Prices. Skimmed milk. Developing countries
(d)	(1) theatres (p) curtains $21 safety (p) flammability	Theatres Safety curtains. Flammability Curtains. Theatres Safety curtains. Flammability Safety curtains. Theatres Flammability Flammability. Safety curtains. Theatres

---

Exercise 7 (p 91)

Two of the terms in the string ('toy bears' and 'glass eyes') contain syncategorematic adjectives. These should not have been differenced. The subject should be indexed as:

String:	*Entries:*
(1) toy bears (p) glass eyes (2) fastening	Toy bears Glass eyes. Fastening Glass eyes. Toy bears Fastening

A (weak) case might be made for supporting the second entry with the reference:

Eyes
See also
Glass eyes

Answers to exercises (cont)

Exercise 8 (p 100)

Strings

(a) (1) iron $v &
(g) bronze $21 cast
(2) cracking $01 fatigue

Entries

Iron
Fatigue cracking

Bronze
Cast bronze. Fatigue cracking

Cast bronze
Fatigue cracking

Cracking. Iron & cast bronze
Fatigue cracking

(b) (2) occupational therapy
(q) basketry $v &
(g) weaving

Occupational therapy
Basketry & weaving

Basketry. Occupational therapy

Weaving. Occupational therapy

(c) (1) primary schools
(p) students $01 normal $v &
(f) handicapped students
(2) integration

Note: There is no point in marking 'students' twice as a lead (once for each focus) since their displays would be identical

Primary schools
Normal students & handicapped students. Integration

Students. Primary schools
Normal students & handicapped students. Integration

Handicapped students. Primary schools
Normal students & handicapped students. Integration

Integration. Normal students & handicapped students. Primary schools

(d) (1) binoculars $v &
(g) telescopes
(p) lenses
(2) grinding $v &
(g) polishing

Note: This approach is valid, but see the comments following Example 5 (p 87)

Binoculars
Lenses. Grinding & polishing

Telescopes
Lenses. Grinding & polishing

Lenses. Binoculars & telescopes
Grinding & polishing

Grinding. Lenses. Binoculars & telescopes

Polishing. Lenses. Binoculars & telescopes

Answers to exercises (cont)

Exercise 9 (p 121)

	Strings	*Entries*
(a)	(1) granite (2) crystallization	Granite Crystallization Crystallization. Granite
(b)	(1) electric motors $01 heavy-duty (p) bearings $21 steel (2) hardening $21 case	Electric motors Heavy-duty electric motors. Steel bearings. Case hardening Bearings. Heavy-duty electric motors Steel bearings. Case hardening Steel bearings. Heavy-duty electric motors Case hardening Hardening. Steel bearings. Heavy-duty electric motors Case hardening Case hardening. Steel bearings. Heavy-duty electric motors
(c)	(2) lawn tennis (p) volleying	Lawn tennis Volleying Volleying. Lawn tennis
(d)	(1) hospitals (p) patients (2) infection $31 cross- (2) prevention	Hospitals Patients. Cross-infection. Prevention Patients. Hospitals Cross-infection. Prevention Infection. Patients. Hospitals Cross-infection. Prevention Cross-infection. Patients. Hospitals Prevention
(e)	(1) building materials (q) concrete $21 ready-mixed (2) delivery $w of (2) timing	Building materials Ready-mixed concrete. Delivery. Timing Concrete. Building materials Ready-mixed concrete. Delivery. Timing Ready-mixed concrete. Building materials Delivery. Timing Timing. Delivery of ready-mixed concrete. Building materials

Answers to exercises (cont)

Exercise 10 (p 130)

	Strings	*Entries*
(a)	(1) Kampuchea (p) jungles	Kampuchea Jungles Jungles. Kampuchea

(b)	(0) Kampuchea
	(1) temples $21 Buddhist
		Kampuchea
		  Buddhist temples
		
		Temples. Kampuchea
		  Buddhist temples
		
		Buddhist temples. Kampuchea

(c)	(0) Kampuchea
	(p) jungles
	(1) temples $21 Buddhist
		Kampuchea
		  Jungles. Buddhist temples
		
		Jungles. Kampuchea
		  Buddhist temples
		
		Temples. Jungles. Kampuchea
		  Buddhist temples
		
		Buddhist temples. Jungles. Kampuchea

(d)	(1) Italy (2) balance of payments	Italy Balance of payments Balance of payments. Italy

(e)	(0) European Economic Community countries
	(2) television $21 commercial
		European Economic Community countries
		  Commercial television
		
		Television.
		  countries
		  Commercial television
		
		Commercial televsion. European Economic Community countries

---

Exercise 11 (p 146)

	Strings	*Entries*

(a)	(1) aircraft
	(2) hijacking $v by $w of
	(3) terrorists
		Aircraft
		  Hijacking by terrorists
		
		Hijacking. Aircraft
		  By terrorists
		
		Terrorists
		  Hijacking of aircraft

Answers to exercises (cont)

Exercise 11 (cont)

(b) (1) plants (2) assimilation $v of $w by (3) ammonium	Plants Assimilation of ammonium Assimilation. Plants Of ammonium Ammonium Assimilation by plants
(c) (1) locomotives $21 steam (2) preservation $w of (2) financial assistance	Locomotives Steam locomotives. Preservation Financial assistance Steam locomotives Preservation. Financial assistance Financial assistance. Preservation of steam locomotives
(d) (2) singing $v by (3) choirs $21 male voice	Singing By male voice choirs Choirs Male voice choirs. Singing Male voice choirs Singing
(e) (1) handicapped persons $21 mentally (2) care $v by $w of (3) local authorities	Handicapped persons Mentally handicapped persons. Care by local authorities Mentally handicapped persons Care by local authorities Local authorities Care of mentally handicapped persons
(f) (2) painting by numbers	Painting by numbers
(g) (1) children (2) dreaming (2) research	Children Dreaming. Research Dreaming. Children Research

Note: It is not necessary to insert a blank field after 'dreaming', or to add a connective to 'dreaming', if 'research' is not marked as a lead.

Answers to exercises (cont)

Exercise 11 (cont)

(h) (1) refineries $21 oil
(2) location $w of
(2)
(3) environmental factors

Refineries
Oil refineries. Location. Environmental factors

Oil refineries
Location. Environmental factors

Environmental factors. Location of oil refineries

Exercise 12 (p 158)

(a) (0) France
(1) civil servants
(3) pensions $w of
(s) effects $v of $w on
(3) inflation

France
Civil servants. Pensions. Effects of inflation

Civil servants. France
Pensions. Effects of inflation

Pensions. Civil servants. France
Effects of inflation

Inflation. France
Effects on pensions of civil servants

(b) (1) firms $21 small
(2) management
(s) participation $v of $w in
(3) employees

Firms
Small firms. Management. Participation of employees

Small firms
Management. Participation of employees

Management. Small firms
Participation of employees

Employees. Small firms
Participation in management

(c) (1) multinational companies
(2) investment $v by $w in
(sub 2↓) (3) Swiss banks
(0) Switzerland
(1) banks

Multinational companies
Investment by Swiss banks

Investment. Multinational companies
By Swiss banks

Switzerland
Banks. Investment in multinational companies

Banks. Switzerland
Investment in multinational companies

Answers to exercises (cont)

Exercise 12 (cont)

(d) (1) mineral resources
(2) prospecting $w for
(s) use $v of $w in
(3) satellites $21 artificial

Mineral resources
  Prospecting. Use of artificial satellites

Prospecting. Mineral resources
  Use of artificial satellites

Satellites
  Artificial satellites. Use in prospecting for mineral resources

Artificial satellites
  Use in prospecting for mineral resources

(e) (1) local authorities
(p) officers
(p) accountability $21 public

Local authorities
  Officers. Public accountability

Officers. Local authorities
  Public accountability

Accountability. Officers. Local authorities
  Public accountability

Public accountability. Officers. Local authorities

(f) (0) West Germany
(1) cars $21 Japanese
(2) sales
(s) effects $v of $w on
(3) advertising

West Germany
  Japanese cars. Sales. Effects of advertising

Cars. West Germany
  Japanese cars. Sales. Effects of advertising

Japanese cars. West Germany
  Sales. Effects of advertising

Sales. Japanese cars. West Germany
  Effects of advertising

Advertising. Japanese cars. West Germany
  Effects on sales

Note: A $w connective was not attached to 'sales' in this case to ensure that 'Japanese cars' appears as the first term in the qualifier (the 'object' position) not only in the entry under 'sales', but also in the entry under 'advertising'. Although 'advertising' was coded '3' in the string (indicating its role as performer of the 'effects'), it refers to a transitive action taking 'cars' as its object.

Answers to exercises (cont)

Exercise 12 (cont)

(g) (1) printing industries (2) automation (s) attitudes $v of $w to (3) trades unions	Printing industries Automation. Attitudes of trades unions Automation. Printing industries Attitudes of trades unions Attitudes. Trades unions. Printing industries To automation Trades unions. Printing industries Attitudes to automation

Note: These entries could be supported by references such as:

Industries
See also
Printing industries

Personnel
See also
Trades unions

Exercise 13 (p 166)

(a) (0) Japan (1) engineers (p) self-image (t) compared with (p) social status	Japan Engineers. Self-image *compared with* social status Engineers. Japan Self-image *compared with* social status Self-image. Engineers. Japan *compared with* social status Social status. Engineers. Japan *compared with* self-image
(b) (1) Christian doctrine (t) $v expounded by $w expounding (sub 3↓) (3) psychoanalytical theories of Jung, C.G. (2) psychoanalysis (s) theories $v of $w of (3) Jung, C. G.	Christian doctrine *expounded by* psychoanalytical theories of Jung, C. G. Psychoanalysis Theories of Jung, C. G. *expounding* Christian doctrine Jung, C. G. Theories of psychoanalysis *expounding* Christian doctrine

Answers to exercises (cont)

Exercise 13 (cont)

(c) (1) universities
(p) students
(2) academic achievement
(t) related to
(p) motivation

Universities
Students. Academic achievement *related to* motivation

Students. Universities
Academic achievement *related to* motivation

Academic achievement. Students. Universities
related to motivation

Motivation. Students. Universities
related to academic achievement

(d) (1) plants
(2) growth
(p) rate
(sub 2↑) (p) growth rate
$w of
(s) effects $v of $w on
(sub 2↓) (3) soil humidity
(1) soil
(p) humidity

Plants
Growth. Rate. Effects of soil humidity

Growth. Plants
Rate. Effects of soil humidity

Soil
Humidity. Effects on growth rate of plants

Humidity. Soil
Effects on growth rate of plants

Note: The subject statement on p 166 simulates a title where an author sets out to convey an element of scientific caution through the use of a phrase such as 'relationship between' or 'related to'. When dealing with a subject of this kind, however, the indexer should be prepared to indicate a causal relationship (operator '2' or 's') rather than an author-attributed association (operator 't'). It is unlikely that 'soil humidity' and 'growth rate of plants' are associated mainly in the mind of the author. Their relationship can be seen instead as a natural phenomenon studied by the author where one of the concepts named in the core ('soil humidity') functioned as the performer. The relationship should then be classed as a one-way action which differs in kind from the vaguely reciprocal relationship expressed in the previous string (Answer 13c) by the use of:

(t) related to

Ascribing causality in this way does not amount to an assertion that the effect actually occurred — only that it was studied.

Answers to exercises (cont)

Exercise 14 (p 183)

(a) (1) industries
(2) management
(s) role $v of $w in
(3) women
(4) feminist viewpoints

Industries
Management. Role of women — *Feminist viewpoints*

Management. Industries
Role of women — *Feminist viewpoints*

Women. Industries
Role in management — *Feminist viewpoints*

Feminist viewpoints
Industries. Management. Role of women

(b) (1) engravings $21 wood $d 1900-
(6) collectors' guides

Engravings
Wood engravings, *1900- — Collectors' guides*

Wood engravings
1900- — Collectors' guides

Collectors' guides
Wood engravings, *1900-*

(c) (1) cities
(p) atmosphere
(2) pollution $v by $w of
(3) lead
(2) measurement
(5) study regions
(q) Illinois
(p) Chicago

Cities
Atmosphere. Pollution by lead. Measurement — *Study regions: Illinois. Chicago*

Atmosphere. Cities
Pollution by lead. Measurement — *Study regions: Illinois. Chicago*

Pollution. Atmosphere. Cities
By lead. Measurement — *Study regions: Illinois. Chicago*

Lead. Cities
Pollution of atmosphere. Measurement — *Study regions: Illinois. Chicago*

Illinois. *Study regions*
Cities. Atmosphere. Pollution by lead. Measurement — *Study regions: Illinois. Chicago*

Chicago. *Illinois. Study regions*
Cities. Atmosphere. Pollution by lead. Measurement

Answers to exercises (cont)

Exercise 14 (cont)

(d) (2) electronics
    (6) dictionaries

Electronics
— *Dictionaries*

Dictionaries
Electronics

Note: In this example, 'dictionaries' was marked as lead for demonstration purposes. The choice of leads in these cases is usually determined by local policies. For example, a policy might require entries under general dictionaries (related to languages), but not under special dictionaries (related to subjects).

(e) (2) semantics
    (6) librarianship $01 for
    (6) programmed instructions

Semantics
— *For librarianship* — *Programmed instructions*

Librarianship
Semantics — *For librarianship* — *Programmed instructions*

Exercise 15 (p 196)

(a) *String:* $z11030$a food
$zp0030$a additives $w to
$zq1030$a protein $21 soy
$zp1030$a nutritional value

Entries: Food
Additives: Soy protein. Nutritional value

Protein. Additives to food
Soy protein. Nutritional value

Soy protein. Additives to food
Nutritional value

Nutritional value. Soy protein. Additives to food

(b) *String:* $z11010$a sailing ships
$zq1030$c Mary Celeste $i (Ship)
$zp1030$a crew
$z20030$a disappearance
$z60030$a dramatizations
$z61030$a videotape recordings

Entries: Sailing ships
Mary Celeste *(Ship)*. Crew. Disappearance — *Dramatizations* — *Videotape recordings*

Answers to exercises (cont)

Exercise 15 (cont)

Mary Celeste *(Ship)*
Crew. Disappearance — *Dramatizations* — *Videotape recordings*

Crew. Mary Celeste *(Ship)*
Disappearance — *Dramatizations* — *Videotape recordings*

Videotape recordings
Sailing ships. Mary Celeste *(Ship)*. Crew. Disappearance — *Dramatizations*

(c) *String:* $z11030$d Asia $21 South-east
$zp1030$a rural regions
$zp1030$a society
$zs0030$a role $v of $w in
$z31030$a women
$z20320$a role of women in society
$zs0030$a effects $v of $w on
$z31030$a economic development

Entries: Asia
South-east Asia. Rural regions. Society. Role of women. Effects of economic development

South-east Asia
Rural regions. Society. Role of women. Effects of economic development

Rural regions. South-east Asia
Society. Role of women. Effects of economic development

Society. Rural regions. South-east Asia
Role of women. Effects of economic development

Women. Rural regions. South-east Asia
Role in society. Effects of economic development

Economic development. Rural regions. South-east Asia
Effects on role of women in society

Exercise 16 (p 197)

(a) Weather
Forecasting. Use of artificial satellites

Forecasting. Weather
Use of artificial satellites

Satellites
Artificial satellites. Use in weather forecasting

Artificial satellites
Use in weather forecasting

Answers to exercises (cont)

Exercise 16 (cont)

(b) Schools
Students. Confidential records. Access. Rights of parents

Students. Schools
Confidential records. Access. Rights of parents

Records. Students. Schools
Confidential records. Access. Rights of parents

Parents. Students. Schools
Rights of access to confidential records on students

(c) Developing countries
Welfare work *compared with* welfare work in developed countries

Welfare work. Developing countries
compared with welfare work in developed countries

Developed countries
Welfare work *compared with* welfare work in developing countries

Welfare work. Developed countries
compared with welfare work in developing countries

Exercise 17 (p 231)

(a) #RI# 0027790 $a Bears#

#RI# 0034584 $a Soft toys#

#RI# 0549916 $a Teddy bears $n 0027790 $o 0034584#

(b) #RI# 0168491 $a Probabilistic models#

#RI# 0009024 $a Mathematical models#

#RI# 0056421 $a Stochastic models $m 0168491 $o 0009024#

(c) #RI# 0067962 $a Office machinery#

#RI# 0022829 $a Sound recording equipment#

#RI# 0067970 $a Dictation machines $o 0067962 $o 0022829#

Exercise 18 (p 232)

(a) Civil Service Commission *(United States) See* United States. *Civil Service Commission*

Answers to exercises (cont)

Exercise 18 (cont)

(b) Propositions. Logic
See also
Hypotheses

(c) Biological rhythms
See also
Circadian rhythms

Diurnal rhythms *See* Circadian rhythms

Exercise 19 (p 248)

(a)

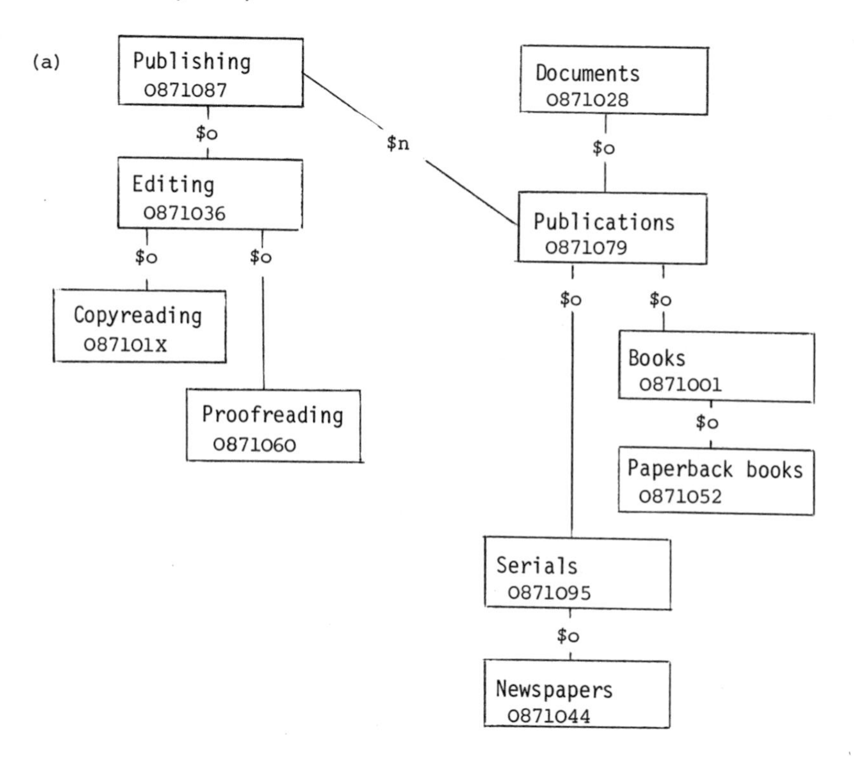

Note: The associative relationship linking 'Publishing' and 'Publications' could justify a reference in each direction. A special technique for constructing these two-way references is described in Chapter 18.

Answers to exercises (cont)

Exercise 19 (cont)

(b)

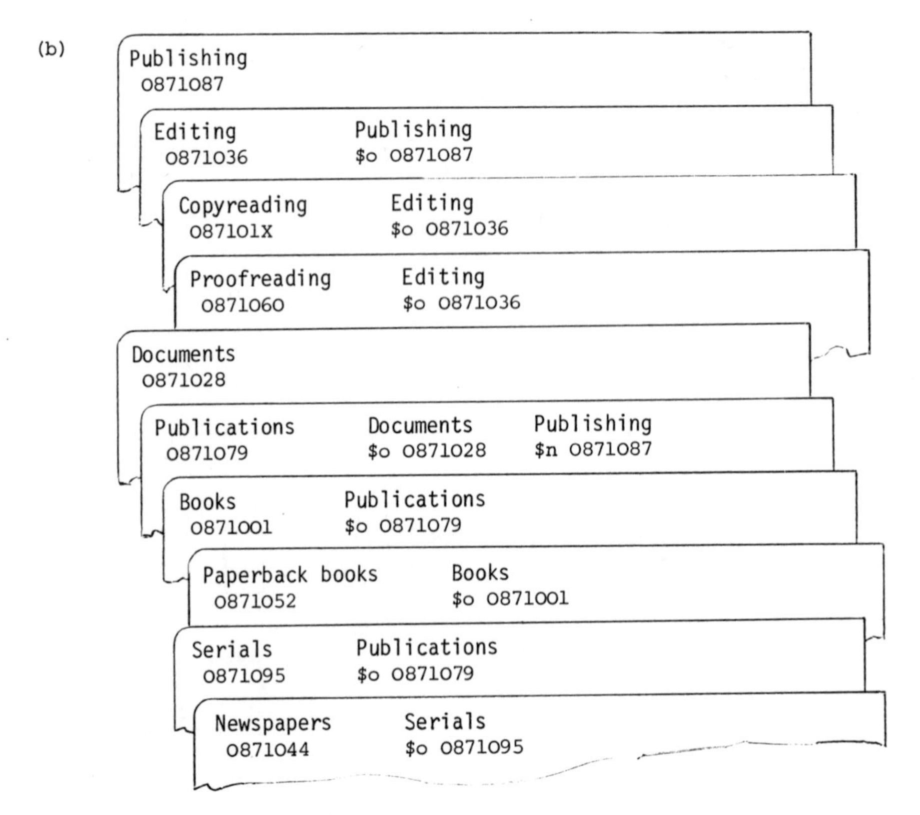

Note: Other input orders will also be capable of satisfying the validation check described on p 238.

Exercise 20

One-step reference produced by $m

Publishing
See also
Publications

By-pass references produced by $o:

Publishing
See also
Proofreading

Editing
See also
Proofreading

Answers to exercises (cont)

Exercise 20 (cont)

Documents
See also
Newspapers

Publications
See also
Newspapers

Serials
See also
Newspapers

Note: Two of these references contain common source terms and would therefore be merged at output:

Publishing
See also
Proofreading
Publications

APPENDIX 5. ALGORITHMS FOR ENTRY CONSTRUCTION AND VALIDATION OF STRINGS

Notes and definitions

1. For the sake of economy, the strings used as examples in these algorithms are written in the conventional form adopted throughout the main part of the *Manual*. For example, operators are written within parentheses, lead foci are marked by √, etc. A note above each algorithm defines the numbered position in a full manipulation code that is occupied by the character controlling that algorithm. These numbers refer to the following diagrams:

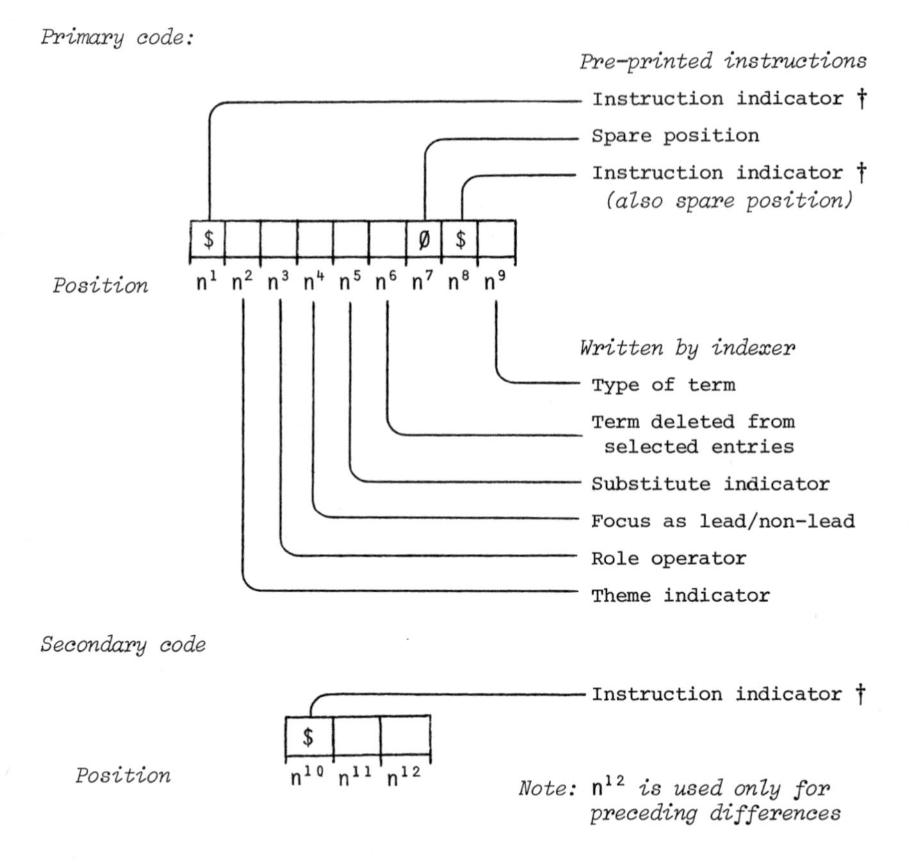

2. The following general definitions apply throughout the algorithms:

— *focus:* the datum, which may consist of one or more words, immediately following a primary manipulation code. Note that a primary code can be followed immediately by another primary code (as opposed to data). This

---

† See Footnote on p 307 concerning the status of the $ symbol as an instruction indicator.

would occur, for example, if the string contained a *blank field insert* (see p 33).

— *term:* a focus plus its differences (if present).

— *downward-reading* (or *earlier-to-later*), and *upward-reading* (or *later-to-earlier*): the direction in which a string is read when its terms are selected and assembled as part of an entry.

Terms that occur with special meanings in particular algorithms are defined in the notes preceding those algorithms. Further definitions are given in the introduction to the *Validation checks* on p 382.

3. The strings used as examples in the algorithms were selected or devised to illustrate the working of this part of the system. They do not necessarily represent the most satisfactory approach to the indexing of these topics. This applies especially to the choice of some leads. It has not been possible to illustrate every step in every algorithm, although each step is explained as a procedure.

4. Some of the algorithms generate outputs that have not been fully described in the narrative part of the *Manual*. For example, Algorithm 8 produces semi-colons, rather than commas, between the terms in a coordinate block if one of the terms in the block is a proper name (n^9 = c *or* d). These situations occur relatively infrequently in practice, and the working of the algorithm does not affect the indexer's approach to the analysis and coding of the subject.

5. Algorithms are introduced in the following order (page numbers are given in parentheses):

This order has been chosen to ensure, as far as possible, that if a step in one algorithm is re-usable in another, the re-usable algorithm is printed first. This is not necessarily (except by coincidence) the order in which the algorithms would be handled by an analyst/programmer.

6. Thanks are due to Mr Fred Smith, of Loughborough University, for checking the algorithms and offering useful insights and suggestions.

ALGORITHM 1. FOCUS IN LEAD

Notes:

(a) The need to print a focus in the lead is indicated by a number in position n^4:

0 = Not printed in lead

1 = Printed in lead.

(b) In the examples in this and the following algorithms, the need for a lead on the focus is indicated by the convention √ written over the term.

Steps	Example
	(1) cameras √ (p) lenses √ (2) assembly
1. Check the number in position n^4. If this is 1, print the focus in the lead, selecting a distinctive typeface †.	Cameras Lenses
2. Assign the rest of the terms in the string to parts of the entry determined by the operator(s) in position n^3 (covered in later algorithms).	Cameras Lenses. Assembly Lenses. Cameras Assembly

† This may be bold face, upper case, etc.

ALGORITHM 2. IDENTIFICATION OF PERMITTED/EXCLUDED TERMS

Notes:

(a) *Permitted terms* are printed in an appropriate part of the entry when an earlier or later term in the string appears in the lead. The selection of permitted terms, and the suppression of *excluded terms*, is controlled by a number in the range 0 to 3 written in position n^6. Each of these numbers carries two instructions:

	Print in an entry under an earlier term?	*Print in an entry under a later term?*
Code 0	No	No
1	Yes	No
2	No	Yes
3	Yes	Yes

(b) In the examples of strings in this and later algorithms, these instructions are indicated by the following conventions written after a term:

(LO) = *Lead only* = Code 0
(NU) = *Not up* = Code 1
(ND) = *Not down* = Code 2

No convention is needed for Code 3, which represents the 'normal' case.

(c) A term coded 0 in position n^6 can *only* appear in the lead. A string in therefore invalid if this coding is used when the number in n^4 = 0 *and* the term does not contain one or more lead differences.

Steps	Examples
	a) (0) London (1) museums (LO) (q) British Museum b) (1) Italy (NU) (p) Rome (2) social life
1. When a term is due to appear in the lead: (a) suppress any *later* term coded 0 or 2; (b) suppress any *earlier* term coded 0 or 1.	a) London British Museum Museums. London British Museum British Museum. London b) Italy Rome. Social life Rome Social life Social life. Rome

ALGORITHM 3. PRECEDING DIFFERENCES

Notes:

(a) The following definitions apply in this algorithm:

Space-generating difference: a difference (e.g. an adjective) separated by a space from the next component of the term as output.
Example: 'leather' in the compound term 'leather handbags'.

Close-up difference: a difference conjoined to the next component of the term as output (i.e. without an intervening space).
Examples: (i) 'hand' in the compound term 'handbags';
(ii) 'arc-' in the compound term 'arc-welding'.

Level: the 'semantic distance' of a difference from its focus:
(i) the focus can be treated as a component at *Level 0;*
(ii) a difference at *Level 1* directly modifies the focus.
Example: 'polystyrene' in the compound term 'polystyrene tiles'.
(iii) a difference at *Level 2* modifies a level 1 difference; it is not related directly to the focus.
Example: 'expanded' in the term 'expanded polystyrene tiles'.
Up to nine levels of differencing are allowed. A term can contain more than one difference on the same level.

(b) Differences that precede their foci in entries are identified by secondary codes in positions n^{10}, n^{11} and n^{12}. These codes are composed as follows:
n^{10} = $: the mark identifying an instruction.
n^{11} = a number in the range 0 to 3 taken from the grid:

	Space-generating	*Close-up*
Non-lead	0	1
Lead	2	3

n^{12} = a number in the range 1 to 9 specifying the level of the difference that follows the code in the string.

(c) If leads are needed under more than one part of a compound term, or under the focus alone, parts of the term are coded and input in the reverse of output order. The term is then assembled for printing by selecting its parts from the string in right-to-left order.

(d) A stage of generalisation is introduced into this algorithm at Step 3. This could have been introduced at Step 2, but was deferred for the sake of more explicit explanations.

Steps	Examples
	a) (1) railways (p) bridges $31 foot $21 concrete $02 reinforced $22 lightweight (p) safety
	b) (2) recidivism (2) (3) factors $21 social $32 psycho
	c) (1) pipes $21 steel $22 welded $33 arc-

Steps	Examples
1. If the focus of the term is marked as a lead ($n^4 = 1$):	
(a) print the focus.	a) Bridges b) Pipes
(b) assemble the term by reading its parts R to L. Print the whole of the term as the 1st component of the display.	a) Bridges Lightweight reinforced concrete footbridges c) Pipes Arc-welded steel pipes
(c) assign any earlier or later terms to appropriate positions.	a) Bridges. Railways Lightweight reinforced concrete footbridges. Safety
2. Select 1st level difference(s) as lead(s):	
(a) read the term in the string from L to R. Identify any part(s) where $n^{11}>1$ and $n^{12} = 1$.	a) *$31 foot* *$21 concrete* b) *$21 social* c) *$21 steel*
(b) print the part identified at the previous step as the 1st component of the lead. If $n^{11} = 2$, print a space. Complete the lead by adding the focus.	a) Footbridges Concrete bridges b) Social factors c) Steel pipes
(c) if the lead does not contain the whole of the term, repeat Step 1(b).	a) Footbridges Lightweight reinforced concrete footbridges Concrete bridges Lightweight reinforced concrete footbridges b) Social factors Psychosocial factors c) Steel pipes Arc-welded steel pipes
(d) repeat Step 1(c).	a) Footbridges. Railways Lightweight reinforced concrete footbridges. Safety Concrete bridges. Railways Lightweight reinforced concrete footbridges. Safety b) Social factors. Recidivism Psychosocial factors

Steps	Examples
3. Select 2nd and higher level difference(s) as lead(s):	
(a) read the term in the string from L to R. Identify any part(s) where $n^{11}>1$ and $n^{12}>1$.	a) *\$22 lightweight* b) *\$32 psycho* c) *\$22 welded* *\$33 arc-*
(b) print the part identified at the previous step as the 1st component of the lead. If $n^{11} = 2$, print a space (symbolized as □).	a) Lightweight□ b) Psycho c) Welded□ Arc-
(c) starting from the part printed at the previous step, read the term in the string R to L. Identify the nearest part on the next lower level (subtracting 1 from the number in n^{12}).	a) *\$21 concrete ... \$22 lightweight* b) *\$21 social \$32 psycho* c) *\$21 steel \$22 welded* *\$22 welded \$33 arc-*
(d) print this part as the next component of the lead. If $n^{11} = 0$ or 2, print a space.	a) Lightweight concrete□ Psychosocial□ Welded steel□ Arc-welded□
(e) check the level (n^{12}) of the part just printed:	
– if $n^{12} = 1$, print the focus.	a) Lightweight concrete bridges b) Psychosocial factors c) Welded steel pipes
– if $n^{12}>1$, repeat Steps 3(c) to 3(e).	c) Arc-welded steel pipes
(f) if the lead does not contain the whole of the term, repeat Step 1(b).	a) Lightweight concrete bridges Lightweight reinforced concrete footbridges c) Welded steel pipes Arc-welded steel pipes
(g) repeat Step 1(c).	a) Lightweight concrete bridges. Railways Lightweight reinforced concrete footbridges. Safety b) Psychosocial factors. Recidivism

ALGORITHM 4. PRECEDING DIFFERENCES ON LEAD-ONLY TERMS

Notes:

(a) A lead-only term is usually written in output order and identified by the following pattern of numbers within the primary manipulation code:

$n^4 = 1$: focus as lead;
$n^5 = 0$: the term is not a substitute;
$n^6 = 0$: the term should be suppressed from entries under other terms.

An example is shown in Algorithm 2, p 343.

(b) In some circumstances, indexers require an entry under part of a compound term, and the whole of the term should then be suppressed from entries generated under earlier and later terms. The programs allow for this:

(i) A term that is coded:

1	0	0
n^4	n^5	n^6

— can be accompanied by one or more preceding differences (lead or non-lead);

(ii) A term can be coded:

0	0	0
n^4	n^5	n^6

— provided that it contains at least one difference where $n^{11} = 2$ or 3.

(c) Terms of this kind are called *differenced lead-only terms*; this is a 'convenience' label, since the whole of the term will appear in the display in certain entries (see example below). These terms can be accompanied *only* by number differences, *not* parenthetical differences ($n, $o) or dates as differences ($d).

Steps	Example
	(O) Surrey (p) Guildford (1) schools $21 grammar (LO) (q) Royal Grammar School
1. Suppress the differenced lead-only term from entries under earlier or later terms.	Surrey Guildford. Royal Grammar School Guildford. Surrey Royal Grammar School Royal Grammar School. Guildford. Surrey
2. When the lead begins with part of a differenced lead-only term, apply Algorithm 3 to construct the lead and the first component of the display; assign remaining terms to appropriate positions.	Schools. Guildford. Surrey Grammar schools: Royal Grammar School Grammar schools. Guildford. Surrey Royal Grammar School

ALGORITHM 5. PARENTHETICAL DIFFERENCES

Notes:

(a) These differences are identified by secondary codes in positions n^{10} and n^{11}. These codes are composed as follows:
n^{10} = $: the mark identifying an instruction;
n^{11} = n *or* o, where:
n = non-lead parenthetical difference;
o = lead parenthetical difference.

(b) A term cannot contain more than one part coded $n or $o.

Steps	Examples
	a) (l) children (p) intelligence $o Wechsler Scale b) (l) children (p) maturity $21 social $n Doll's Vineland Scale
1. When an earlier or later term appears in the lead:	a) & b) Children
(a) organise the parts of the compound term in the order: — preceding differences (if any); — the focus; — the parenthetical difference printed within parentheses.	
(b) print the compound in the appropriate part of the entry (qualifier or display).	a) Children Intelligence (Wechsler Scale) b) Children Social maturity (Doll's Vineland Scale)
2. When the focus appears in the lead:	
(a) if no preceding difference is present, print the parenthetical difference after the focus.	a) Intelligence (Wechsler Scale)
(b) if a preceding difference is present, print the focus in the lead and assign the whole term, organised as in Step 1(a), to the display.	b) Maturity Social maturity (Doll's Vineland Scale)
(c) assign earlier or later terms (if any) to appropriate positions.	a) Intelligence (Wechsler Scale). Children b) Maturity. Children Social maturity (Doll's Vineland Scale)

Steps	Examples
3. When a preceding difference is selected as the lead:	
(a) if the term contains no other preceding difference, print the parenthetical difference after the focus in the lead.	b) Social maturity (Doll's Vineland Scale)
(b) if the lead does not contain all the preceding differences - — organise the parts of the term as in 1(a); — print the whole term in the display.	
(c) assign earlier or later terms to appropriate positions.	b) Social maturity (Doll's Vineland Scale). Children
4. When a parenthetical difference prefixed by $o appears in the lead:	
(a) print this part without parentheses.	a) Wechsler Scale
(b) print the rest of the term, without the parenthetical difference, as the first component of the qualifier.	a) Wechsler Scale. Intelligence
(c) assign earlier or later terms to appropriate positions.	a) Wechsler Scale. Intelligence. Children

ALGORITHM 6. DATES AS DIFFERENCES

Notes:

(a) A date as a difference is input as the final part of the term and prefixed by the secondary code $d.

(b) A date prefixed by $d -
- is printed in italic in all entries;
- does not appear as part of the lead in any entry.

Steps	Example
	(0) Thames River (1) barges $21 sailing $d 1900-1914 (2) restoration
1. When an earlier or later term appears in the lead:	Thames River Restoration
(a) assemble preceding and/or parenthetical differences (if any) according to Algorithms 3 and 5.	
(b) assign the part prefixed by $d to the final position in the term following a comma.	
(c) assign the term to the appropriate position.	Thames River Sailing barges, *1900-1914*. Restoration Restoration. Sailing barges, *1900-1914*. Thames River
2. When part of the term containing $d appears in the lead:	Barges
(a) assemble the term as in Steps 1(a) and 1(b).	
(b) print the full term as the first component of the display.	Barges Sailing barges, *1900-1914*
(c) assign any earlier or later terms to appropriate positions.	Barges. Thames River Sailing barges, *1900-1914*. Restoration
3. When the lead contains all preceding/parenthetical differences:	Sailing barges
(a) print the date, without a preceding comma, as the first component of the display.	Sailing barges *1900-1914*
(b) assign any earlier or later terms to appropriate positions.	Sailing barges. Thames River *1900-1914*. Restoration

ALGORITHM 7. PROPER NAMES

Notes:

(a) A proper name is identified by a letter *(term code)* in n^9:
c = the proper name of a class-of-one *other than* a place name;
d = a place name.

(b) When n^9 = c or d, the term can include one or more secondary codes in positions n^{10} and n^{11}; these control the typography, punctuation and filing characteristics of the parts of the term:

$e = non-filing part in italic preceded by comma
$f = filing part in italic preceded by comma
$g = filing part in roman, no preceding punctuation
$h = filing part in italic preceded by full point
$i = filing part in italic, no preceding punctuation.

The code $e cannot be used unless the next part is prefixed by $g.

Steps	Examples
	n^9 = c a) Molière b) Edward I $f King of England c) Beecham $e Sir $g Thomas d) Great Britain $h Army. Royal Sussex Regiment e) Smith, John $f 1921- n^9 = d f) Germany $i (Federal Republic)
1. When a proper name appears in the qualifier or display: (a) print the parts in input order (b) print the 1st part in roman (c) typeface & punctuation of other parts controlled by the secondary codes listed above.	a) Molière b) Edward I, *King of England* c) Beecham, *Sir* Thomas d) Great Britain. *Army. Royal Sussex Regiment* e) Smith, John, *1921-* f) Germany *(Federal Republic)*
2. When a proper name appears in the lead: (a) print the parts in input order (b) print the 1st part, and any part prefixed by $g, in a distinctive face (e.g. bold) (c) print other parts with typefaces and punctuation determined by the secondary codes listed above.	a) Molière b) Edward I, *King of England* c) Beecham, *Sir* Thomas d) Great Britain. *Army. Royal Sussex Regiment* e) Smith, John, *1921-* f) Germany *(Federal Republic)*

ALGORITHM 8. CONNECTIVES

Notes:

(a) A connective (usually a preposition or conjunction) is identified by a secondary code in positions n^{10} and n^{11}:

n^{10} = $: the mark identifying an instruction.

n^{11} = *either* V: downward-reading connective (also called a *$v connective*)

or W: upward-reading connective (also called a *$w connective*).

(b) A downward-reading connective is suppressed from entries generated under terms later in the string. An upward-reading connective is suppressed from entries generated under terms earlier in the string. A connective (usually $v) can occur as the first component of the display, but the qualifier never begins with a connective.

(c) Both kinds of connective can be attached to the same term, in which case they must be input in the order *$v before $w*.

(d) In these algorithms, the term to which a connective is attached is referred to as a *gated term* — the connective opens a 'gate' to another term in the string, and incorporates the other term into a phrase.

Steps	Examples
	a) (1) hospitals (p) patients (NU) (q) children $w in (2) visits $v by $w to (3) parents b) (1) Iceland (p) rocks (2) erosion $v by $w of (3) glaciers (2) measurement
1. When the lead consists of a term or part of a term earlier in the string than a gated term containing $v:	a) Hospitals Patients Children b) Iceland Rocks
(a) identify other permitted terms earlier in the string than the gated term containing $v. Assign these to appropriate positions. If any of these terms is accompanied by a $w connective, organise a phrase by applying Steps 2(a) to 2(c).	a) Hospitals Patients: Children Patients. Hospitals Children Children. Hospitals b) Iceland Rocks Rocks. Iceland

Steps	Examples
(b) assemble a phrase consisting of (i) the gated term containing $v; (ii) the $v connective; (iii) the next permitted term later in the string. The connective and next permitted term are printed without preceding punctuation, and with lower case initials unless input with u.c. initials.	a) *Visits by parents* b) *Erosion by glaciers*
(c) if the last component of the phrase assembled at the previous step is also accompanied by a $v connective, continue to assemble the phrase by adding: (i) the new $v connective; (ii) the next later permitted term.	
(d) repeat Step 1(c).	
(e) print the phrase assembled in Steps 1(b) to 1(d) in the appropriate part of the entry (partly constructed at Step 1(a)).	a) Hospitals Patients: Children. Visits by parents Patients. Hospitals Children. Visits by parents Children. Hospitals Visits by parents b) Iceland Rocks. Erosion by glaciers Rocks. Iceland Erosion by glaciers
(f) assign any remaining permitted terms to appropriate positions. If any of these terms is accompanied by a connective, construct a phrase by applying: (i) Steps 1(b) to 1(d) if the connective is $v; (ii) Steps 2(a) to 2(c) if the connective is $w.	b) Iceland Rocks. Erosion by glaciers. Measurement Rocks. Iceland Erosion by glaciers. Measurement
2. When the lead consists of a term or part of a term later in the string than a gated term containing $w:	
(a) assemble a phrase consisting of (i) the gated term; (ii) the connective; (iii) the next permitted term earlier in the string. The connective and next permitted term are printed without intervening punctuation, and with lower case initials unless input with u.c. initials.	a) *Visits to children* b) *Erosion of rocks*

Steps	Examples
2 cont.	
(b) if the last component of the phrase assembled at the previous step is also accompanied by a $w connective, continue to assemble the phrase. Add: (i) the new $w connective; (ii) the next earlier permitted term.	a) *Visits to children in hospitals*
(c) repeat Step 2(b).	
(d) print the phrase assembled in Steps 2(a) to 2(c) in the appropriate position.	a) Parents Visits to children in hospitals b) Glaciers Erosion of rocks
(e) Repeat Step 1(f).	b) Glaciers. Iceland Erosion of rocks. Measurement
3. When a gated term accompanied by $v is due to appear in the lead:	a) *Visits* b) *Erosion*
(a) check the term for preceding and/or parenthetical differences. If only part of the term is present in the lead †, print the whole term as the 1st component of the display; assemble a phrase in the display, applying Steps 1(b) to 1(d).	
(b) if all parts of the gated term are in the lead †, print the following parts as a phrase, with no intervening punctuation, in the display: (i) the $v connective; (ii) the next permitted term later in the string. An u.c. initial is printed only on the 1st word (and later words input with u.c. initials).	a) Visits b) Erosion a) Visits By parents b) Erosion By glaciers

† ... or the heading, in the case of terms with parenthetical differences.

Steps	Examples
(c) if the last component of the phrase assembled at the previous step is also accompanied by a $v connective, continue to assemble the phrase in the display by adding: (i) the new $v connective; (ii) the next permitted term later in the string.	
(d) repeat Step 3(c).	
(e) repeat Step 1(f).	a) Visits. Children in hospital By parents b) Erosion. Rocks. Iceland By glaciers. Measurement

ALGORITHM 9. COORDINATE CONCEPTS

Notes:

(a) A coordinate concept is identified by a letter in position n^3. Two letters are used to indicate this relationship:
n^3 = *either* f: bound coordinate concept;
or g: 'standard' coordinate concept.

(b) Any term introduced by one of the following operators in n^3:
— primary operators 0 to 4;
— secondary operators p, q, r or u –
— may be followed by one or more coordinate concepts. The first concept, plus its associated coordinate concept(s), are referred to altogether as the *block*.

(c) Coordinate concept codes must be consistent within a block; i.e. they must all be either 'g' or 'f'. Some of the steps in the algorithm call for a distinction between:
— *f blocks* (n^3 = f for all coordinate terms);
— *g blocks* (n^3 = g for all coordinate terms).

(d) The typography of terms within a block, and the position of the block within an entry, are determined by the operator assigned to the first concept in the block.

(e) Punctuation within the block is determined by the class of terms comprising the block. This is explained and illustrated in Step 1(c).

(f) The connective code $v, followed by a sign of conjunction (e.g. &) should be attached to the penultimate term in a block. Other terms in the block may also be accompanied by $v connectives.

Steps	Examples
	a) (1) gardens (p) plants $01 annual (g) shrubs $21 flowering $v & (g) trees b) (1) tales $21 French $v & (f) legends $21 French (2) textual criticism c) (2) television (2) (3) cameramen (q) Finch, Gordon (g) Gordon, John $v & (g) Jones, Harry
1. When the lead consists of a term or part of a term that precedes or follows the block in the string:	a) Gardens b) Textual criticism c) Television Cameramen

Steps	Examples
(a) assemble the terms in the block in input order.	
(b) insert $v conjunctions at appropriate positions within the block (see Algorithm 8).	
(c) insert the following punctuation marks between the other terms in the block: (i) a comma if all the terms in the block are common nouns (n^9 = a); (ii) a semicolon if any one of the terms in the block is a proper name (n^9 = c *or* d).	
(d) print the block in the appropriate position in the entry. This is determined by the operator (n^3) assigned to the first term in the block. The first word in the block is printed with an u.c. initial; other terms are in l.c. unless input with u.c. Assign any earlier or later terms to appropriate positions.	a) Gardens Annual plants, flowering shrubs & trees b) Textual criticism. French tales & French legends c) Television Cameramen: Finch, Gordon; Gordon, John & Jones, Harry Cameramen. Television Finch, Gordon; Gordon, John & Jones, Harry
2. When the 1st term in a *g block* is due to appear in the lead:	a) *plants $01 annual* c) *Finch, Gordon*
(a) check this term for differences. If present, apply algorithms 3 to 5. Print the term(s) produced.	a) Plants Annual plants c) Finch, Gordon
(b) suppress all other terms comprising the *g block;* assign any earlier or later terms to appropriate positions.	a) Plants. Gardens Annual plants c) Finch, Gordon. Cameramen. Television
3. Repeat Step 2 for each successive term in the *g block.*	a) Shrubs. Gardens Flowering shrubs Flowering shrubs. Gardens Trees. Gardens

Steps	Examples
3 *cont*	c) Gordon, John. Cameramen. Television Jones, Harry. Cameramen Television
4. When the 1st term in an *f block* is due to appear in the lead:	b) *tales $21 French*
(a) check the term for differences. If present, apply Algorithms 3 to 5 to construct the lead(s).	b) Tales French tales
(b) print the whole of the *f block* in input order as the 1st component of the display †.	b) Tales French tales & French legends French tales French tales & French legends
(c) assign any earlier or later terms to appropriate positions.	b) Tales French tales & French legends. Textual criticism French tales French tales & French legends. Textual criticism
5. Repeat Step 4 for each successive term in the *f block*.	b) Legends French tales & French legends. Textual criticism French legends French tales & French legends. Textual criticism

† This overrides any instruction in algorithms 3 to 5 which calls for the whole of the term to be printed (separately) as the first component of the display if only part of the term appears in the lead.

ALGORITHM 10. STANDARD FORMAT

Notes:

(a) The standard format is controlled by the role operator in position n^3 of the primary manipulation code.

(b) This format is applied to any set of consecutive terms prefixed by primary operators in the range 0 to 3, including their dependent elements (identified by operators p, q and r — see Algorithm 11). A consecutive set of these terms is referred to as the *sequence*. Later algorithms deal separately with the format of entries under terms prefixed by the operator 3 when they immediately follow action concepts (identified by operators 2, s, t and u).

(c) When a term introduced by an operator in the range 0 to 3 appears in the qualifier or display, it is -
— printed in standard roman;
— preceded by a full point except when it is the first component of the display.

Steps	Example
	(0) London $01 east (1) children (2) games $21 street
1. When a term in the sequence appears in the lead:	
(a) check for differences associated with the term. If present, apply Algorithms 3 to 6.	London East London Children Games Street games Street games
(b) permitted terms earlier in the sequence are printed in the qualifier in the reverse of input order. If any of these terms is accompanied by a $w connective, check Algorithm 8, Steps 2(a) to 2(c), and construct a phrase if necessary.	Children. East London Games. Children. East London Street games Street games. Children. East London
(c) permitted terms later in the sequence are printed in the display in input order. If any of these terms is accompanied by a $v connective, check Algorithm 8, Steps 1(b) to 1(d), and construct a phrase if necessary.	Children. East London Street games

ALGORITHM 11. DEPENDENT ELEMENTS

Notes:

(a) A dependent element is identified by one of the secondary operators p, q or r written in position n^3 of the manipulation code.

(b) Part of a string that consists of a term prefixed by a numbered operator followed immediately by one or more terms introduced by dependent element operators is referred to as the *sequence*.

(c) The typeface, and the position within an entry, of a term prefixed by a dependent element operator are determined by the numbered operator at the start of the sequence.

(d) When a term prefixed by the operator q, plus the next earlier permitted term in the sequence, appear together in the display they are separated by a colon.

Steps	Example
	(1) metals $21 non-ferrous (p) hardness (5) study examples (q) copper
1. Terms within a dependent element sequence are dealt with in accordance with the standard entry format (Algorithm 10).	Metals Non-ferrous metals. Hardness — *Study examples: Copper* Non-ferrous metals Hardness — *Study examples: Copper* Hardness. Non-ferrous metals — *Study examples: Copper* Copper. *Study examples* Non-ferrous metals. Hardness

ALGORITHM 12. PREDICATE TRANSFORMATION

Notes:

(a) The predicate transformation is initiated when an entry is generated under a term that represents a performer (n^3 = 3) and the next preceding term in the string represents either an action (n^3 = 2) or the dependent element of an action. This also covers strings where the performer term is followed by its own dependent element(s).

(b) The following definitions apply in this algorithm:

— *sequence:* a set of consecutive terms prefixed by primary operators in the range 0 to 2, including their dependent elements prefixed by operators p, q and r (e.g. terms *A* to *D* in the diagram below);

— *2-block:* an action concept prefixed by the operator 2 together with its dependent element(s) (e.g. terms *C* and *D* in the diagram below);

— *3-block:* a performer concept prefixed by the operator 3 together with its dependent element(s) (e.g. terms *E* and *F* in the diagram below).

sequence — [(0) *A*, (1) *B*, (2) *C*, (q) *D*]
2-block — [(2) *C*, (q) *D*]
3-block — [(3) *E*, (p) *F*]

(c) The predicate transformation is also involved in some later algorithms:
— Two-way interactions (Algorithm 13);
— Role definers; directional properties (Algorithm 14);
— Author-attributed associations (Algorithm 15).

Steps	Examples
	a) (0) East Anglia (1) crops (2) damage \$v by \$w to (3) wind b) (2) skiing \$21 cross-country (q) racing (p) training \$v by \$w for (3) Danes (q) women
1. When the lead consists of a term forming part of the sequence:	
(a) check the term for differences. If present, apply Algorithms 3 to 6.	a) East Anglia Crops Damage b) Skiing Cross-country skiing Cross-country skiing Racing

Steps	Examples
Step 1 cont.	
(b) apply Algorithm 8 to any terms linked by connectives.	
(c) generate entries in the standard format.	a) **East Anglia** Crops. Damage by wind **Crops.** East Anglia Damage by wind **Damage.** Crops. East Anglia By winds b) **Skiing** Cross-country skiing: Racing. Training by Danes: Women **Cross-country skiing** Racing. Training by Danes: Women **Racing.** Cross-country skiing Training by Danes: Women
2. When a performer concept ($n^3 = 3$) appears in the lead, *and* the next earlier permitted term is specified as an action ($n^3 = 2$):	a) *wind*
(a) check for differences associated with the performer term. If present, apply Algorithms 3 to 6.	a) **Wind**
(b) if the performer concept is followed in the string by one or more dependent elements (n^3 = p, q or r), print the dependent element(s) as the next component(s) of the display.	
(c) print the action term as the next component of the display.	a) **Wind** Damage
(d) if the action term is accompanied by a $w connective, apply Algorithm 8, Steps 2(a) to 2(c).	a) **Wind** Damage to crops
(e) assign the remaining terms to appropriate positions.	a) **Wind.** East Anglia Damage to crops
3. When the performer concept ($n^3 = 3$) is due to appear in the lead, *and* this term is preceded by a 2-block in the string:	b) *(3) Danes*
(a) check for differences associated with the performer concept. If present, apply Algorithms 3 to 6.	b) **Danes**

Steps	Examples
(b) if the performer term is the first component of a 3-block: (i) check the block for $v connectives. If present, apply Algorithm 8, Steps 1(b) to 1(d). (ii) print these terms, including the $v phrase(s), as the first/next component(s) of the display.	b) Danes Women
(c) process the terms in the 2-block: (i) check the block for $w connectives. If present, apply Algorithm 8, Steps 2(a) to 2(c); (ii) assemble the components of the block (including $w phrases constructed at the previous step) *in input order* †; (iii) print these as the next component(s) of the display.	b) Danes Women. Cross-country skiing. Training for racing
(d) assign any remaining terms to appropriate positions.	
4. When the first/next dependent element in the 3-block is due to appear in the lead:	b) *women*
(a) check for differences associated with this term. If present, apply Algorithms 3 to 6;	b) Women
(b) apply the standard format (Algorithm 10) to the rest of the terms in the 3-block;	b) Women. Danes
(c) repeat Steps 3(c) and 3(d).	b) Women. Danes Cross-country skiing. Training for racing
(d) check the 3-block for further dependent elements. If present, repeat Steps 4(a) to 4(d).	

† Imposing input order at this stage maintains the general principles which call for *whole-before-part*, and *general-before-specific*, in the display position.

ALGORITHM 13. TWO-WAY INTERACTIONS

Notes:

(a) A two-way interaction is identified by the operator u in position n^3 of the primary manipulation code. This concept is sometimes referred to as the *u-term*.

(b) A *u-term* —

— may be followed by one or more coordinate concepts (where n^3 = f or g). If a coordinate concept is present, it is regarded as part of the u-term when references are made to earlier or later terms in the string.

— must be accompanied in the string by both an earlier and later term where n^3 =
- *either* a primary operator in the range 1 to 3;
- *or* one of the secondary operators p, q or r.

(c) The concepts on either side of a u-term share a common relationship (usually indicated by a common character in n^3). Consequently, if a term prefixed by the operator u is followed by a dependent element (where n^3 = p, q or r), this is not a dependent element of the two-way interaction. Instead, it possesses the same dependency relationship as the concept which precedes the u-term in the string.

(d) The following definition applies in this algorithm:

u-block: a sequence of terms that consists of the two-way interaction (including its coordinate concept(s), if present), and the next later term in the string, e.g. terms *C* to *E* in *Diagram 1*. The next later term may be followed by one or more coordinate concepts, in which case these are included within the u-block, e.g. terms *C to E* in *Diagram 2*.

(1)
(1) *A*
(p) *B*
(u) *C* ⎤
(g) *D* ⎬— *u-block*
(p) *E* ⎦
(2) *F*

(2)
(1) *A*
(2) *B*
(u) *C* ⎤
(2) *D* ⎬— *u-block*
(g) *E* ⎦

Steps	Examples
	a) (1) Australia (u) cultural relations $v & (g) economic relations $v with $w with (1) China b) (1) hospitals (p) doctors (u) interpersonal relationships $v with $w with (p) nurses $v & (g) patients

Steps	Examples
1. When the lead consists of a term outside the u-block:	a) *Australia* b) *hospitals* *doctors*
(a) check the term for differences. If present, apply Algorithms 3 to 6.	a) Australia b) Hospitals Doctors
(b) apply Algorithm 8 to any terms linked by connectives.	
(c) generate entries in the format appropriate for each lead.	a) Australia Cultural relations & economic relations with China b) Hospitals Doctors. Interpersonal relationships with nurses & patients Doctors. Hospitals Interpersonal relationships with nurses & patients
2. If the term prefixed by the operator u is marked as a lead:	a) *cultural relations* b) *interpersonal relationships*
(a) check the term for differences. If present, apply Algorithms 3 to 6.	a) Cultural relations b) Interpersonal relationships
(b) taking each lead as a starting point, generate two entries:	
2.1 First entry	
(a) generate entries in the standard format (Algorithm 10), taking account of algorithms associated with the operators/codes in the string (connectives, coordinate terms, etc.)	a) Cultural relations. Australia With China b) Interpersonal relationships. Doctors. Hospitals With nurses & patients
2.2 Second entry	
(a) print the $w connective attached to the u-term as the first/next component of the display, followed by the next permitted term that precedes the u-block in the string. If this term is also accompanied by a $w connective, apply Algorithm 8, Steps 2(a) to 2(c).	a) Cultural relations With Australia b) Interpersonal relationships With doctors

Steps	Entries
Step 2.2 cont.	
(b) check the term which follows the u-term in the string. If this term is accompanied by a $v connective, apply Algorithm 8, Steps 1(b) to 1(d). Print the result in the qualifier.	a) *China* b) *nurses* b) *nurses & patients* a) Cultural relations. China With Australia b) Interpersonal relationships. Nurses & patients With doctors
(c) assign any remaining terms to appropriate positions.	b) Interpersonal relationships. Nurses & patients. Hospitals With doctors
3. If the term prefixed by the operator u is followed by a coordinate concept (n^3 = f or g), and the coordinate concept is marked as a lead, apply Step 2 to the coordinate concept. Repeat this step if necessary.	a) Economic relations. Australia With China Economic relations. China With Australia
4. If the later term in the u-block (see Note b) is marked as lead, apply the predicate transformation (Algorithm 12).	a) China Cultural relations & economic relations with Australia b) Nurses. Hospitals Interpersonal relationships with doctors
5. If the term selected as a lead in the previous step is accompanied by a coordinate concept marked as a lead, repeat Step 4. Repeat this step if necessary.	b) Patients. Hospitals Interpersonal relationships with doctors

ALGORITHM 14. ROLE DEFINERS; DIRECTIONAL PROPERTIES

Notes:

(a) Concepts that function as *role definers* or *directional properties* are identified by the secondary operator s in position n^3. Both kinds of concept are referred to as *role definers* in this algorithm.

(b) A role definer must occur as part of a *sequence* (illustrated below). This can consist of:

Term 1, where n^3 =
- *either* a primary operator in the range 1 to 3;
- *or* one of the dependent element operators p, q or r.

Term 2: the role definer (n^3 = s);

Term 3, where n^3 = 3.

Terms 1 and 2 in the sequence are obligatory. Term 3 (sometimes called the *3-term*) can be omitted; see Example (c) below. When all three terms are present in the sequence, the role definer must be accompanied by both $v and $w connectives. When terms 1 and 2 are present, the role definer must be accompanied by a $w connective. If the 3-term is accompanied by one or more dependent elements, these are referred to together as the *3-block* and regarded as part of the sequence.

Example:

(1)
sequence { (2) (s) (3) (p) } — with (3) (p) forming the *3-block*

(c) A role definer cannot possess a dependent element, and it cannot be followed by a coordinate concept.

Steps	Examples
	a) (2) marriage (s) attitudes $v of $w to (3) adolescents (q) girls
	b) (1) documents (2) indexing $w of (s) applications $v of $w in (3) computer systems $31 micro (p) software packages
	c) (1) whales (2) conservation $w of (s) policies $w on (6) bibliographies
1. When a term outside the sequence is marked as a lead:	b) *documents* c) *whales*
(a) check the term for differences. If present, apply Algorithms 3 to 6.	b) Documents c) Whales

Steps	Examples
Step 1 cont.	
(b) apply Algorithm 8 to any terms linked by connectives.	
(c) generate entries in the format appropriate for the role of the term in the lead.	b) Documents Indexing. Applications of microcomputer systems. Software packages c) Whales Conservation. Policies — *Bibliographies*
2. When the first term in the sequence is marked as a lead:	a) *marriage* b) *indexing* c) *conservation*
(a) check the term for differences. If present, apply Algorithms 3 to 6.	a) Marriage b) Indexing c) Conservation
(b) apply Algorithm 8 to any terms linked by connectives.	
(c) generate entries in the standard format (Algorithm 10).	a) Marriage Attitudes of adolescents: Girls b) Indexing. Documents Applications of microcomputer systems. Software packages c) Conservation. Whales Policies — *Bibliographies*
3. If the role definer is marked as a lead †:	a) *attitudes* c) *policies*
(a) check the term for differences. If present, apply Algorithms 3 to 6.	a) Attitudes c) Policies
(b) print the $w connective attached to the role definer as the first/next component of the display, followed by the earlier term in the sequence. If the earlier term is also accompanied by a $w connective, apply Algorithm 8, Steps 2(a) to 2(c).	a) Attitudes To marriage c) Policies On conservation of whales

† This step generally repeats the generation of the 2nd entry when a two-way interaction appears in the lead; see Algorithm 13, Steps 2 and 2.2.

Steps	Examples
(c) if the sequence contains a 3rd term with $n^3 = 3$, check for the presence of a *3-block*.	a) *adolescents*
(i) if the 3-term does not start a block, print it in the qualifier. If the 3-term is accompanied by a $v connective, apply Algorithm 8, Steps 1(b) to 1(d); add the result(s) to the qualifier.	
(ii) if the 3-term begins a 3-block, check the block for $w connectives. If present, apply Algorithm 8, Steps 2(a) to 2(c). Print the parts of the block, including $w phrases (if any) in the qualifier *in the reverse of input order* †.	a) Attitudes. Girls. Adolescents To marriage
(d) assign any remaining terms to appropriate positions.	c) Policies On conservation of whales — *Bibliographies*
4. If a 3-term following the role definer is marked as a lead:	a) *adolescents* b) *computer systems $31 micro*
(a) check the 3-term for differences. If present, apply Algorithms 3 to 6.	a) Adolescents b) Computer systems Microcomputer systems Microcomputer systems
(b) apply the predicate transformation; refer to Algorithm 12, Steps 2(b) to 2(e), replacing *action term* by *role definer* where necessary.	a) Adolescents Girls. Attitudes to marriage b) Computer systems Microcomputer systems. Software packages. Applications in indexing of documents Microcomputer systems Software packages. Applications in indexing of documents
5. If the 3-term is followed by a dependent element marked as a lead, apply Algorithm 12, Step 4, replacing *action term* by *role definer* where necessary.	a) *girls* b) *software packages* a) Girls. Adolescents Attitudes to marriage b) Software packages. Microcomputer systems Applications in indexing of documents

† Imposing the reverse of input order at this stage maintains the general principles which call for *part-before-whole* and *specific-before-general* in the qualifier (see also footnote on p 363).

ALGORITHM 15. AUTHOR-ATTRIBUTED ASSOCIATIONS

Notes:

(a) Author-attributed associations are identified by the secondary operator t in position n^3. They are referred to in this algorithm as *t-terms*.

(b) A t-term must be accompanied in the string by both an earlier and a later term where n^3 =
- *either* a primary operator in the range 1 to 3;
- *or* one of the secondary operators p, q or r.

These three terms together comprise a *sequence*.

(1) *A*
(p) *B* ⎤
(t) *C* ⎬ *sequence*
(p) *D* ⎦
(2) *E*

If the term on either side of the t-term is part of a coordinate block (see Note (b), p 356), the block is regarded as part of the sequence.

(c) A t-term *cannot* -
- occur as a lead;
- be accompanied by a difference;
- possess a dependent element;
- form part of a coordinate block.

Consequently, if a t-term is followed by a term where n^3 = p, q or r, this is not a dependent element of the t-term. Instead, it possesses the same dependency relationship as the concept preceding the t-term in the string.

(d) A t-term may be associated with $v and $w connectives. Whether or not connectives are attached, the t-term is always:
- printed in italic, with a lower case initial, in any part of the entry (this also applies to any connective(s) attached to a t-term);
- printed as part of a phrase that contains one or both of the other terms in the sequence. The first word in the phrase has an u.c. initial; other terms have l.c. initials unless input with upper case. The phrase is printed without intervening punctuation.

Steps	Example
	(1) in✓dexing systems (p) pe✓rformance factors (q) pr✓ecision (t) related to (q) re✓call (2) st✓atistical analysis
1. When the lead consists of any term(s) earlier than the sequence:	a) *indexing systems* b) *performance factors*
(a) check the term(s) for differences. If present, apply Algorithms 3 to 6.	

Steps	Example
(b) apply Algorithm 8 to any terms linked by connectives.	
(c) print these terms in positions determined by their roles.	Indexing systems Performance factors Performance factors. Indexing systems
(d) assemble a phrase consisting of: (i) the first term in the sequence; (ii) the t-term and its $v connective (if present); (iii) the final term in the sequence.	
(e) print this phrase as the first/next component of the display.	Indexing systems Performance factors: Precision *related to* recall Performance factors. Indexing systems Precision *related to* recall
(f) assign any remaining terms to appropriate positions.	Indexing systems Performance factors: Precision *related to* recall. Statistical analysis Performance factors. Indexing systems Precision *related to* recall. Statistical analysis
2. When the first term in the sequence appears in the lead:	*precision*
(a) check the term for differences. If present, apply Algorithms 3 to 6.	Precision
(b) print in the next position in the display: (i) the t-term and its $v connective (if present); (ii) the final term in the sequence.	Precision *related to* recall
(c) assign any remaining terms to appropriate positions.	Precision. Performance factors. Indexing systems *related to* recall. Statistical analysis
3. When the third term in the sequence appears in the lead:	*recall*
(a) check the term for differences. If present, apply Algorithms 3 to 6.	Recall
(b) print in the next position in the display: (i) the t-term and its $w connective (if present); (ii) the first term in the sequence.	Recall *related to* precision

Steps	Example
Step 3 cont.	
(c) assign any remaining terms to appropriate positions.	Recall. Performance factors. Indexing systems *related to* precision. Statistical analysis
4. When the lead is occupied by a term that is: (i) later than the sequence; (ii) prefixed by a primary operator or the dependent element of a primary operator:	*statistical analysis*
(a) check the term for differences. If present, apply Algorithms 3 to 6.	Statistical analysis
(b) assemble a phrase by repeating Step 1(d).	
(c) print this phrase in the appropriate part of the entry, determined by the role of the term in the lead.	Statistical analysis. Precision *related to* recall
(d) assign any remaining terms to appropriate positions.	Statistical analysis. Precision *related to* recall. Performance factors. Indexing systems

ALGORITHM 16. INVERTED FORMAT

Notes:

(a) This format is initiated when a term is prefixed by a primary manipulation code where n^3 = 4, 5 or 6. The format and typographic instructions associated with these operators also apply to dependent elements of these terms (where n^3 = p, q or r), except when special conditions occur in certain steps.

(b) Terms prefixed by primary operators in the range 4 to 6, together with their dependent elements (if present) are referred to as the *sequence:*

(1) *A*
(2) *B*
(5) *C* ⎤
(q) *D* ⎬— *1st sequence*
(p) *E* ⎦
(6) *F* }— *2nd sequence*

(c) Terms in the sequence should be printed in a de-emphasising typeface (e.g. italic) in the qualifier and display (but note an exception in Step 3(b)). The first term in the sequence (where n^3 = 4, 5 or 6) is preceded by a long dash in the display. Other terms in the sequence are preceded by the punctuation marks usually associated with their operators: operator q generates a preceding colon, and operators p and r generate preceding full points.

Steps	Examples
	a) (1) Cornwall (p) coastal waters (NU) (2) tides (6) tables b) (2) mathematics (6) surveying $01 for (6) bibliographies c) (1) urban regions (2) social planning (5) study regions (q) Finland (p) Helsinki
1. When the lead consists of any term or part of a term earlier than the sequence:	a) *Cornwall* *coastal waters* *tides* b) *mathematics* c) *urban regions* *social planning*

Steps	Examples
Step 1 cont.	
(a) assign these terms to positions determined by their roles. Print the terms in the sequence (or sequences) as the first/next components of the display.	a) Cornwall Coastal waters. Tides — *Tables* Coastal waters. Cornwall Tides — *Tables* Tides. Cornwall — *Tables* b) Mathematics — *For surveying* — *Bibliographies* c) Urban regions Social planning — *Study regions: Finland. Helsinki* Social planning. Urban regions — *Study regions: Finland. Helsinki*
2. When a term that begins a sequence (including a single-term sequence) appears in the lead:	a) Tables b) Surveying Bibliographies
(a) print in the display, in input order, permitted terms in the string up to (but excluding) the term in the lead.	a) Tables Cornwall. Coastal waters. Tides b) Surveying Mathematics Bibliographies Mathematics — *For surveying*
(b) if the term in the lead: — is complete (i.e. contains all differences); — *and* is the final permitted term in the string - the entry is complete.	a) *tables* b) *bibliographies*
(c) if the term in the lead: — is not complete; — *or* is not the final permitted term in the string - print the remaining permitted terms in input order.	b) *surveying* b) Surveying Mathematics — *For surveying* — *Bibliographies*
3. When a dependent element forming part of a sequence appears in the lead:	c) Finland Helsinki

Steps	Examples
(a) print in the display, in input order, permitted terms in the string up to (but excluding) the sequence that contains the term in the lead.	c) Finland Urban regions. Social planning Helsinki Urban regions. Social planning
(b) if the sequence contains one or more earlier dependent elements (n^3 = p, q or r), print these in the qualifier: — in roman; — in the reverse of input order. (That is, apply the standard format).	c) Helsinki. Finland Urban regions. Social planning
(c) complete the qualifier by adding, in italic, the first term in the sequence (i.e. the term with n^3 = 4, 5 or 6)	c) Finland. *Study regions* Urban regions. Social planning Helsinki. Finland. *Study regions* Urban regions. Social planning
(d) if the term in the lead is complete; — *and* the heading (lead + qualifier) contains all the terms in the sequence; — *and* the sequence is the final part of the string — — the entry is complete.	c) *Helsinki*
(e) if the term in the lead is not complete: — *or* the heading does not contain all the terms in the sequence; — *or* the sequence is not the final part of the string —	c) *Finland*
— print the remainder of the string in input order in the display.	c) Finland. *Study regions* Urban regions. Social planning — *Study regions: Finland. Helsinki*

ALGORITHM 17. COORDINATE THEMES

Notes:

(a) Coordinate themes within a string are marked by primary codes in position n^2:

x = first term in coordinate theme;
y = second or subsequent term in coordinate theme;
z = common term.

(b) The following definitions apply in this algorithm:

coordinate theme: one of two or more independent themes embedded within a single string. The start of a coordinate theme is marked by a term with n^2 = x (an *x-term*). Later terms belonging to that theme (independent of any other coordinate theme) have n^2 = y (*y-terms*). A string must not contain only one x-term.

common term: a term prefixed by n^2 = z. One or more common terms can occur at the beginning or end of a string containing coordinate themes; they are then treated as part of each coordinate theme (see diagram below). Common terms cannot occur between one coordinate theme and another.

Example (using the conventions adopted throughout the *Manual*):

Codes	Term	
(z)(0)	*A*	*common terms*
(z)(p)	*B*	
(x)(1)	*C*	*1st coordinate theme*
(y)(p)	*D*	
(x)(1)	*E*	*2nd coordinate theme*
(y)(2)	*F*	
(z)(6)	*G*	*common term*

This string can be regarded as the amalgamation of two independent strings:

String 1:		*String 2:*	
(0)	*A*	(0)	*A*
(p)	*B*	(p)	*B*
(1)	*C*	(1)	*E*
(p)	*D*	(2)	*F*
(6)	*G*	(6)	*G*

(c) This algorithm does not deal with the generation of entries from a string where all terms have n^2 = z. This is regarded as a 'normal' case.

Steps	Examples
	a) (x)(1) plants (y)(2) growth (x)(1) wood (y)(2) damage $v by $w to (y)(3) fungi (z)(6) time-lapse films
	b) (z)(1) universities (x)(p) students (y)(2) academic achievement (y)(2) assessment (x)(p) courses (y)(2) evaluation (z)(4) students' viewpoints

Steps	Examples
1. When a term coded $n^2 = z$ appears in the lead:	a) *time-lapse films* b) *universities* *students' viewpoints*
(a) check the term for differences. If present, apply Algorithms 3 to 6.	a) Time-lapse films b) Universities Students' viewpoints
(b) identify a set of terms containing: (i) any adjacent permitted terms where $n^2 = z$; (ii) the nearest/next x-term, plus its y-terms (if any); (iii) any term(s) beyond the coordinate themes with $n^2 = z$. Treat the set as a single string. Assign permitted terms to appropriate positions.	a) Time-lapse films Wood. Damage by fungi b) Universities Students. Academic achievement. Assessment — *Students' viewpoints* Students' viewpoints Universities. Students. Academic achievement. Assessment
(c) repeat Step (b) as many times as there are x-terms in the string.	a) Time-lapse films Plants. Growth b) Universities Courses. Evaluation — *Students' viewpoints* Students' viewpoints Universities. Courses. Evaluation
2. When a term coded $n^2 = x$ is marked as a lead:	a) *plants* *wood* b) *students* *courses*
(a) check the term for differences. If present, apply Algorithms 3 to 6.	a) Plants Wood b) Students Courses
(b) identify a set of terms containing: (i) any adjacent following terms where $n^2 = y$; (ii) any preceding or following terms where $n^2 = z$. Treat the set as a single string. Assign permitted terms to appropriate positions.	a) Plants Growth — *Time-lapse films* Wood Damage by fungi — *Time-lapse films*

Steps	Examples
Step 2 cont.	b) Students. Universities Academic achievement. Assessment — *Students' viewpoints* Courses. Universities Evaluation — *Students' viewpoints*
3. When a term coded $n^2 = y$ is marked as a lead:	a) *growth* *fungi* b) *academic achievement* *evaluation*
(a) check the term for differences. If present, apply Algorithms 3 to 6.	a) Growth Fungi b) Academic achievement Evaluation
(b) identify a set of terms containing: (i) any adjacent preceding and/or later y-terms; (ii) the next preceding x-term; (iii) any preceding or following terms where $n^2 = z$. Treat the set as a single string. Assign permitted terms to appropriate positions.	a) Growth. Plants — *Time-lapse films* Fungi Damage to wood — *Time-lapse films* b) Academic achievement. Students. Universities Assessment — *Students' viewpoints* Evaluation. Courses. Universities — *Students' viewpoints*

ALGORITHM 18. SUBSTITUTES

Notes:

(a) A substitute is indicated by a number, in the range 1 to 9, in position n^5. The number in this position specifies how many terms should be suppressed and replaced by the substitute when an earlier or later term appears in the lead. Terms that do not function as substitutes have $n^5 = 0$.

(b) The following definitions and conventions are used in this algorithm:

— *sequence:* the substitute plus the term(s) it replaces.

— *sub-string:* the terms replaced by a downward-reading substitute. The operators assigned to the terms in a sub-string (in position n^3) -
- — may differ from any of the operators assigned to earlier terms;
- — can begin again from '0' (location) if necessary.

— *upward-reading* and *downward-reading:* these refer to the direction in which the sequence is read when terms in the string are selected for assembly as an entry:
- — an *upward-reading substitute* is inserted when the sequence is read in a later-to-earlier direction. It is indicated by the figure 2 in n^6, and is conveyed in the examples by the convention (sub n ↑), where n is a number in the range 1 to 9.
- — a *downward-reading substitute* is inserted when the sequence is read in an earlier-to-later direction. It is indicated by the figure 1 in n^6, and is conveyed in the examples by the convention (sub n ↓), where n is a number in the range 1 to 9.

Example:

```
              (2) A  ]
              (p) B  ]
 (sub 2 ↑)    (2) C  ]
              (s) D
 (sub 2 ↓)    (3) E     ]
              (1) F  ]  ]
              (p) G  ]  ]
```

Terms *A–B–C* and *E–F–G* form *sequences*.

Terms *F* + *G* form a *sub-string*.

(c) A substitute cannot -

— function as a lead. Consequently, if $n^5 > 0$, then n^4 must be 0.

— contain a difference.

— be associated with coordinate concepts.

(d) The two kinds of substitute are handled by separate algorithms:

— 18A deals with upward-reading substitutes;

— 18B deals with downward-reading substitutes.

Algorithm 18A Upward-reading substitutes

Steps	Example
	(2) medicine (p) research (sub 2 ↑) (2) medical research (2) planning
1. When the role of the term in the lead calls for the sequence to be read in an earlier-to-later direction:	*medicine*
(a) ignore the substitute;	
(b) print any other permitted terms in appropriate positions.	Medicine Research. Planning
2. When the role of the term in the lead calls for the sequence to be read in a later-to-earlier direction:	*planning*
(a) print the substitute in the appropriate part of the entry (this is determined by its operator in n^3);	
(b) suppress all other terms comprising the sequence.	Planning. Medical research

Algorithm 18B. Downward-reading substitutes

Steps	Example
	(1) London (p) atmosphere (2) pollution $v by $w of (sub 2 ↓) (3) car exhaust fumes (1) cars (p) exhaust fumes (6) research reports
1. When the role of the term in the lead calls for the sequence to be read in an earlier-to-later direction:	*London* *atmosphere* *research reports*
(a) print the substitute in the appropriate part of the entry (this is determined by its operator in n^3);	

Steps	Example
(b) suppress the terms that comprise the sub-string.	London Atmosphere. Pollution by car exhaust fumes — *Research reports* Atmosphere. London Pollution by car exhaust fumes — *Research reports* Research reports London. Atmosphere. Pollution by car exhaust fumes
2. When a term in the sub-string appears in the lead:	Cars Exhaust fumes
(a) assign the other permitted terms in the sub-string to positions determined by their roles;	Cars Exhaust fumes Exhaust fumes. Cars
(b) identify the next permitted term that precedes the sequence. Assign this to a position determined by its relationship to the *substitute* (expressed by the operators in n^3). *The next earlier permitted term in the example, i.e. 'pollution', has* $n^3 = 2$. *The substitute has* $n^3 = 3$. *This* 2-3 *operator pattern initiates the predicate transformation (see Algorithm 12, Step 2).*	Cars Exhaust fumes. Pollution Exhaust fumes. Cars Pollution
(c) if the term that precedes the substitute is accompanied by a $w connective, apply Algorithm 8, Steps 2(a) to 2(c).	Cars Exhaust fumes. Pollution of atmosphere Exhaust fumes. Cars Pollution of atmosphere
(d) assign any remaining terms to appropriate positions.	Cars. London Exhaust fumes. Pollution of atmosphere — *Research reports* Exhaust fumes. Cars. London Pollution of atmosphere — *Research reports*

VALIDATION OF STRINGS

Definitions:

String: a sequence of *concepts* starting with a *primary manipulation code* and ending with a string termination symbol (#).

Concept: the set of *data* and *codes* beginning with one primary manipulation code and ending at either the next primary code or the termination symbol.

Data (used here as singular or plural): a word or words written between the codes in a string; covers both *terms* and *connectives*.

Term: a *focus* together with its *difference(s)* (if present).

Focus: a noun or noun phrase (including typographic instruction codes, if present) immediately following a primary manipulation code.

Difference: part of a term introduced by a differencing code.

Connective: an adjunct that connects terms into phrases in some entries.

Theme: a string of terms expressing a subject. A single-theme string consists of concepts where every primary code contains n^2 = z, e.g.

n^2	n^3	Term
z	1	*A*
z	p	*B*
z	6	*C*

A string containing *coordinate themes* has a minimum of two concepts where n^2 = x, e.g.

n^2	n^3	Term
z	0	*A*
x	1	*B*
y	p	*C*
x	2	*D*
y	2	*E*
z	6	*F*

For validation purposes, this should be checked as two separate themes: (i) *A-B-C-F*; (ii) *A-D-E-F*.

Blocks. For some validation purposes, a theme must be divided into blocks of concepts as follows:

0-block, beginning with a concept where n^3 = ∅. This may contain concepts where n^3 = f, g, p, q or r.

1-2 block, beginning with a concept where n^3 = 1 or 2. This may contain concepts where n^3 = 3, f, g, p, q, r, s, t or u.

4-block, beginning with a concept where n^3 = 4. This may contain concepts where n^3 = f or g.

5-block, beginning with a concept where n^3 = 5, followed by a concept where n^3 = q. This may contain later concepts where n^3 = f, g, p, q or r.

6-block, beginning with a concept where n^3 = 6.

A. General validation

1. Primary manipulation codes

A concept must begin with a primary code consisting of 9 characters:

n^1	n^2	n^3	n^4	n^5	n^6	n^7	n^8	n^9

— where:
n^1 (instruction indicator) = $
n^2 (theme interlink) = x *or* y *or* z.
n^3 (role operator) = *either* a number in the range Ø to 6,
- *or* one of the letters f, g, p, q, r, s, t *or* u.

n^4 (focus as lead/non-lead) = Ø *or* 1.
n^5 (substitute) = a number in the range Ø to 9.
n^6 (permitted term) = a number in the range Ø to 3.
n^7 (spare) = Ø
n^8 (spare) = $
n^9 (type of term) = a *or* c *or* d.

2. Secondary manipulation codes

These occur in two forms:

(a) Two-character codes:

n^{10}	n^{11}

— where:
n^{10} (instruction indicator) = $.
n^{11} = one of the letters —
d (date as a difference).
e to i (typographic instruction).
n *or* o (parenthetical difference).
v *or* w (connective).

(b) Three-character codes:

n^{10}	n^{11}	n^{12}

— where
n^{10} (instruction indicator) = $
n^{11} (type of preceding difference) = a number in the range Ø to 3.
n^{12} (level of difference) = a number in the range Ø to 9.

3. A primary code or a connective code ($v *or* $w) can be followed by 'no data' — that is, the following character can be an instruction indicator ($).

4. If a concept consists of several parts, they must be in the order:
1) primary code (n^1 to n^9);
2) focus;
3) preceding difference(s), where: n^{11} = Ø to 3;
n^{12} = Ø to 9;
4) parenthetical difference, where n^{11} = n *or* o;
5) date, where n^{11} = d;
6) connective(s), where n^{11} = v *and/or* w.

B. Strings/Themes

1. The first primary code in every theme must have n^3 = Ø *or* 1 *or* 2.

2. At least one primary code in every theme must have n^3 = 1 *or* 2.

3. If n^2 = x, the string must contain at least one other concept where n^2 = x.

4. If n^2 = y, the theme must contain an earlier concept where n^2 = x.

5. A string containing concepts where n^2 = x can also contain concepts where n^2 = z. If these concepts are present, they must occur *before* the first concept where n^2 = x *and/or after* the final concept where n^2 = y.

C. Blocks

1. Every string must contain a 1-2 block. Other blocks are optional.

2. A 1-2 block must contain at least one part coded as a lead, i.e. a concept where n^4 = 1 *and/or* n^{11} = o (the letter) *or* 2 *or* 3.

3. A concept where n^3 = 1 can occur only once in a theme *unless* the second/subsequent concept where n^3 = 1:
— has n^5>Ø *and* n^6 = 2;
— *or* is preceded by a concept where n^5>Ø *and* n^6 = 1;
— *or* is preceded by a concept where n^3 = t *or* u.

4. A Ø-block cannot follow a 1-2 block in the same theme *unless* the 1-2 block contains a concept where n^5>Ø *and* n^6 = 1.

5. A 1-2 block cannot follow a 4-block or 5-block in the same theme.

6. A 4-block cannot follow a 5-block or 6-block in the same theme.

7. A 5-block is repeatable, but cannot follow a 6-block in the same theme.

8. A 6-block is repeatable. It cannot be followed by any other kind of block.

D. Coordinate concepts

1. A concept where n^3 =
— *either* a number in the range Ø to 4;
— *or* one of the letters p, q, r *or* u;
— can begin a *coordinate block* where subsequent concepts have n^3 = f *or* g.

Example: In the string: n^3 = Ø *A*
n^3 = 1 *B*
n^3 = g *C*
n^3 = g *D*
n^3 = 2 *E*

— the concepts *B–C–D* comprise a coordinate block.

2. If the second concept in a coordinate block has n^3 = f, all subsequent concepts in the same block must have n^3 = f.

3. If the second concept in a coordinate block has n^3 = g, all subsequent concepts in the same block must have n^3 = g.

4. Every concept in a coordinate block must have $n^5 = \emptyset$.

5. Every concept in a coordinate block must have the same number in n^6.

6. Any concept in a coordinate block can have n^{11} = v.

7. Only the final concept in a coordinate block can have n^{11} = w.

E. Connectives

1. A concept can contain:
   — only one part where n^{11} = v;
   — only one part where n^{11} = w.

2. If a concept contains both connectives, they must be input in the order $v *before* $w.

3. If n^{11} = v, then n^6 must be 2 *or* 3.

4. If n^{11} = w, then n^6 must be 1 *or* 3.

5. If n^{11} = v, the block must contain a later concept where n^6 = 1 *or* 3 †.

6. If n^{11} = w, the block must contain an earlier concept where n^6 = 2 *or* 3 †.

F. Differences

1. A concept can contain —
   — only one part where n^{11} = n *or* o.
   — only one part where n^{11} = d.

2. If a concept contains a difference where n^{12} = *'n'* (where *'n'* is a number in the range 2 to 9), the concept must also have at least one earlier part where n^{12} = *'n'-1*.
Example: If part of a term has n^{12} = 4, the term must have an earlier part where n^{12} = 3; this, in turn, must be preceded by a part where n^{12} = 2, and this must be preceded by a part where n^{12} = 1.
Parts on lower levels need not be adjacent. A term can contain more than one part on the same level.

---

† A *0-block* and a *1-2 block* are treated as a single block for this purpose.

F. Differences *cont*

4. If a concept contains $n^4 = \emptyset$ *and* $n^6 = \emptyset$, it must contain at least one difference where $n^{11} = 2$ *or* 3.

G. Substitutes

1. If $n^5 > \emptyset$, then n^4 must be $\emptyset$, and n^6 must be 1 *or* 2.

2. If $n^5 > \emptyset$ and $n^6 = 1$, the theme must contain a number of later concepts equal to or exceeding the number in n^5.

3. If $n^5 > \emptyset$ and $n^6 = 2$, the theme must contain a number of earlier concepts equal to or exceeding the number in n^5.

4. If $n^5 > \emptyset$, the concept cannot include a secondary code where n^{11} =
— *either* n *or* o;
— *or* a number in the range $\emptyset$ to 3.

H. Proper names

1. If a proper name (where n^9 = c *or* d) has a part preceded by n^{11} = e, the next part of the same concept must be preceded by n^{11} = g.

I. Special classes of actions (operators s, t and u).

1. A concept where n^3 = s *or* t *or* u can occur only in a 1-2 block.

2. A concept where n^3 = s must include a connective where n^{11} = w, and must be preceded by a concept where -
— n^3 is a number in the range 1 to 3 or one of the letters f, g, p, q *or* r;
— *and* $n^6 = 2$ *or* 3.

3. A concept where n^3 = s may also include a connective where n^{11} = v. If this connective is present, the adjacent concept later in the block must have $n^3 = 3$, *and* the block must contain a later concept where $n^6 = 1$ *or* 3.

4. If a concept has n^3 = t *or* u, it must be accompanied in the block by:
— an adjacent earlier concept where $n^6 = 2$ *or* 3;
— *and* an adjacent later concept where $n^6 = 1$ *or* 3.
Both the earlier and the later concept must have n^3 =
— *either* a number in the range 1 to 3;
— *or* one of the letters f, g, p, q *or* r.

5. A concept where n^3 = t:
— cannot have $n^4 = 1$;
— cannot contain secondary codes *except* $v *and/or* $w.

Index